PALGRAVE STUDIES IN THEATRE AND PERFORMANCE HISTORY is a series devoted to the best of theatre/performance scholarship currently available, accessible, and free of jargon. It strives to include a wide range of topics, from the more traditional to those performance forms that in recent years have helped broaden the understanding of what theatre as a category might include (from variety forms as diverse as the circus and burlesque to street buskers, stage magic, and musical theatre, among many others). Although historical, critical, or analytical studies are of special interest, more theoretical projects, if not the dominant thrust of a study, but utilized as important underpinning or as a historiographical or analytical method of exploration, are also of interest. Textual studies of drama or other types of less traditional performance texts are also germane to the series if placed in their cultural, historical, social, or political and economic context. There is no geographical focus for this series, and works of excellence of a diverse and international nature, including comparative studies, are sought.

The editor of the series is Don B. Wilmeth (Emeritus, Brown University), Ph.D., University of Illinois, who brings to the series over a dozen years as editor of a book series on American theatre and drama, in addition to his own extensive experience as an editor of books and journals. He is the author of several award-winning books and has received numerous career achievement awards, including one for sustained excellence in editing from the Association for Theatre in Higher Education.

Also in the series:

Undressed for Success by Brenda Foley
Theatre, Performance, and the Historical Avant-garde by Günter Berghaus
Theatre, Politics, and Markets in Fin-de-Siècle Paris by Sally Charnow
Ghosts of Theatre and Cinema in the Brain by Mark Pizzato
Moscow Theatres for Young People by Manon van de Water
Absence and Memory in Colonial American Theatre by Odai Johnson
Vaudeville Wars: How the Keith-Albee and Orpheum Circuits Controlled the Big-Time and Its Performers by Arthur Frank Wertheim
Performance and Femininity in Eighteenth-Century German Women's Writing by Wendy Arons
Operatic China: Staging Chinese Identity across the Pacific by Daphne P. Lei
Transatlantic Stage Stars in Vaudeville and Variety: Celebrity Turns by Leigh Woods
Interrogating America through Theatre and Performance edited by William W. Demastes and Iris Smith Fischer
Plays in American Periodicals, 1890–1918 by Susan Harris Smith
Representation and Identity from Versailles to the Present: The Performing Subject by Alan Sikes
Directors and the New Musical Drama: British and American Musical Theatre in the 1980s and 90s by Miranda Lundskaer-Nielsen

Beyond the Golden Door: Jewish-American Drama and Jewish-American Experience by Julius Novick

American Puppet Modernism: Essays on the Material World in Performance by John Bell

On the Uses of the Fantastic in Modern Theatre: Cocteau, Oedipus, and the Monster by Irene Eynat-Confino

Staging Stigma: A Critical Examination of the American Freak Show by Michael M. Chemers, foreword by Jim Ferris

Performing Magic on the Western Stage: From the Eighteenth-Century to the Present edited by Francesca Coppa, Larry Hass, and James Peck, foreword by Eugene Burger

Memory in Play: From Aeschylus to Sam Shepard by Attilio Favorini

Danjūrō's Girls: Women on the Kabuki Stage by Loren Edelson

Mendel's Theatre: Heredity, Eugenics, and Early Twentieth-Century American Drama by Tamsen Wolff

Theatre and Religion on Krishna's Stage: Performing in Vrindavan by David V. Mason

Rogue Performances: Staging the Underclasses in Early American Theatre Culture by Peter P. Reed

Broadway and Corporate Capitalism: The Rise of the Professional-Managerial Class, 1900–1920 by Michael Schwartz

Lady Macbeth in America: From the Stage to the White House by Gay Smith

Performing Bodies in Pain: Medieval and Post-Modern Martyrs, Mystics, and Artists by Marla Carlson

Early-Twentieth-Century Frontier Dramas on Broadway: Situating the Western Experience in Performing Arts by Richard Wattenberg

Staging the People: Community and Identity in the Federal Theatre Project by Elizabeth A. Osborne

Russian Culture and Theatrical Performance in America, 1891–1933 by Valleri J. Hohman

Baggy Pants Comedy: Burlesque and the Oral Tradition by Andrew Davis

Transposing Broadway: Jews, Assimilation, and the American Musical by Stuart J. Hecht

The Drama of Marriage: Gay Playwrights/Straight Unions from Oscar Wilde to the Present by John M. Clum

Mei Lanfang and the Twentieth-Century International Stage: Chinese Theatre Placed and Displaced by Min Tian

Hijikata Tatsumi and Butoh: Dancing in a Pool of Gray Grits by Bruce Baird

Staging Holocaust Resistance by Gene A. Plunka

Acts of Manhood: The Performance of Masculinity on the American Stage, 1828–1865 by Karl M. Kippola

Acts of Manhood

The Performance of Masculinity on the American Stage, 1828–1865

Karl M. Kippola

ACTS OF MANHOOD
Copyright © Karl M. Kippola, 2012.

Softcover reprint of the hardcover 1st edition 2012 978-0-230-34045-9

All rights reserved.

The author gratefully acknowledges permission to publish portions of the manuscript (in some cases now revised) that have appeared in the following journals as these articles:

"'The Battle-Shout of Freemen:' Edwin Forrest's Passive Patriotism and Robert T. Conrad's *Jack Cade.*" *The Journal of American Drama and Theatre* 13 (Fall 2001).

"Suppressing the Female Voice: Edwin Forrest's Silencing of Women in *Jack Cade.*" Reprinted with permission from *Theatre Symposium*, Volume 10: Representations of Gender on the Nineteenth-Century American Stage (2002). *Theatre Symposium* is the annual scholarly publication of the Southeastern Theatre Conference (www.setc.org).

"The Masculine Transformations of 'Genial' John McCullough." *Theatre History Studies* 27 (2007).

First published in 2012 by
PALGRAVE MACMILLAN®
in the United States—a division of St. Martin's Press LLC,
175 Fifth Avenue, New York, NY 10010.

Where this book is distributed in the UK, Europe and the rest of the world, this is by Palgrave Macmillan, a division of Macmillan Publishers Limited, registered in England, company number 785998, of Houndmills, Basingstoke, Hampshire RG21 6XS.

Palgrave Macmillan is the global academic imprint of the above companies and has companies and representatives throughout the world.

Palgrave® and Macmillan® are registered trademarks in the United States, the United Kingdom, Europe and other countries.

ISBN 978-1-349-34304-1   ISBN 978-1-137-06877-4 (eBook)

DOI 10.1057/9781137068774

Library of Congress Cataloging-in-Publication Data
Kippola, Karl M., 1966–
   Acts of manhood : the performance of masculinity on the American stage, 1828–1865 / Karl M. Kippola.
     p. cm.—(Palgrave studies in theatre and performance history)
     (Introduction: a new race of men—Act like a man: images and rhetoric of reconstructed manhood—A glorious image of unperverted manhood: Edwin Forrest as masculine ideal—A masculine identity worth dying for: the Astor Place Riot—Decorum and delicacy: the feminized manliness of Edwin Booth—Impossibly genial: the masculine transformations of John McCullough conclusion: affirming white masculinity by deriding the Other.)

     1. Masculinity in the theater—United States—History—19th century.
2. Theater and society—United States—History—19th century. 3. Male actors—United States. I. Title.
PN2260.M37K56 2012
792.0811′0973—dc23   2012002518

A catalogue record of the book is available from the British Library.

Design by Newgen Imaging Systems (P) Ltd., Chennai, India.

First edition: August 2012

For my wife and son

Contents

List of Illustrations	ix
Acknowledgments	xi
Introduction: A New Race of Men	1
1 Act Like a Man: Images and Rhetoric of Reconstructed Manhood	21
2 "A Glorious Image of Unperverted Manhood": Edwin Forrest as Masculine Ideal	53
3 A Masculine Identity Worth Dying For: The Astor Place Riot	89
4 Decorum and Delicacy: The Feminized Manliness of Edwin Booth	117
5 Impossibly Genial: The Masculine Transformations of John McCullough	147
Conclusion: Affirming White Masculinity by Deriding the Other	173
Notes	191
Works Cited	229
Index	245

Illustrations ∞

0.1 Richard Caton Woodville, *War News From Mexico,* 1848. Image courtesy of the author. 6

1.1 Andrew Jackson. The Library Company of Philadelphia. 36

1.2 Edwin Forrest. The Library Company of Philadelphia. 36

1.3 Frederick Douglass. Image courtesy of the author. 36

1.4 Ulysses S. Grant. The Library Company of Philadelphia. 36

1.5 John Quincy Adams. The Library Company of Philadelphia. 44

1.6 Judge Robert T. Conrad—dramatist of Edwin Forrest vehicle *Jack Cade* and Whig mayor of Philadelphia. The Library Company of Philadelphia. 44

1.7 "Abraham Lincoln, President of the United States, Signing the Emancipation Proclamation" (1864), engraved by John Serz after a painting by W. E. Winner. The Library Company of Philadelphia. 44

1.8 Henry Ward Beecher. The Library Company of Philadelphia. 44

2.1 Edwin Forrest as Spartacus in *The Gladiator.* The Library Company of Philadelphia. 63

2.2 Cartoon of Edwin Forrest as Spartacus in *The Gladiator.* Image courtesy of the author. 63

2.3 "Downfall of Mother Bank" (1833), by Henry R. Robinson. The Library Company of Philadelphia. 69

3.1 William Charles Macready. The Library Company of Philadelphia. 94

4.1	Edwin Booth on the cover of *Harper's Weekly: A Journal of Civilization* (January 13, 1866). The Library Company of Philadelphia.	126
4.2	Edwin Booth as Hamlet. Image courtesy of the author.	129
4.3	Edwin Forrest on the cover of *Vanity Fair* (September 20, 1862). The Library Company of Philadelphia.	140
4.4	Edwin Booth on the cover of *Vanity Fair* (November 1, 1862). The Library Company of Philadelphia.	140
5.1	"Genial John" McCullough. Image courtesy of the author.	148
6.1	John Vanderlyn, *The Death of Jane McCrea,* 1804. Image courtesy of the author.	174

Acknowledgments

I am grateful for the opportunity to thank a few of the many people who made this book possible. While space and memory will not allow me to name everyone, I honor each individual who contributed to my intellectual, artistic, and personal journey. This long list includes the teachers and fellow students at Seabeck Elementary, Bremerton Christian, and Central Kitsap Junior and Senior High Schools; Olympic College; University of Washington; University of Montana; Wayne State University; and University of Georgia, who molded my development. I wish to convey special appreciation to everyone at the University of Maryland for supporting me in the early stages of this project. Actors, directors, and designers at theatres, who are too numerous to mention, encouraged the marriage of intellectual, artistic, and personal passions. I applaud the patience, enthusiasm, generosity, and creative contributions of the staffs of libraries and archives throughout the country, although I will single out the extraordinary support of the people at the Library Company of Philadelphia, who provided a Mellon Fellowship and most of the images contained in this work. I thank administrators, colleagues, and students at American University for a decade of support, as well as for intellectual, academic, and artistic inspiration.

This project would not exist without the sense of humor, keen intellect, and perpetual selflessness of Heather Nathans. I wish to acknowledge Aaron Tobiason and Gordon Kippola for providing tough love in the manuscript's later stages. I thank my parents, Wallace and Clara, for the love, sacrifices, and encouragement that allowed me to pursue my dreams, however misguided. I thank Gordon, Diane, and Steven for generally being what siblings should be. I thank my dear, dear friends, past and present, from every walk of life—far too numerous to mention. However, my biggest debt of gratitude goes to my wife, Antoinette, and my son, Wally. Every day they teach me what it is to be a man.

Introduction: A New Race of Men ❦

> *What then is the American, this new man?... [L]eaving behind him all his ancient prejudices and manners, [he] receives new ones from the new mode of life he has embraced, the new government he obeys, and the new rank he holds... Here individuals of all nations are melted into a new race of men.... The American is a new man, who acts upon new principles; he must therefore entertain new ideas, and form new opinions."*
>
> Hector St. John de Crevecoeur, 1782[1]

In his oft-quoted 1802 parody of audience behavior, 19-year-old law student Washington Irving (writing as Jonathan Oldstyle) detailed the social behavior of three distinct groups of men in the playhouse. First, the working class, which sat up in the gallery: "The noise in this part of the house is somewhat similar to that which prevailed in Noah's ark...stamping, hissing, roaring, whistling,...and groaning in cadence." In the boxes were "the votaries of fashion...the beaus of the present day, who meet here to lounge away an idle hour, and play off their little impertinencies for the entertainment of the public...They even *strive* to appear inattentive." And finally, there were "the honest folks in the pit...a host of strapping fellows, standing with their dirty boots on the seats of the benches."[2] Irving spent the least amount of time speaking about the pittites, likely because he surveyed the spectacle of the playhouse (physically and philosophically) as one of them and also because they inspired less fascination than the manly extremes of the gallery gods or the beaux critics.

These three competing masculine models—the rowdy, the dandy, and the honest man—also shared the stage in the first American-written comedy, Royall Tyler's *The Contrast* (1787), which was inspired by national tensions that emerged from the Shays' Rebellion (1786–1787). The first group was embodied by Jonathan, the naïve, rustic bumpkin, whose plain-spoken pragmatism endeared him to the gallery gods and established the stage Yankee as a fixture of the American drama for the next 100 years: "I am a true blue son of liberty... no man shall master me." In his demand to be known as a waiter rather than as a servant to his colonel, Jonathan laid strong claims to republican equality: "Why, I swear we don't make any great matter of distinction in our state between quality and other folks."[3] The effete, duplicitous, Anglophilic Billy Dimple earns the scorn of his unwilling fiancée, Maria, "a depraved wretch, whose only virtue is a polished exterior; who is actuated by the unmanly ambition of conquering the defenseless." Maria resists Dimple's seductive artifice, claiming she would prefer "awkwardness," "deformity," "poverty," and even weakness to Dimple's insincere posing.[4] The honest man is elevated and idealized in Colonel Manly, a hero of the Revolution and a staunch, if somewhat stiff, defender of honor and country: "I have learned that probity, virtue, honour, though they should not have received the polish of Europe, will secure to an honest American the good graces of his fair countrywomen, and I hope, the applause of the public."[5]

As these three disparate models suggest, it is impossible to talk of one American masculine model. Limiting and reductive assumptions of a single, hegemonic, timeless, "natural" masculinity disregard varieties and complexities. Far from being stable and fixed, masculinities are man-made, fluid constructs, which are continually adjusting to evolving expectations and demands. In 1964, the late Supreme Court Justice Stewart once famously said of pornography that he could not precisely define it, but "I know it when I see it."[6] The ubiquity of masculinity makes its definition equally illusive. On the most basic level, the parameters of masculinity, as a cultural invention, are established by characteristics and behaviors that are identified as manly (and just as importantly identified as unmanly, animalistic, or effeminate). In his performance of gender, a man "assumes" a role, to borrow from Judith Butler—meaning a role both taken on and taken for granted.[7] Assuming this role also represents an "act"—meaning both performance and subterfuge—as a man contrives, consciously or not, to recreate a masculine ideal. If the role is assumed and acted effectively, the individual male is rewarded with inclusion and acceptance.

To further complicate historical inquiry, an exemplar of manhood differs from the "multiplicities of masculinities" that are actually performed, which creates a constant double vision of male identity that is identified by Michael Kimmel as "the history of the changing 'ideal' version of masculinity and the parallel and competing versions that coexist with it."[8] I will primarily examine two dominant strains of masculinity, which are based on conflicting ideal models, and many of the ways these ideals were pursued and enacted onstage and offstage. I identify these dueling strains as *intellectual self-control* and *passionate action*, although many men fell between or outside these classifications or embraced elements of both at different times. In her examination of Manifest Destiny, Amy S. Greenberg similarly examines the contrast between what she terms *restrained manhood* and *martial manhood*. I frequently equate the former with the middle classes and elites of the Whig and Republican parties and the latter with working-class Democrats, although these generalizations and limitations were not always in place. Restrained men valued domesticity and feminine virtues, refinement and moderation, emotional self-control and moral stature. Martial men rebelled against these moral and social constraints, privileging physical power and dominance and at times embracing excess and violence.[9] These bifurcated ideals are mutually constructed by (theatrical, political, and social) performers and audiences (both supporters and detractors), who validate and vilify specific values and models.

Attempting to cover all the manly models that span over 40 years is impossible, and I limit my study almost exclusively to the construction and representation of white masculinities. While not ignorant of the range of African American, Native American, and other nonwhite masculine models, I focus on a group whose size and complexity leaves little room for the adequate treatment of nonwhites.[10] The study of white men clearly does not address an underrepresented group. Their lives and artistry fill the pages of nineteenth-century American theatre scholarship, but their masculinity is typically taken for granted and too frequently becomes invisible. Very few works address these men *as men*, nor do they directly deal with the multiple ways in which masculinity was performed, nor with the reciprocal relationships of theatre and society in constructing models of maleness.[11] The dangerous temptation is to treat men as a monolithic and universal (nongendered) group, but a recent proliferation of works scrutinizes these limiting assumptions and presents more complex and nuanced pictures of males as individuals and groups. Multiple works have examined the history of American manhood from literary, cultural, and political perspectives.[12] Others have explored issues of masculinity in popular media, but only Robert Vorlicky's and Carla J. McDonough's studies of post–World War II drama have focused exclusively, let alone predominantly, on theatre.[13] My study represents the first book-length exploration of masculinity on the antebellum American stage.

While a surprising amount of language that specifically references manliness is used to describe the men I examine, I also read between the lines to highlight issues of masculine behavior and identity that are inextricably linked to nationality, class, race, culture, education, and gender. Even when masculinity or masculine motives are not overtly articulated, they frequently have a direct and determining impact. Similarly, moving beyond the dramatic script, I must rely on literary artifacts to communicate performative acts by sifting through biased and conflicting historical accounts. Similar to Paul Connerton's theorization of social memory, acting represents an *incorporating practice* communicated through bodily activity only when the body is present, while the *inscribing practice* of recording or critiquing that performance transforms it through the selection, omission, and interpretation of the chronicler.[14] We read the "factual" details of these men and their performances, but their memory remains tantalizingly incomplete.

ACTS OF MANHOOD

Though frequently at odds, discrete and disparate groups of American men shared the early Republic's theatres and enjoyed a vast array of entertainments on a single bill. With urban growth and viable transcontinental travel, socially segregated theatres became both desirable and financially viable, and the entertainments that were presented mirrored the increasingly divergent taste and tenor of their devotees. As the Civil War approached and, to borrow Dana Nelson's term, the illusion of America's "fraternal sameness" began to disintegrate, obvious social, political, and economic divisions contributed to a national fragmentation.[15] David Grimsted notes that the gradual social and economic fragmentation of American society mirrored schisms in theatre audiences: "One roof, housing a vast miscellany of entertainment each evening, could no longer cover a people growing intellectually and financially more disparate."[16] Divided by class, education, politics, race, nationality—but most importantly by social behavior—urban audiences patronized theatres that catered to their niche and demanded entertainments and stars that reflected their values.

In *Acts of Manhood: The Performance of Masculinity on the American Stage, 1828–1865,* I examine how theatre artists and audiences reflected and manipulated ideal, manly models. American men, who were seemingly in a perpetual crisis of masculine identity, sought the proper performance of gender—an inspirational but unrealizable ideal. The pursuit of this reassuring but false monolithic archetype, by its very nature, inevitably creates crisis. All manner of overlapping but distinct exemplars of masculine behavior are simultaneously in play. A single vision of American manhood does not, nor can it ever, exist; however, its ultimate impossibility did not prevent people from seeking it and believing that they had found it. Within the wide range of American manly models, warring factions of egalitarianism and individualism vied for supremacy as men relentlessly hunted elusive perfections, which resulted in what Tocqueville called the "strange unrest of so many happy men, restless in the midst of abundance."[17]

The election of Andrew Jackson over John Quincy Adams in 1828 can be seen as part of a shifting conception of masculinity. That same year, the passionate and muscular Edwin Forrest cemented his reputation as America's preeminent native actor. His playwriting competitions fostered American drama that appealed to working-class sensibilities, which resulted in works that promoted nationalism and consciously created distinctly American, uniquely masculine characters. By the late 1850s, scandals and changing tastes had diminished Forrest's popularity, and Edwin Booth— his father was the famous British actor Junius Brutus Booth, who named his son after Forrest—eventually supplanted his namesake as the country's most celebrated actor. Most famous for his tortured and sensitive Hamlet, Edwin Booth and his middle-class audiences mutually constructed an ideal of genteel restraint. The conclusion of the Civil War and Lincoln's death in 1865 marked a national turning point and a profound shift in perceptions of Edwin Booth. Major actors and political figures represent men who are publicly portraying a calculated masculine image (both representing an ideal to be emulated and emulating a representation that is demanded by their audiences) and sharing a popularity that is validated by popular appeal, whether at the box office or at the ballot box.

The rugged masculinity of Forrest and the effete intellectualism of Booth, the two great stars that bookend this period, represent diametrically opposed visions of manhood. How and why did the performance of masculinity change so dramatically? In fact, each dominant masculine model contains intriguing contradictions. While they are more similar than a cursory glance would suggest, audiences read these visions of manhood as antithetical. Intentionally reductive views of complex identities emerged from an audience desire to clarify and simplify their own social positions and gendered aspirations. I expand significantly beyond these two familiar, narrow, limiting masculine poles to understand the concurrent multiplicity of models on and off the American stage. Most actors of the nineteenth century fell somewhere between (or even outside) the artistic extremes of the Forrest-Booth spectrum, reflecting significant and widening social divisions. These other performers offer alternate visions that reflect or respond to the dominant antitheses, suggesting subtle shifts or conflicts within the discourse on masculinity. In limiting my study to

Figure 0.1 Richard Caton Woodville, *War News From Mexico*, 1848. Image courtesy of the author.

As a visual representation of the range of men sharing social and theatrical stages, Woodville's painting places multiple masculine images and viewpoints on the porch/stage of the "American Hotel." American victory in the Mexican-American War, which was prompted by the annexation of Texas in 1845, resulted in Mexico ceding most of what is now the American Southwest. Response to the war revealed sharp political and sectional divisions. Democrats who supported President Polk saw the war as the next logical step in American expansion, and editor John O'Sullivan coined the now-famous term in urging the country to embrace "the fulfillment of our *manifest destiny* to overspread the continent allotted by Providence for the free development of our yearly multiplying millions" ("Annexation," *United States Magazine and Democratic Review* 17 [July 1845]: 5–10). Whig opponents feared the rise of a Slave Power that would upset the uneasy balance between North and South, and poet James Russell Lowell condemned the war as an excuse for "stealin' bigger pens to cram with slaves" ("The Biglow Papers [June 1846]," in *The Poetical Works of James Russell Lowell* [Boston, MA: Fields, Osgood, 1869], 185). Henry David Thoreau was famously jailed for refusing to pay taxes to support the war and penned *Civil Disobedience*. The white men in the image (varying in class, age, and deportment) provide diverse responses, some unreadable. In addition to the men taking the stage, dimly visible to the viewer's far right, an interested woman watches from the wings of the domestic sphere. Two African American figures in the foreground, although not included in the group or on the stage, remain invested in the news and conversation. Woodville captures multiple men and masculine models, hinting at an enormous range of potential masculinities that share the American stage.

the most visible theatrical exemplars of antebellum white masculinity, I privilege the popular. While examining any of the less successful manly models that simultaneously shared the stages would likely shed light on the nation's trial-and-error journey through the century, I focus on the masculine performances that were perceived as being the most effective and affective—those that were celebrated on- and offstage and significantly influenced and reflected the behaviors of their audiences. While this choice may initially appear limiting, the same range of qualities and behaviors exhibited in less popular actors can also be seen operating in the more successful ones. Exploring the complexity and contradictions within these persuasive and pervasive models challenges gender assumptions and reveals the vast range of manly possibilities.

Acts of Manhood spans six chapters in which I map different portrayals of American masculinity. Integrating social, political, and cultural histories with an examination of those texts (dramatic, literary, and instructional) that shaped the American male, I explore a range of archival materials, political cartoons, popular novels, portraiture, conduct manuals, melodramas, and burlesques to trace the shifting meanings and signifiers of manhood in antebellum America. My introduction briefly examines a selection of dramatic and performance practices before 1828, to provide a foundational context for the rest of the study. In my conclusion, in addition to looking at the journey of masculine performance beyond the Civil War, I examine the process of exclusion that is necessary for the construction of privileged white manhood. Scrutinizing the ways in which white stages framed Native Americans, African Americans, and immigrants reveals the importance of marginalization, denigration, derision, and stigmatization in the construction of masculine identity.

My first chapter, "Act Like a Man: Images and Rhetoric of Reconstructed Manhood," explores the theatricalization of the newly American male and the ways he perceived the inextricable link between nationality and gender. The pivotal 1828 presidential election featured sharply contrasting opponents in John Quincy Adams and Andrew Jackson. The country was torn between the familiar, fixed hierarchical structure of an aristocratic model and the uncharted territory of a "true democracy." Public figures adapted their performance of gender to meet the changing needs of the country and of their constituents. To provide concrete direction to men seeking success in this contradictory world, advice literature promoted a system of codified social behavior that reflected the country's democratic equality as well as its ambition. Whereas artifice and conscious representation were thought to be negative, they were paradoxically essential to the social and economic success everyone desired. The ideal performance of gentility and masculinity was an invisible one, performed so seamlessly that audiences were unaware that they were seeing an actor, rather than a genuine human being. This complex, theatricalized social performance of American manhood would be reflected and expanded on the dramatic stage.

My second chapter, "'A Glorious Image of Unperverted Manhood': Edwin Forrest as Masculine Ideal," investigates Forrest's often belligerent, hypermasculine performance on- and offstage. He exerted influence over working-class audiences, providing a theatrical template of the ideal Jacksonian male. His involvement in the Astor Place Riot and a very public divorce from a socially ambitious Englishwoman placed him in the public spotlight as a source of American pride or embarrassment, depending on the audience's increasingly class-bound perspective. Capitalizing on the democratic fervor and nationalistic sentiment that brought Jackson to office, a 22-year-old Forrest announced the first of his drama competitions in 1828. Forrest's prize plays showcased his strengths and presented him as a symbol of American nationalism. By examining Robert T. Conrad's *Jack Cade* (1835), which Forrest adapted for performance, I explore the ways in which Forrest and his audience mutually constructed masculine identity and proper behavior.

In chapter 3, "A Masculine Identity Worth Dying For: The Astor Place Riot," I examine the 1849 riot both as a theatrical and as a political spectacle of conflicting masculinities, one triggered by the personal and professional feud between Edwin Forrest and England's most respected star, William Charles Macready. Within an uncertain social, economic, and political climate, men of all classes sought to affirm and to stabilize their individual and collective masculine identities. The urban, working-class male demanded recognition and respect through intimidation and popular sovereignty, while the middle and upper classes ultimately exerted dominance through legal means. This simmering showdown between incompatible masculine identities suggests that no single model could satisfy a nation that was already splintering along political and economic lines.

As the American middle class became a dominant social, political, and economic force in the years before the Civil War, their values, expectations, and social roles were reflected in the restraint and moderation of Edwin Booth. My fourth chapter, "Decorum and Delicacy: The Feminized Manliness of Edwin Booth," explores Booth's subdued, genteel brand of masculinity as a reflection of the "invisible" performance of ideal manhood. The elevation of women as models of purity and the performance of masculinity as a devotion to the feminine ideals of refinement, repression, and sentiment lay at the heart of a changing middle-class manhood. Booth's admirers praised the moral superiority of his masculine self-control and derided the weakness of unchecked emotion (even on stage) as unmanly. As Lincoln's audience learned to appreciate the softer intellectual quality he brought to political oratory, Booth and his audience transformed the theatre experience from riotous to thoughtful.

My final chapter, "Impossibly Genial: The Masculine Transformations of John McCullough," examines the career of the Irish-born tragedian who achieved theatrical success as protégé to Edwin Forrest. As audience tastes changed, McCullough adapted his acting style to embrace the principles of the Delsarte system and the emotional restraint associated with Edwin Booth. His systematic efforts at self-improvement matched a middle-class desire to adjust behavior to achieve social acceptance. Shunning the theatrical extremes of Forrest and Booth, McCullough's agreeable-but-bland nature lacked the dynamism to inspire emulation in others. McCullough too closely embodied the emerging middle class, which secretly longed to see passion and inspiration beneath the controlled, genteel, and genial mask.

These changes in masculine performance should not be read as a teleological progression or decline. The shift from Forrest to Booth did not reflect a linear development toward national or theatrical refinement, nor is it possible to discuss the changing tastes of a monolithic audience. One ideal of manhood did not supplant the other; rather, a multitude of masculinities simultaneously fought for dominance and recognition. The national stage not only mirrored but magnified that process, simultaneously providing models of behavior and creating physical characters upon which contemporary ideals of manhood could be inscribed. Whereas both Forrest and Booth provide "texts" for reading masculinity, other models demand consideration. The ever-changing face of the American man can be viewed as a cultural palimpsest—like a parchment written on multiple times to make room for alternate messages, the previous text, which is imperfectly erased, remains partly visible.

FOUNDING FATHERS OF AMERICAN ACTING: BRITISH STARS IN AMERICA'S HEAVENS

Rather than one school or style supplanting another, a variety of acting approaches coexisted and coevolved throughout the nineteenth century. Changes in theory and practice were gradual and provided only finely nuanced variations on dominant models. In fact, multiple performance philosophies could share the stage of a single performance. The range of approaches, which differed from one another both subtly and radically, provided a rich and evolving tapestry of acting methods and masculine behaviors. An "American" style of acting, if such a separate category truly existed, emerged from the established traditions of British actors in colonial America and the early Republic. Two dominant performance strains filled period stages. Whereas most actors predominantly fell into one school or another, these generalized categories were not rigid, and the qualities noted in individual actors often melded elements from both acting styles. The "classical" school of John Philip Kemble (1757–1823) featured a declamatory and elevated style, and the "romantic" approach associated with Edmund Kean (1789–1833) relied on tempestuous passions intended to simulate nature. "Natural," "true to life," or "realistic" acting are relative terms used to describe performance that goes back to the Greeks, as the qualities that comprise what is considered natural continually evolve. Spontaneity on stage represented an illusion, according to Edmund Kean, whose unbridled passion typified romantic acting: "Because my style is easy and natural they think I don't study, and talk about the 'sudden impulse of a genius.' There is no such thing as impulsive acting; all is premeditated and studied beforehand."[18] This craft under the guise of nature, which David Garrick (1717–1779) put into practice on the English-speaking stage and Diderot debated in *Le paradoxe sur le comedien* (1773), dominated nineteenth-century stages. The uneasy relationship between the conscious and the calculated, yet seemingly artless and inspired, also marked social, political, and gender performances. And in all forums it proved crucial not to be caught acting.

From the late-eighteenth century through the first quarter of the nineteenth century, the theatre space was largely a heterogeneous mixture of classes, although it was stratified spatially within the playhouse itself. A range of audiences initially patronized and enjoyed both acting schools, but as the nineteenth century progressed, theatrical patronage became increasingly divided along class lines. The reserved dignity of the classical actor typically drew the upper and growing middle classes, which were eager to separate themselves from the perceived vulgarities of a working class that was viscerally connected to the fervor of the romantics. This growing audience fragmentation, which was accelerated by industrialization and the country's subsequent urbanization—not to mention drastically reduced admission prices in the 1820s—led to a concentration of working-class males in urban centers that were fully able to sustain the growing number of theatres dedicated to entertaining this new and demanding audience.[19] Of course, no one class or social group during this (or any) period was entirely homogenous, nor did they operate in concert. This lack of cohesion especially held true for the lower classes, where the constant infusion of new immigrants changed the demographics throughout the century.

Before the first native-born star (Edwin Forrest) garnered national acclaim, English actors represented the best performers available on the American stage. Most were second-tier performers who played supporting roles in London and enjoyed occasional starring opportunities in the provinces. All risked the danger, uncertainty, and stigma of traveling to the New World for a chance at theatrical acclaim and an opportunity to make their fortune. After the Revolutionary War, actors with established reputations cautiously trod American boards, inspiring the American actors to follow.[20] A brief examination of the most influential visiting and emigrating theatrical figures reveals the spectrum of performance and masculine models on American stages before 1828.

Thomas Abthorpe Cooper (1776–1849) debuted successfully as Hamlet at Covent Garden in London but, unable to capitalize on this success, agreed to try America (debuting in Baltimore in 1796). Cooper, America's leading actor until Forrest, embraced the idealized poeticism of John Philip Kemble—elegant deportment, grand declamation, and formalized gesture. Actor James E. Murdoch's description draws similarities to Cooper's most famous emulator, Edwin Forrest: "Cooper depended upon a certain imposing bearing and the power of his well-modulated voice."[21] The *New York Commercial Advertiser* (1798) described the inspiring impact of Cooper's physical presence:

> We look for something uncommonly attractive or imposing, in a hero. How much soever we may have rationally persuaded ourselves that greatness of character is not appropriate to this or that size, we always experience something like disappointment in finding nothing remarkable in his appearance of whom we have heard much and often. Few performers will permit the spectator to depart with so little disappointment of this kind, as Mr. Cooper.

Lacking Kemble's studious attention to detail, Cooper relied on his natural gifts and the power of his considerable personal magnetism: "His person, countenance, voice, gesture and manners, were admirably calculated to impress on the audience the liveliest realization of the personage he represented."[22] Extremely popular into the 1820s, Cooper also earned admiration offstage for his charm and vitality. Henry Dickinson Stone in his *Personal Recollections of the Drama* (1873) admired Cooper's courage and athleticism:

> The physical powers of endurance of this eminent actor were most remarkable... He frequently played at the Park Theatre, New York, and at the Walnut Street Theatre, Philadelphia, alternate nights in the week,... [He journeyed on horseback,] which was considered through the heavy sand roads of New Jersey a Herculean performance.²³

According to actor-manager Frances Wemyss, American audiences embraced Cooper as a native son, "the pride and boast of the America stage...whose style of declamation was held up as worthy of imitation, both by the pulpit and the bar."²⁴ Cooper's social success—his daughter married President Tyler's son, and President Polk appointed him Inspector of the New York Customs House—was extraordinary for anyone associated with the theatre. Cooper served as a prototype of Forrest's muscular masculinity, embodying the magnitude and unbridled passion of the country and providing the force of personality and the physical and moral stature to effectively embody and reinforce the noble characters he portrayed.

George Frederick Cooke (1756–1812), a legitimate rival to Kemble in England, agreed to tour America in 1810. In contrast to the regulated, declamatory style and noble sentiments of Kemble, Cooke anticipated Kean and initiated a romantic style characterized by feverish attack and sudden shifts in tempo and pitch, which represented a marked advance toward "natural" acting. James Murdoch praised Cooke's performance for "the actor's mastery over his voice and his skill in adapting it to the play of feature and bodily action in the familiar expression of every-day life and character." Although Murdoch particularly admired Cooke's energetic portrayal of stage villains—"[H]is unassumed personal malignity was the crowning-point of artistic delineation"—alcohol, ill health, and irresponsible behavior often marred Cooke's performances, and he died suddenly from drink and prolonged, untreated illness.²⁵ Cooke was not admired as a man—but strictly as a performer. Dunlap lauds Cook, the first major British star to visit America, as the biggest theatrical sensation yet experienced: "[R]eiterated plaudits expressed the fullness with which expectation had been realized and taste and feeling gratified."²⁶ Cooke's arrival provided the American theatre with much-needed cultural status.

The diminutive Edmund Kean (1787–1833), the leading actor of the English stage, idolized Cooke and shared many of his excessive, self-destructive behaviors. Kean made his American debut in New York in 1820 and, although in the country for a relatively short period of time, exerted more influence than any other individual on the early American stage. Hailed as the theatrical personification of romantic naturalism, critic William Hazlitt (who composed 21 reviews of Kean's performances from 1814 to 1820) marveled at the often uneven performances, which were imbued with violent intensity, passion, and power, through which Kean's distinctive personality was always present: "[His] acting is like an anarchy of the passions, in which each upstart humor, or frenzy of the moment, is struggling to get violent possession of some bit or corner of his fiery soul and pigmy body."[27] This not atypical physical description did not suggest a wholly appealing masculine image. In his debut, the *New York Evening Post* (1820) instantly recognized Kean's greatness: "[W]e saw the most complete actor...that ever appeared on our boards...We are desirous that all should witness the exhibitions of Kean, because we believe he will introduce a new and better taste in acting...and thus materially improve the judgment of the public."[28] Audiences initially responded with equal enthusiasm, but when Kean refused to play to a small house in Boston, the *Boston Galaxy* (1821) vilified Kean as an "insolent pretender," an "inflated, self-conceited, unprincipled vagabond."[29] Although this attack used the language of the elite, Kean offended across class lines. The upper class chastised him for stepping above his station, and the lower class condemned him as a conceited Englishman. Reports of Kean's arrogance and his attack against the Kemble style of acting practiced by Cooper (America's adopted son with friends in high places) further poisoned America's response. Growing tensions on Kean's second trip to America eventually led to the nation's most violent theatre riot to date (December 21, 1825).[30] Kean's erratic lifestyle and a well-publicized affair with a London alderman's wife also contributed to his troubling masculine image. The uninhibited and unschooled passion of his dramatic portrayals, however, largely harmonized with the American sensibility. Physician and historian John Francis extolled Kean's tenacity and versatility: "The drudgery of his early life had given a pliability to his muscular powers that rendered him the most dexterous harlequin, the most graceful fencer, the most finished gentleman, the most insidious lover, the most terrific tragedian."[31] Like his idol Cooke, Kean fulfilled a masculine model only onstage, and then, only when his personal demons did not follow him there.

Junius Brutus Booth (1796–1852), a serious rival and sometime imitator of Kean who abandoned a wife and son in England to begin another family in America, spent the last 30 years of his life performing throughout the country. Kean's acting inspired him, but the *Spirit of the Times* (1848) praised the elder Booth for a suppler vocal instrument and a greater knack for subsuming his own personality in performance: "We say [Booth was Kean's] superior because Booth sustains a character from the first line to the end of the play, impressing it with the grandness of a wonderful conception subdued practically."[32] The *National Advocate* (1821) applauded the intensity of Booth's passion: "[H]is eyes flashed fire;... and he rushed upon the foe like a lion, animating his followers with a voice of thunder."[33] Because he performed in almost every viable theatre community in the country over three decades, Booth imposed the greatest practical impact of any of the traveling British stars, but his improper family life, intemperance, and bouts of mental instability made him more of a curiosity than an ideal model of masculine behavior.

William Charles Macready (1793–1873), the "Eminent Tragedian," shared the high-minded ideals and the offstage decorum that were typically associated with the classical school, but his performance style borrowed heavily from both dominant acting traditions and direct observation of Kemble and Kean. Historian John Francis alluded to Macready's success in capturing the natural feel of the romantic school while maintaining the dignity of the classical: "He cannot be entirely classed with the exclusive followers of nature, though he borrowed largely from her resources; and it would be unjust to his original powers to attribute his excellencies to his adoption of the cold and formal school of actors."[34] As Macready described his own performance, "Acted Hamlet, if I may trust my own feeling, in a very Shakespearian style; most courteous and gentlemanly, with high bearing, and yet with abandonment and, I think, great energy."[35] Macready borrowed from the classical style a meticulous, finely detailed, premeditated approach to acting and characterization, but he deplored the lifeless artificiality often associated with the Kemble school. Inspired by Kean, Macready attempted naturalistic readings and sought the appearance of sincere passion and spontaneous emotion. J. Sheridan Knowles, who wrote *William Tell* (1873) for Macready, applauded the tragedian's apparent sense of abandon:

> Mr. Macready excels in passages of tender emotion, but he absolutely transcends himself in those of high and impetuous feeling. You see the passion flashing in his eye and flaming on his cheek, and you hear it in the thunder of his voice—the finest voice upon the stage. Here he never thinks of his delivery, but gives his utterance the rein, and lets it bound along with all the freedom of wild and headlong nature.[36]

Macready intellectually controlled and justified his sudden shifts, using what came to be known as the "Macready pause" to give the impression of thinking within soliloquy. Macready privileged passion that was closely governed by intellect over unbridled power: "I was most attentive to the necessity of subduing my voice, and letting the passion rather than the lungs awaken the audience."[37] Self-chastisements over failing to inhabit a character in performance filled his diaries: "I cannot act Macbeth without *being Macbeth*."[38] Macready's struggles and frustrations over the pursuit of artless subtlety mirrored the invisible performance of genteel decorum that was sought by middle-class men. Just as Macready sought the *effect* of nature, rather than attempting somehow to (re)create it onstage, the image-conscious men of the middle classes manufactured outward signs of proper manliness.

Cooke, Kean, and the elder Booth practiced similar approaches to acting—an inspired, intuitive, and impulsive intensification of nature. Their style thrilled because it exhibited an inherently individual air of spontaneity. British critic and philosopher George Henry Lewes derided the shallow, surface emulators of Kean: "His imitators have been mostly ridiculous, simply because they reproduced the manner and the mannerism, but could not reproduce the power which made these endurable."[39] In performances marked by a passionate fire that is impossible to train or teach, the singularity of these British stars, and the fledgling American actors whom they inspired, strongly appealed to a working-class faith in individual greatness, which invariably led to social success. This passionate individual expression, however, often prohibited the social acceptance of the romantic actor by genteel audiences. The decorous manner and ennobling performance of classical actors, such as Cooper and Macready, more naturally matched the expectations of image-conscious elite audiences. Visiting British stars faced the impossible challenge of being "all things to all men." These performers appeared during a transitional period, when masculine identities were in flux. If audiences had yet to separate along class lines in the 1810s and the 1820s, how could *one* man possibly appeal to every masculine identity in the playhouse? Ironically, masculine representation on stage became simpler as America's class relationships became more complex. As audiences began to fragment, spectators and actors mutually constructed appealing modes of behavior. This collaboration between the men on stage and the men in the audience continued throughout the remainder of the nineteenth century.

MASCULINITY IN CONTRAST: THEATRICAL MANHOOD IN THE EARLY REPUBLIC

Understanding the gradual democratization of the eighteenth-century theatrical world contextualizes my exploration of the nineteenth century. The physical configuration of the colonial theatre mirrored the deferential hierarchy and social separation of the British model of box, pit, and gallery. Patrons of the box were primarily composed of gentry, including women, with servants and slaves being typically relegated to the gallery.[40] Tradesmen, artisans, and laborers, while not excluded from the playhouse, certainly did not comprise a substantial presence. Theatres were associated with the British aristocracy, and as anti-British sentiments grew, the perceived aristocratic extravagance of theatre became a target. In the early Republic, however, theatre became a more accessible form of amusement, one that more fully represented the full social spectrum. New playhouses like the Chestnut Street Theatre (1794) in Philadelphia featured an enlarged pit and a reduction in the number of boxes, and ticket prices decreased dramatically, making the theatre more accessible to working-class audiences. This arrangement created a less hospitable environment for respectable ladies, effectively banishing them from the auditorium and into the domestic sphere.

Edwin Forrest and the dramas he championed did not spring fully formed onto American stages in 1828. Representative plays, characters, and masculine models of the early Republic foreshadowed developments that I will explore in the following chapters. In revisiting the manly voices from Tyler's *The Contrast*, Dimple aped the British and their flowery insincerity, Jonathan spoke (or at least aspired to) the simple common sense of Thomas Paine, and Manly invoked the elevated eloquence of the Founding Fathers. Actually, Maria's father, Van Rough, provides a fourth dominant masculine model. The social-climbing, self-made urban businessman continually spouts his cautious and greedy mantra: "[I]t is money makes the mare go; keep your eye on the main chance."[41] Michael S. Kimmel convincingly argues that it is Van Rough who "would emerge triumphant in the nineteenth century, and [that] the mobility and insecurity of the Self-Made Man came to dominate the American definition of manhood."[42] However, neither Jonathan's rustic rowdiness, nor Dimple's effete pretensions to aristocracy, nor Van Rough's obsessive self-interest provided wholly appealing models of male behavior. The independent, hard-working, and honest spirit of Manly seems to represent what Tyler felt to be the proper manly aspiration. Even Tyler's allegorical naming of his hero, an established and popular convention of the day, suggested the desire for a new, uniquely American model of masculine behavior.

The *Pennsylvania Journal* praised the play "for exhibiting in such true colors the pernicious maxims of the Chesterfieldian system, of all others the most dangerous to the peace of society."[43] Chesterfield represented a unifying target for fear of insincere social behavior. Published posthumously in 1774, the collection of *Letters to His Son by the Earl of Chesterfield on the Fine Art of Becoming a Man of the World and a Gentleman* comprised the legacy of British statesman and diplomat Philip Dormer Stanhope, 4th Earl of Chesterfield.[44] While filled with sound advice on life, conduct, and self-improvement, Chesterfield's letters of advice to his illegitimate son emphasize appearance that encourages both dissimulation (concealing undesirable characteristics) and simulation (feigning desirable characteristics that do not, in fact, exist). Samuel Johnson's condemnation of this work ("They teach the morals of a whore, and the manners of a dancing-master") captured a pervasive American attitude toward the dangers of following in the footsteps of English manhood.[45] Although prevalent, this attitude was not universal. Hard and fast distinctions about topics that are bound up with issues of nationalism were rarely clear-cut. A significant group, while never formally aligned with the loyalist cause, was not quite ready to vilify their former countrymen and culture.

Royall Tyler's attack on the emotional detachment and insincerity of the Chesterfield model suggests that, from the nation's first significant dramatic effort, Americans needed to separate from the calculated manipulation of the British and their insidious, feminizing influence on America's elite. As American minister James Dana warned in 1779, "Nothing hath a darker aspect on rising states than effeminate manners."[46] An inability to establish a masculine identity that was separate from the mother country—the only model he knew—stymied the emerging republican male. However, Tyler's cry for something uniquely American comprised a lone, if manly, voice in the theatrical wilderness. A paucity of American drama, which was coupled with a persistent mistrust of the fledgling American aesthetic, limited theatre's contribution to evolving gender identities.

A range of audiences, however, became aware of theatre's potential power as an increasingly politicized tool that would be useful in establishing social dominance and legitimacy. Dramas such as *Cato* (1712), *Andre* (1798), and *Gustavus Vasa* (1739) encouraged male spectators to identify themselves with the positive traits embodied by the hero. These plays celebrated republican virtues and passionately demonstrated the need to fight for freedom. Because of their potential for inspiration, productions of these works overcame many of the prejudices and suspicions against drama. As articulated by the Charleston *National Gazette* (1793), a properly regulated theatre possessed the potential to "inculcate an observance of the moral and social duties, or in some shape tend to better the heart, without vitiating the understanding by an overstrained address to fancy."[47] Whereas this formal defense of theatre does not address a need to entertain, the most effective works reached the intellect through the emotions.

Plays such as *Cato* (1712) by Englishman Joseph Addison inspired passionate responses. The upright Marcus Porcius Cato Uticensis (Cato the Younger), along with Numidian prince Juba, virtuously fights for liberty and freedom against the tyranny of Julius Caesar. *Cato* likely provided literal inspiration for the rhetoric of prominent Revolutionary-era figures such as Patrick Henry, whose "Give me liberty or give me death" draws from Act II, scene iv: "It is not now a time to talk of aught / But chains or conquest, liberty or death," and Nathan Hale's "I regret that I have but one life to give for my country" from Act IV, scene iv: "[W]hat pity is it / That we can die but once to serve our country!" In fact, despite a Continental Congress ban on theatrical productions in 1774, General George Washington requested that the play, his favorite, be performed for the Continental Army while at Valley Forge.

Washington was actually placed onstage as a masculine model in two plays by American William Dunlap (1766–1839). *Andre* (1798) portrayed Washington as a staunch and inflexible defender of the nation's honor:

> I likewise am
> A soldier; entrusted by my country.
> What I shall judge most for that country's good
> That shall I do.[48]

Only showing emotion or uncertainty when alone, Dunlap's Washington exuded a somewhat cold, forbidding presence in his unwavering resolve to execute the condemned titular British spy for his role in Benedict Arnold's treasonous plan. Most dramatists of the early Republic focused entirely on citizenship as the ultimate goal of masculine behavior. Through the character of George Washington, Dunlap argued that no matter how charismatic or compelling the individual, nothing was more important than the state. *Andre* did not enjoy great success until Dunlap converted the tragedy into a patriotic musical pageant, *The Glory of Columbia, Her Yeomanry* (1803), which remained popular until the middle of the century. One of Dunlap's lesser-known plays, an interlude entitled *Darby's Return* (1789), features an Irish rustic (played by comic actor Thomas Wignell, a favorite of George Washington and the original Jonathan in *The Contrast*), who describes the president:

> A man who'd fought to free the land from woe,
> *Like me* had left his *farm a-soldiering* to go;
> But having gain'd his point, he had, *like me,*
> Return'd his own *potatoe ground* to see.
> But there he couldn't rest; with one accord
> He's called to be a kind of—not a lord;
> I don't know what: he's not a great man, sure,
> For poor men love him, just as he was poor!
> They love him like a father or a brother.[49]

Dunlap presented Washington as a model of masculine behavior in both pieces, yet in both works, this model remains idealized and unattainable. Darby's repeated *like me* ironically underscores the impossibility of comparing the mythic image of Washington to that of a common man, while simultaneously emphasizing the unpretentious performance of American masculinity, even in its most exalted form. In *The Contrast,* Royall Tyler explicitly connects Manly to Washington from his first entrance: "I have humbly imitated our illustrious WASHINGTON, in having exposed my health and life in the service of my country, without reaping any other reward than the glory of conquering in so arduous a contest." Of the four masculine models in *The Contrast,* Manly represented the most admirable but likely the least emotionally compelling model, at least as described by a comic coquette: "the essence of everything that is *outre* and gloomy."[50] Dunlap's Washington and Tyler's Manly represented heroes of noble sentiment and impeccable behavior. They were admirable but their very lack of weakness deprived them of the humanity and dramatic fire needed to elicit passionate response.

Irishman Henry Brooke's *Gustavus Vasa, The Deliverer of his Country* (1739) would also forever be associated with Washington. Brooke's thinly veiled attack on the British government, the first drama to be banned under the Licensing Act in England, not surprisingly appealed to Americans. Vasa, who was chosen to lead Sweden to victory against Christian II (king of Norway, Sweden, and Denmark), mercifully allows the Danes to return to their country. Vasa (now King Gustav I) represents both a patriotic and a patriarchal hero:

> Come, come, my Brothers all! Yes I will strive
> To be the Sum of ev'ry Title to ye,
> And you shall be my Sire, my Friend reviv'd,

> My Sister, Mother, all that's kind and dear,
> For so *Gustavus* holds ye—Oh I will
> Of private Passions all my Soul divest,
> And take my dearer Country to my Breast.
> To publick Good transfer each fond Desire,
> And clasp my *Sweden* with a Lover's Fire.
> Well pleas'd, the Weight of all her Burdens bear;
> Dispense all Pleasure, but engross all Care.
> Still quick to find, to feel my People's Woes;
> And wake that Millions may enjoy Repose.[51]

American audiences saw this selfless devotion to country embodied in their own leader, Washington. A 1778 Philadelphia printing of the play was "Inscribed to His Excellency General Washington Commander in Chief of the Forces of the Thirteen United States of America." In the early Republic, *Gustavus Vasa* became a theatrical fixture that was performed on patriotic occasions and to commemorate the birthday of the country's champion.

Celebrating a self-made manhood that Edwin Forrest's prize-winning dramas would come to embrace, Scotch clergyman John Home's *Douglas* (1756) provided one of the more popular vehicles for young male actors, which served as a proving ground for histrionic ability and masculine sentiment. In the story, Lady Douglas has lost both her husband and her son and remarries a Lord Randolph, who is rescued in battle by the brave Young Norval. Norval, raised by a shepherd, turns out to be Lady Randolph's lost son, Douglas. Lord Randolph, who has turned against Douglas, helps murder him, and the young man dies in his mother's arms. The role not only provided dramatic opportunities for heroism, bravery, and tragic death, but it also underscored the inherent value of unpolished, native worth ("stamp'd a hero by the sovereign hand of nature!") within a theatrically viable frame.[52] The success of a 14-year-old Edwin Forrest as Young Norval at Philadelphia's Walnut Street Theatre in 1820 launched the career of America's first great actor.

1. Act Like a Man: Images and Rhetoric of Reconstructed Manhood ∾

> *The patriots of the revolution did not make speeches to be unattended by their brethren in Congress and fill up the columns of newspapers. They only spoke when they had something to say, and preferred* acting *to* talking.[1]
>
> Hezekiah Niles, 1822

Dedicated to the "young men of the United States...that they may be encouraged to adhere to the simplicity of truth...and emulate the noblest deeds," *Weekly Register* editor Hezekiah Niles attempted to collect stirring speeches of the revolutionary period 46 years after the Declaration of Independence.[2] Although he managed to fill 500 pages, Niles still lamented the impossibility of chronicling the words of men who, of necessity, privileged action over oratory. On the centennial of independence, Ralph Waldo Emerson praised this same quality, suggesting that speech "is not to be distinguished from action. It is the electricity of action. It is action, as the general's word of command or chart of battle is action." Emerson pared down the ultimate power of eloquence to its essence: "If I should make the shortest list of the qualifications of the orator, I should begin with manliness; and perhaps it means here presence of mind. Men differ so much in control of their faculties!"[3] I would argue that the delicate marriage, or the deliberate divorce, of passionate action and manly self-control provides the key to understanding masculine leadership and identity in the nation's first 100 years.

Rather than following a strictly chronological or even thematic framework, in this chapter I provide a broad context for understanding antebellum masculine performance by addressing a wide range of contributing factors. Examining the rhetorical style and the perceived manly image of some of the most visible and influential figures of the period reveals an evolving, diverse, and complex web of masculinities. The changing of the guard from John Quincy Adams to Andrew Jackson in the presidential election of 1828 validated a rough, self-made model. Future presidential aspirants, whether admirers or detractors of Jackson, were forced to contend with the popular appeal of this masculine paradigm. The "Great Triumvirate" (John C. Calhoun, Henry Clay, and Daniel Webster) represented diverse attempts to establish or maintain manly alternates to Jackson that appealed across class, political, and sectional divisions. Abraham Lincoln presented a masculine image that combined the self-made appeal of Jackson and the intellectual persuasion of Adams, while also incorporating an accessible sensitivity. From the pulpit, Henry Ward Beecher's Gospel of Love radically reframed religion's role in life, and his sentimental, emotional model of manhood reflected middle-class passions and priorities. With each of these figures, it is the perception of the masculine ideal he represents (a perception mutually constructed with admirers and detractors), rather than the fully nuanced, self-contradictory individual, that serves as positive or negative model. In addition to these multiple potential ideals, middle-class men also sought more overt, pragmatic instruction in proper social decorum from conduct manuals. Each of these disparate, sometimes contradictory, inspirations influenced behavior. This complexity contextualizes the range of theatrical performances.

Although patriots of the revolution may have preferred acting to talking, the words they used to establish their independence and their unique identity influenced the newly American man. In his study of eighteenth-century rhetoric, Jay Fliegelman examines the implementation of vernacular speech:

> Preoccupied with the spectacle of sincerity and an intensified scrutiny of the body as an instrument of expression, the quest for a natural language led paradoxically to a greater theatricalization of public speaking, to a new social dramaturgy, and to a performative understanding of selfhood.

In "spectacle of sincerity," Fleigelman suggests a conscious, deliberate performance, which eliminates all signs of artifice and privileges the credibility of the speaker over the content of the argument. Fliegelman positions the blurring of the natural and the theatrical in America as "[an] awareness of the impossibility of separating the doing of things for effect from the doing of things to effect, the doubleness, that is, of being an effectual historical 'actor' in both the general sense of agent and the specific sense of performer."[4] In a document intended to be read aloud and performed, Thomas Jefferson used the theatricalized "natural language" of a gentleman to justify the necessity to fight in his Declaration of Independence.

In *Common Sense* (1776), Thomas Paine implemented a more fully realized version of this theoretically natural language—one that diverged sharply from the comparatively elevated rhetoric of Washington, Adams, and Jefferson—directing his appeal to the artisans rather than the elite: "And however our eyes may be dazzled with show, or our ears deceived by sound; however prejudice may warp our wills, or interest darken our understanding, the simple voice of nature and of reason will say, it is right."[5] The contrast between the common sense of Paine and the exclusionary nature of traditional oratory suggested diverging paths of expression and persuasion that would grow wider throughout the nineteenth century. The Revolutionary-era newspaper the *Massachusetts Spy* suggested a conscious pragmatism in the implementation of image and language: "[C]ommon sense in common language is necessary to influence one class of citizens, as much as learning and elegance of compositions are to produce an effect upon another."[6] A single oratorical or masculine model was insufficient to meet the multiplicity of tastes and demands. These evolving modes of speech represented more than purely rhetorical preferences, as Kenneth Cmiel argues in *Democratic Eloquence: The Fight for Popular Speech in Nineteenth-Century America*:

> Telling people to speak one way instead of another is a way of telling them to be a certain kind of person, of saying that certain skills and practices are valued while others are not. The nineteenth-century debate over language was a fight over what kind of personality was needed to sustain a healthy democracy.[7]

Speech determined masculine identity, status, and self-worth, and effective public speakers reflected the personality of their audiences.

As America woke from what Paine called its "unmanly slumbers" and declared its independence from the patriarchal protection and the aristocratic control of the English Crown, it boldly declared that "all men are created equal."[8] The Founding Fathers established idealistic democratic and egalitarian laws for self-government. In the wake of the American Revolution, however, both the nation and its citizens faced a crisis of identity, as the newly, and somewhat precariously, united states sought a character that was distinct from their British past and was appropriate to their singular nature. In *Letters from an American Farmer*, the French American Crèvecoeur struggled to identify this new breed: "What, then, is the American, this new man? He is neither an European nor the descendant of an European; hence that strange mixture of blood, which you will find in no other country."[9] America's "new man" faced an open horizon of possibilities—an exciting and terrifying freedom—and he would spend the next several decades simultaneously creating and rebelling against parameters of masculine identity. The country, likewise, was torn between the comfortable familiarity and the fixed hierarchical structure of an aristocratic history and the uncharted future of true democracy.

THE PRESIDENTIAL ELECTION OF 1828: A MASCULINE REVOLUTION

The War of 1812 and the "Era of Good Feelings" that followed (roughly between 1815 and 1825) revived the robust patriotism of the Revolution and masked the country's growing social, political, and sectional divisions. However, escalating tensions between and within the political parties of the 1820s, which were aggravated by the "corrupt bargain" of 1824, culminated in a drastic shift in political rhetoric before the election of 1828. The nomination of presidential candidates in 1824 was a hybrid process, using both the old caucus procedure and nomination by legislatures. The caucus, which was poorly attended and derided as undemocratic, nominated William H. Crawford, who was plagued by health problems. Neither Adams nor Jackson, the presidential front-runners, could muster an outright majority of votes, although Jackson received a higher number of electoral and popular votes.[10] The House of Representatives, voting by state, chose between the top three candidates: Adams, Jackson, and Crawford. Henry Clay, the final candidate and a distant fourth in electoral votes, was Speaker of the House and wielded much influence. Adams decisively won the House vote and, upon taking office, promptly appointed Clay Secretary of State (considered a natural stepping stone to the presidency, given that Adams, Monroe, and Madison each served in the post immediately before becoming President). Jackson's supporters excoriated the appointment as a "corrupt bargain." In 1825, mere months after Adams's inauguration, the Tennessee legislature selected Jackson as their presidential candidate for the 1828 election, and Old Hickory's political followers began his campaign three years before the next election.

The 1828 election featured sharply contrasting opponents and parties. Incumbent John Quincy Adams (1767–1848)—with his perceived aristocratic image, direct hereditary link to the nation's Founding Fathers, eloquent calls to expand the power of federal government, and neoclassical style of oratory—differed in almost every imaginable way from his opponent, Andrew Jackson (1767–1845)—with his rough-hewn image, martial heroism, impassioned demands for Democratic egalitarianism, and unpolished-yet-charismatic oratorical style. Following the federalist tenets of the American System championed by Henry Clay, Adams sought to place expansive power for social improvement in the hands of the federal government and pushed for economic expansion, protective tariffs, and the privileging of legislative power over the presidency.[11] Jackson's Democratic Party championed states' rights and sought to limit the power of the federal government while simultaneously increasing the power of the executive branch. Whereas Adams had assumed an international political role since the age of 14, Jackson presented himself as a man of the people. Although each man was far more complicated than a simple binary would suggest, political audiences perceived their behaviors and modes of communication as fundamentally opposite. As is often the case in political life, the *perception* of contrasts proves far more important than do genuine differences.[12]

John Quincy Adams presented an elegant and dignified oratorical style that was self-consciously patterned on classical Roman models.[13] His mode of speaking ultimately reinforced perceptions of a hierarchical separation that privileged the intellectual elite. Adams's oratorical philosophy, which was a descendent of eighteenth-century Federalism and was in harmony with what would become the Whigs' public agenda until the election of 1840, suggested that as the mind must govern the body's baser passions, the learned leadership of a nation must guide the commons. In *Democratic Eloquence,* Kenneth Cmiel argues the incompatibility of democracy with this rhetorical approach: "When eighteenth-century linguists located linguistic authority in the speech of gentlemen, . . . it certainly wrote off the language of at least nine tenths of the human race as 'vulgar' and not to be taken seriously."[14] This patriarchal approach to government and aloof image of privileged aristocracy combined with the failed promise of his administration and contributed to Adams's limited appeal.

Although intellectually persuasive, the perceived formality of Adams's speech was out of step with his time and often served to emotionally distance his audience: "I disclaim not one particle of what I have done; not a single word of what I have said do I unsay; nay, I am ready to do and say the same again tomorrow."[15] An image of stubborn resolve, staunch individualism, and unwillingness to compromise (both as president and later when he fought against slavery and the "gag rule" in the House of

Representatives) earned grudging admiration but also alienated many listeners and likely undermined his persuasive power. Unable to overcome widespread popular discontent with the government and lacking the support of Congress, Adams did little to strengthen his reputation or his party's position. Thurlow Weed campaigned for Adams's election and expressed disappointment at receiving no political favors in return: "Mr. Adams during his administration failed to cherish, strengthen, or even recognize the party to which he owed his election; nor, so far as I am informed, with the great power he possessed did he make a single influential friend."[16] This conception of virtuous republican leadership spoke strongly of Adams's character, but his unwillingness to play the political game hurt him. In stark contrast, Jackson's presidencies encouraged the growth of a spoils system, one that used political appointments to reward (and cultivate) loyal followers.

Political audiences made sharp distinctions between Jackson's common sense and Adams's intellectualism. The *Address of the Republican General Committee of Young Men of the City and County of New York* (1828) outlined the contrast:

> That he [Adams] is learned we are willing to admit; but his wisdom we take leave to question.... We confess our attachment to the homely doctrine...:
> That not to know of things remote
> From use, obscure and subtle, but to know
> That which before us lies in daily life,
> Is the prime wisdom.
> That wisdom we believe Gen. Jackson possesses in an eminent degree.[17]

The *New York Times* (1834) continued to praise, possibly with a hint of irony, Jackson's pragmatic intelligence well into his second term:

> He arrives at conclusions with a rapidity which proves that his process is not through the tardy avenues of syllogism, nor over the beaten track of analysis, or the hackneyed walk of logical induction. For, whilst, other minds, vigorous and cultivated, are pursuing these routes, he leaves them in the distance, and reaches his object in much less time, and with not less accuracy.[18]

A mistrust of European aristocracy and East Coast intellectualism privileged native wisdom and encouraged a rejection of education. In his address to Yale's Society of Phi Beta Kappa in 1844, Whig lawyer and politician Willis Hall declared, "The age of *philosophy* has passed.... That of *utility* has commenced."[19] Davy Crockett, the Whig equivalent of the Jacksonian hero, championed a typical pride in native intelligence and guileless masculine performance: "I had never taken any degree, and did not own to any, except a small degree of good sense not to pass for what I was not."[20] The political benefits that were derived from the performance of rustic simplicity gradually diminished, but certainly did not abate, as the problems facing the nation grew increasingly complex.

While Jackson's public image encouraged the idea of president as man of the people, his speeches typically communicated authority and paternalism: "[L]et me not only admonish you as the first magistrate of our common country, not to incur the penalty of its laws, but to use the influence that a father would over his children whom he saw rushing to certain ruin."[21] In this single sentence, Jackson blends elevated language with a domestic metaphor, deliberately illustrating the dual nature of the role he performed—both exalted leader and familiar father.[22] The increasingly egalitarian nature of society required a combination of high and low in language and decorum.[23] Jackson's everyday conversation contained elements of the rustic and the vulgar, but these elements were largely absent from his official speeches, almost all of which were penned by others. His advisors expunged from presidential speeches his most colloquial tone, perhaps in an effort to combat an illiterate image that was encouraged by his rivals. (In an 1833 diary entry, Adams referred to Jackson as "a barbarian and savage who can scarcely spell his own name."[24]) However, Jackson also exhibited the rage of a soldier when crossed, introducing a touch of melodrama—bombast that suggested a clear binary of right and wrong. In response to South Carolina's threatened nullification of federal law in 1832, Old Hickory warned: "If a single drop of blood is shed in defiance of the laws of the United States I will hang the first man I lay hands on engaged in such treasonable conduct upon the first tree I can reach."[25] Jackson spoke plainly, passionately, and often combatively in support of democratic freedoms, as was evinced by his veto of the rechartering of the Bank of the United States in 1832:

> Equality of talents, of education, or of wealth cannot be produced by human institutions. In the full enjoyment of the gifts of Heaven and the fruits of superior industry, economy, and virtue, every man is equally entitled to protection by law; but when the laws undertake to add to these natural and just advantages artificial distinctions,... to make the rich richer and the potent more powerful, the humble members of society—the farmers, mechanics, and laborers—who have neither the time nor the means of securing like favors to themselves, have a right to complain of the injustice of their government.[26]

Jackson pledged equal access to opportunity, presenting himself as a representative champion of the working-class male by curtailing preferences to the wealthy, yet he simultaneously defended social and economic inequality as natural.

The cool logic of Adams's oratory contrasted with the colloquial passion of Jackson. Adams refused to adjust his behavior to appeal to his audience, whereas Jackson manipulated his persona to match the values of a range of audiences. The Whigs remained confined to a formal image until they learned to "out-folksy" the Democrats in the 1840 election . Writing on eloquence in the 1840s, Ralph Waldo Emerson suggests a mixture of high and low, privileging the vernacular over the formal: "The orator must command the whole scale of the language, from the most elegant to the most low and vile. Every one has felt how superior in force is the language of the street to that of the academy." However, Emerson emphasizes that the power of persuasion is not limited to a technical use of language:

> That which he wishes, that which eloquence ought to reach, is not a particular skill in telling a story, or neatly summing up evidence, or arguing logically, or dexterously addressing the prejudice of the company,—no, but a taking sovereign possession of the audience. Him we call an artist who shall play on an assembly of men as a master on the keys of the piano,—who, seeing the people furious, shall soften and compose them, shall draw them, when he will, to laughter and to tears.[27]

Onstage and offstage, a stronger emotional connection to (and manipulation of) the audience, which is built on a sympathetic relationship to the performer, dictates victory for political and theatrical artists.

The 1828 election marked an abrupt shift in what had been a gradual transformation. Jackson's conspicuous performance of virility sharply contrasted with Adams's reserved manner and bearing. Adams talked the talk of an eighteenth-century gentleman whose relevance was fading, championing an elevated speech and comportment that, Cmiel argues, soon would be self-defeating: "By the mid-nineteenth century...the very decorum that 'gentlemen of the old school' saw as essential to principled behavior was viewed by large segments of the democratic republic as 'aristocratic'."[28] In contrast to these firmly entrenched traditions, Jackson was a war hero who was known for his temper and willingness to take political and personal action, which included assaulting and dueling men who insulted him. Representing both an average and an ideal, Jackson walked the walk of a self-made manhood that would dominate the second quarter of the nineteenth century, suggesting that strength of character and singular force of will were sufficient to achieve greatness. The 1828 choice between Adams and Jackson highlighted an obvious dichotomy between two distinct masculine ideals—the intellectual self-control of a restrained manhood versus the passionate action of a martial manhood—that continued to evolve and compete through the rest of the century. Jackson created a distinct style—one that ultimately made him both impossible to challenge and impossible to copy. Edwin Forrest employed a similar uniqueness that was often imitated but rarely with complete success. Rivals could ape superficial physical and vocal traits but not the passion, charisma, and (at least perceived) flashes of inspiration that attracted public devotion.

JACKSONIAN ALTERNATIVES: COMPETING MASCULINITIES OF THE GREAT TRIUMVIRATE

As the viability of Adams's masculine model faded, political performers and audiences in (political or philosophical) opposition to Jackson adjusted their behavior and expectations to find alternative manly possibilities. The Great Triumvirate of Henry Clay, Daniel Webster, and John C. Calhoun, each of whom passionately (and unsuccessfully) campaigned for president, dominated political oratory between 1812 and 1852. Each provided a persuasive masculine image, which was somewhat limited by perceptions of ambition and calculation, as well as sectional issues and perspectives. Calhoun, who campaigned for president in 1824, served as vice-president in 1824 and 1828, under both Adams and Jackson. Clay, also a nominee in the 1824 election, suffered from the taint of the "corrupt bargain" with Adams and lost to Jackson in 1832 and again to James K. Polk in 1844. Webster failed to reach the presidency three times (1836, 1848, and 1852) in elections that were won by Martin Van Buren, Zachary Taylor, and Franklin Pierce, respectively. Calhoun, Clay, and Webster all served in the House of Representatives and the United States Senate and assumed the office of Secretary of State. Although all three ultimately joined forces against the perceived tyrannies of Andrew Jackson, the triumvirate employed differing methods of achieving goals and represented a broad range of rhetorical styles, which shifted according to their strengths, personal desires, and regional demands. Although eloquently articulating devotion to the Union and fighting to avert the approaching devastation of civil conflict, each was inextricably linked with the region he represented and so ardently championed: the intellectual Calhoun with the South, the erudite Webster with New England and the East, and the charismatic Clay with the West. Each man also provided a more nuanced and elevated masculine model than did Jackson, which, in combination with perceptions of a biased sectional agenda, somewhat limited their widespread appeal. All three men died within two years of the Compromise of 1850 (determining slave status of territories acquired in the Mexican-American War and enacting a new fugitive slave law), which likely postponed but could not prevent the Civil War.[29]

"The Great Nullifier," John C. Calhoun (1782–1850) exuded an aristocratic air and employed cold logic and metaphysical reasoning:

> [T]hat power which reduces the most complex idea into its elements, which traces causes to their first principle, and, by the power of generalization and combination, unites the whole in one harmonious system...it is the highest attribute of the human mind. It is the power which raises man above the brute.[30]

Whereas Calhoun's skill in demonstrating the power of the human mind could alienate, he exhibited a passionate defense of the South—as in his response to the "Force Bill," which authorized use of federal troops to enforce tariffs in the South and purportedly provided a "measure of peace" to the sectional crisis of 1833:

> Yes, such a peace as the wolf gives to the lamb—the kite to the dove! Such peace as Russia gives to Poland, or death to its victim!...It is to South Carolina a question of self-preservation; and I proclaim it that should this bill pass, and an attempt be made to enforce it, it will be resisted at every hazard—even that of death itself. Death is not the greatest calamity: there are others still more terrible to the free and the brave, among which may be placed the loss of liberty and honour.[31]

Calhoun combined intellect and passion more effectively than did John Quincy Adams; but, like Adams, perceptions of intellectual superiority distanced listeners and drew unfavorable comparisons to Jackson's accessible "folksiness." Introducing the idea of a *concurrent majority*, Calhoun framed the sectional crisis as an issue of a minority (property-owning white Southerners) having the right to coexist independent of a majority's will. President Jackson, who supported states' rights but feared the threat of nullification (allowing an individual state to invalidate federal laws deemed unconstitutional), provided the following toast at the Jefferson Day dinner of 1830: "Our federal Union, it must be preserved." Vice President Calhoun responded: "The Union, next to our liberty, the most dear. May we all remember that it can only be preserved by respecting the rights of the States and distributing equally the benefits and burdens of the Union."[32] The inflexible position established in Jackson's concise and simple toast contrasted both in opinion and in mode of expression to Calhoun's more nuanced appeal.

Calhoun adjusted his political position on key issues, which included a change from championing a strong national government and protective tariffs to states' rights, nullification, and free trade. Rather than apologizing for slavery as a "necessary evil," Calhoun framed it as a "positive good" in an 1837 speech before the Senate, claiming that "the black race of Central Africa, from the dawn of history to the present day, [never] attained a condition so civilized and so improved, not only physically, but morally and intellectually."[33] When politically expedient, though, Calhoun moderated his proslavery stance: "I am no panegyrist of slavery. It is an unnatural state, a dark cloud which obscures half the luster of our free institutions."[34] His skill in arguing both sides of these political extremes, which was necessitated by sectional tensions, suggested political expediency. Although Calhoun fought a losing battle in his defense of slavery and the South, abolitionist congressman John Wentworth claimed, "If he could but talk with every man, he would have the whole United States on his side."[35] The austere passion of Calhoun, the era's most skilled logician, helped postpone the inevitable, violent conflict between the states. As a manly model, perceptions of intellectual superiority and calculated use of logic to privilege a sectional agenda intimidated rather than inspired, doing little to encourage a sympathetic or emotional bond with his audience.

Providing a comparatively accessible masculine image, the magnetic personality of Henry Clay (1777–1852) could influence even one Jacksonian representative, who jokingly justified his practice of avoiding sessions of the House when no voting was to take place: "I am willing to do my duty when I can, but I'm damned if I can listen to Henry Clay speak and believe he is wrong."[36] Clay's conservatism and moderation frequently allowed him to operate as a peacekeeper between various political, economic, social, and sectional tensions:

> I go for honorable compromise whenever it can be made....All legislation, all government, all society is founded upon the principle of mutual concession, politeness, comity, courtesy; upon these everything is based....Let him who elevates himself above humanity, above its weaknesses, its infirmities, its wants, its necessities, say, if he pleases, I never will compromise, but let no one who is not above the frailties of our common nature disdain compromise."[37]

Clay, "The Great Compromiser," exerted significant political influence on key issues—as a "War Hawk" encouraging America into the War of 1812, as creator of the "American System" that supported manufacturing, and as principal player in the Missouri Compromise, the nullification crisis, and the Compromise of 1850. His political skill inspired affection, but the man never garnered unqualified respect: "[T]here were thousands who voted against Clay on grounds of his moral delinquency."[38] Clay was charged—not without basis—of gambling, womanizing, and intemperance. Additionally, his role in the "corrupt bargain" that brought Adams to office forever stigmatized him as a political opportunist. Although generally well liked, Clay's perceived hypocrisy and reluctance to commit to issues ultimately suggested an improper model of masculine behavior.

Although detractors accused Clay of political opportunism, he was willing (or at least willing to threaten) to sacrifice his reputation in defense of the Union, as he sought to eliminate an 1833 tariff on South Carolina before Jackson sent troops to enforce it: "Pass this bill, tranquillize the country, restore confidence and affection in the Union, and I am willing to go home to Ashland and renounce public service forever."[39] No one demanded that Clay fulfill his heat-of-the-moment promise to leave office when the bill was passed. Clay served as a political and oratorical inspiration to a fellow Kentuckian (transplanted to Illinois), Abraham Lincoln, who called Clay, "my ideal of a great man."[40] Clay actually coined the term *self-made man* in 1832 while speaking to the Senate in defense of a protective tariff: "[A]lmost every manufactory known to me is in the hands of enterprising, self-made men, who have whatever wealth they possess by patient and diligent labor."[41] Although a pragmatic speaker who lacked substantial formal education, the slave-owning Clay comported himself like a well-bred gentleman and capitalized on his ability to persuade: "There is no power like that of oratory; Caesar controlled men by exciting their fears, Cicero by captivating their affections and swaying their passions; the influence of the one perished with its author, that of the other continues to this day."[42] However, Clay ultimately provided a manly model with too many contradictions. His geniality and magnetic personality was tempered by a calculated moderation. Whereas his background promised the accessibility of a self-made man, his elevated airs suggested pretense. Above all, his reputation for excessive self-indulgence indicated a lack of self-restraint that limited his masculine and political appeal.

Ponderous and imposing, with broad shoulders, a massive brow, and dark, deep-sunken eyes, "The Godlike Daniel" Webster (1782–1852) was an elitist and, even by the relaxed ethical standards of the time, was criticized for taking money to support a lavish lifestyle.[43] However, Webster exhibited an oratorical style that was noted for its simplicity, clarity, and noble sentiment. Nathaniel Parker Willis describes the power of Webster's deep, unaffected voice: "[W]ith no impression but the unencumbered profoundness of its truth..., as monotonous as thunder—but it is because thunder has no need to be more varied and musical, that Webster leaves the roll of his bass unplayed upon by the lightning that outstrips it."[44] Emphasizing the natural gifts of the performer and his uncalculated impact upon auditors, "unencumbered profoundness" suggests an innate sense of truth and an artless sincerity, although this image contrasted with his elitist reputation. Webster sought the presidency three times (in 1836, 1848, and 1852), turned down vice-presidential offers twice (from William Henry Harrison and Zachary Taylor—both of whom died in office), and served as Secretary of State under three presidents (Harrison, John Tyler, and Millard Fillmore).

Webster used the forcefulness of his presence and his political influence in passionate defense of the Constitution and efforts to avert civil war. In supporting the Fugitive Slave Act in 1850, an action that likely eliminated his hopes of reaching the White House, he presented the following passionate plea:

> And now, Mr. President, instead of speaking of the possibility or utility of secession, instead of dwelling in those caverns of darkness, instead of groping with those ideas so full of all that is horrid and horrible, let us come out into the light of day; let us enjoy the fresh air of Liberty and Union.[45]

Webster brilliantly employed repetition, and his skillful and persuasive oratorical strategies frequently achieved their desired effect, but Webster's craft often suggested calculation. Webster constructed great speeches with an eye toward posterity, such as his eulogy of John Adams:

> True eloquence, indeed, does not consist in speech.... It must exist in the man, in the subject, and in the occasion.... It comes, if it comes at all, like the outbreaking of a fountain from the earth, or the bursting forth of volcanic fires, with spontaneous, original, native force.... The clear conception, out running the deductions of logic, the high purpose, the firm resolve, the dauntless spirit, speaking on the tongue, beaming from the eye, informing every feature, and

urging the whole man *onward*, right ONWARD to his object,—this, this is ELOQUENCE; or rather it is something greater and higher than eloquence—it is ACTION—NOBLE, SUBLIME, GODLIKE ACTION.[46]

Eloquence, then, requires the inspiration of the right man at the right moment, as illustrated by Adams's emotional impact on Webster. Webster's style of performance—and his oratory certainly appeared as detailed, calculated, and theatrical a presentation as any given on the stage—rarely relied on spontaneous improvisation, but exuded the passionate air of immediate, creative genius. His masculine performance relied on the *illusion* of responding instantly to the unimpeded, honest promptings of the heart rather than the detached shrewdness of the brain. And awareness of this craft, coupled with his oligarchic reputation, complicated his masculine image.

Each member of the Great Triumvirate swayed his individual, regional audience but failed to reach the presidency he so ardently desired. By the middle of the nineteenth century, success in America required a flexibility of image to meet the varied demands of the full spectrum of a democratic public. The inability of all three persuasive orators to win the trust and approval of the entire country suggests that no single masculine model could possibly embody the divergent expectations of a nation that was increasingly fragmenting along sectional, social, economic, and political lines.

ABRAHAM LINCOLN: AN UNLIKELY MASCULINE MODEL

Following the Compromise of 1850, issues related to the "peculiar institution" dominated the political stage, dwarfing personalities and rhetorical skills. Positions on slavery and secession became so polarized and entrenched that oratorical powers alone could no longer postpone civil conflict. Similar tensions divided political parties as the Democrats and Whigs (and other emerging parties like the Free-Soilers) sought candidates to further delay disunion. This political chaos ultimately culminated in the election of 1860, when bickering between a hopelessly fractured Democratic party (divided between the nomination of Illinois' Stephen A. Douglas and Kansas' John C. Breckinridge) and the remnants of the Whig and Know-Nothing parties (nominating John Bell of Tennessee) virtually assured the election of the relatively unknown Republican from Illinois, Abraham Lincoln (1809–1865).

According to *U.S. Presidents as Orators,* between the administrations of Jackson and Lincoln, no American president made a lasting rhetorical impression:

> In fact, during what is generally accepted as America's 'Golden Age or Oratory' from the 1830s to the Civil War, one remembers for their oratory Senators Daniel Webster, Henry Clay, Thomas Hart Benton, and John C. Calhoun, but no U.S. president, save John Quincy Adams, Andrew Jackson, and Abraham Lincoln, comes to mind for oratorical prominence.[47]

Not until the dawn of the twentieth century, with the popular appeal of Theodore Roosevelt, does another president warrant recognition. Jackson represented something of a political and cultural aberration, which was out of place in a formerly exclusive presidential line of distinguished statesmen, and his success inspired emulation. Between the presidencies of Jackson and Lincoln, however, conservative figures assumed the presidency as the country sought to avoid conflict. Each suffered from a perceived deficiency in passionate charisma or forcefulness of character that was required to overcome the country's divisiveness. Such a swing toward the ordinary may seem puzzling. Consciously or not, these statesmen diluted the power and passion of their rhetoric to avoid controversy. Van Buren, Harrison, Tyler, Polk, Taylor, Fillmore, Pierce, and Buchanan often sought a middle ground to salve burning social and political issues and to avert disunion.[48] After Jackson, political figures and voters mutually exuded what could be described as a *fear* of charisma, finding safety in the moderate and the unexciting. In a nation already on the verge of implosion, these candidates embodied a safe masculinity, eliminating anything potentially confrontational or incendiary.

In speech, physical presence, and comportment, Lincoln failed to live up to presidential expectations. In stark contrast to the elocutionary perfection and oratorical flourishes of the era's great speakers, a high and often unpleasant tone (which an 1860 *Boston Daily Journal* described as "fifey and shrill") marked Lincoln's vocal delivery.[49] Statesman and journalist Carl Shurz characterized Lincoln as unusually tall, thin, and awkward:

> On his head he wore a somewhat battered "stovepipe" hat. His neck emerged, long and sinewy, from a white collar turned down over a thin black necktie. His lank, ungainly body was clad in a rusty black dress coat with sleeves that should have been longer...His black trousers, too, permitted a very full view of his large feet....I had seen, in Washington and in the West, several public men of rough appearance; but none whose looks seemed quite so uncouth, not to say grotesque, as Lincoln's.[50]

Figure 1.1 Andrew Jackson. The Library Company of Philadelphia.

Figure 1.2 Edwin Forrest. The Library Company of Philadelphia.

Figure 1.3 Frederick Douglass. Image courtesy of the author.

Figure 1.4 Ulysses S. Grant. The Library Company of Philadelphia.

The figures in these four masculine images share an austerity in dress, a formal and self-conscious dignity, and a sense of gravitas. The image of Jackson dates from his presidency (1829–1837). Forrest's image (1851) was disseminated shortly after his scandalous association with the Astor Place Riot and a very public divorce. The Douglass portrait was done immediately after the Civil War as African American men were attempting to establish a free masculine identity. Grant's presidential-era portrait (1869–1877) draws comparison to that of Jackson, the previous popular war hero to complete two terms in office. The striking similarity of these portraits suggests attempts, conscious or not, to capture (and capitalize on) Jackson's masculine ideal.

In the Illinois Senatorial debates with Stephen A. Douglas, Lincoln encouraged and cultivated this "grotesque" performance, heightening the sharp contrast with his more aristocratic opponent. As early as 1839, the Democratic *Illinois State Register* accused Lincoln of intentionally propagating a ridiculous image:

> Mr. Lincoln...has, however, a sort of *assumed clownishness* in his manner which does not become him. It is *assumed*—assumed for effect. Mr. L will sometimes make his language correspond with this *clownish* manner, and he can thus frequently raise a loud laugh among his Whig hearers; but this entire game of buffoonery convinces the mind of no man, and is utterly lost on the majority of his audience.[51]

Similar remarks followed him throughout his career, although both fans and detractors generally acknowledged his sincerity, even if they mocked his appearance. At a New Hampshire Republican rally in 1860, young Republican leader Edward H. Rollins found Lincoln "a unique specimen of the human family...long, lank and awkward...the real Yankee.... These oddities and peculiarities which would seem to detract from the efficiency of an orator all go to gain the sympathy of his hearers."[52] Here, "sympathy" suggests understanding rather than pity, although both responses may have occurred simultaneously. Framing Lincoln as a true "Yankee" invites comparisons to the socially awkward Jonathan character (introduced in *The Contrast*), a dramatic fixture on the American stage, who similarly spoke plainly and had no idea of what to do with his hands and feet. Even in his bid for reelection in 1864, the *Comic Monthly* derided his inelegance: "His anatomy is composed mostly of notes, and when walking he resembles the off-spring of a happy marriage between a derrick and wind-mill.... His hands and feet are plenty large enough and in society he has the air of having too many of them."[53] Yet Lincoln's unprepossessing manner masked intelligence and political acumen.

Simplicity and poetry, idealism and humility, folksy humor and compelling argument marked Lincoln's speeches. Although self-educated and of humble beginnings, Lincoln proved to be a powerful storyteller, stump speaker, and courtroom lawyer. An influential Illinois Whig until the party dissolved due to sectional tensions and divisions, he assumed a prominent role in the fledgling Republican Party. Early in his national visibility, Lincoln argued the incompatibility of slavery and democracy: "'A house divided against itself cannot stand.' I believe this government cannot endure permanently half slave and half free. I do not expect the

Union to be dissolved—I do not expect the house to fall—but I do expect it will cease to be divided. It will become all one thing or all the other."[54] In dealing with such an inflammatory subject, Lincoln sought a quality that was simple and logical but also resolute. In his first inaugural address, Lincoln's conciliatory tone absolved men of the South from responsibility for the seemingly inevitable conflict, placing blame on events and institutions rather than on individuals:

> We are not enemies, but friends. We must not be enemies. Though passion may have strained, it must not break our bonds of affection. The mystic chords of memory, stretching from every battlefield and patriot grave to every living heart and hearthstone all over this broad land, will yet swell the chorus of the Union when again touched, as surely they will be, by the better angels of our nature.[55]

In comparison to Clay's earlier quoted plea for compromise, Lincoln's straightforward brevity combined with an affecting plea communicated a similar message, but Lincoln appealed more than Clay both to logic and to emotion. Lincoln eschewed obvious and theatrical rhetorical pyrotechnics in favor of a perceived simplicity and earnestness that proved more effective. Because Lincoln's style of speech frequently defied the era's oratorical expectations, most American critics did not praise Lincoln until after sentimentalized perceptions following his assassination.[56]

Shortly after his death, the *New York Herald* (1865) made Lincoln remarkable for being unremarkable:

> He may not have been, and perhaps was not, our most perfect product in any one branch of mental or moral education, but taking him for all in all, the very noblest impulses, peculiarities and aspirations of our whole people—what may be called our continental idiosyncracies—were more collectively and vividly reproduced in his genial and yet answering nature than in that of any other public man of whom our chronicles bear record.[57]

Frequently identified as emerging from humble beginnings, Lincoln furnished urban workers with an illusory connection to frontier, log-cabin roots. Lincoln at least outwardly retained the image and behavior of a simple, honest, country man unspoiled by success—continuing to eschew the trappings of wealth or position—seemingly propelled purely by hard work and native wisdom. Relatively unknown nationally until campaigning began for the 1860 election, supporters branded Lincoln as "Rail Splitter" and "Honest Abe," framing him as a simple laborer to appeal to growing populations (and increasing votes) of the West. Of course, many in the South, including vice president of the Confederate States Alexander Hamilton Stephens, viewed Lincoln in quite a different light: "And yet, notwithstanding all these distinguishing, amiable and high qualities of his private character, he is by the general consent of mankind looked upon as the destroyer of the liberties of Rome!"[58]

Bookending this political period, Jackson and Lincoln arguably established stronger, more intimate connections with common men than any other presidents of the nineteenth century. Ultimately constructions of their respective periods and political audiences, each answered the fearful call of a desperate nation in desperate times, serving as an anchor in the uncertainty of turbulent republican seas. Jackson provided the country with a mythic yet pragmatic hero and a sense of direction as it foundered in search of national identity, reclaiming the egalitarian freedom idealistically suggested by the Founding Fathers. Jackson reigned forcefully, fiercely championing state and individual rights. Whereas both provided more accessible masculine models than most politicians of the era, Lincoln brought a persuasive, articulate intelligence to the presidency that had not been seen since Adams, while simultaneously adding vulnerability to Jackson's image of the frontier man. Rather than asserting Jacksonian authority, a role for which Lincoln was temperamentally unsuited and hardly in a position to fulfill, he exuded a comparatively sympathetic and empathetic air. Firm but humane, Lincoln led the nation through the devastation of the Civil War, a brutal military conflict far more costly than anything the martial Jackson had experienced, and ultimately provided a sacrifice in atonement for slavery's (and the nation's) offences against God and man. His resolve in committing the country to war suggests a masculine image of strength tempered by sensitivity. The log-cabin ethos of Jackson and Lincoln suggested that the advantages of a noble birth and a college education were not prerequisites to strength of character, moral fortitude, and (in conjunction with earnest devotion and self-sacrifice) lofty position. Both leaders emanated proud nobility while remaining true to the essence, or at least the perception, of their rustic and simple natures and exuding the social and intellectual accessibility of an attainable masculine model. Although not guaranteeing similar success, their accomplishments motivated American men toward seemingly attainable goals.

HENRY WARD BEECHER: A SOFTER RELIGION AND MANHOOD

While Jackson and Lincoln fought to sway votes, Henry Ward Beecher (1813–1887) sought to save souls and in the process redefined Christian citizenship as an active, vital role of masculine identity that was integrally connected to the life of the nation. Beecher was born into an important but poor family, but his preaching departed from the conservative Calvinist model of his minister father and ultimately transformed religion's role in life: "The thing the preacher aims at all the while is *reconstructed manhood*, a nobler idea in his congregation of how people ought to live and what they ought to be."[59] Beecher presented a sharp contrast to the harsh and unforgiving Puritanical history of "Angry God" and "Calvinistic Moloch" that dominated eighteenth-century religion:

> To tell me that back of Christ there is a God, who for unnumbered centuries has gone on creating men and sweeping them like dead flies—nay, like living ones—into hell, is to ask me to worship a being so much worse than the conception of any mediaeval devil as can be imagined; but I will not worship the devil, though he should come dressed in royal robes and sit on the throne of Jehovah.[60]

Jonathan Edwards (1703–1758), the most famous minister of the Great Awakening that peaked in the 1740s, represented the quintessential doctrine of punishment and retribution that dominated Puritan ideology. It provided an anchor for colonial America and demanded an inflexible moral code—with horrific, eternal damnation awaiting those who failed to live up to religious or societal expectations. After the Revolution, religion became increasingly sentimental and emotional as was reflected in the revival frenzies of the Second Great Awakening (beginning in the 1790s and continuing at least through the late 1830s). Based on personal salvation, which was coupled with social belonging, ministers transformed the mode of persuasion, as Jon Butler in *Awash in a Sea of Faith* argues, "deliberately using theatricality to promote conversion."[61] One hundred years after Edwards' death, social ostracism replaced hell's fire in incentivizing proper behavior. Religion became a refuge rather than a threat. Beecher presented a God with "the power of loving erring creatures," and rather than focusing on theological dogma, he embraced a nonsectarian freedom, tolerance, and universal salvation—the "Gospel of Love."[62]

Although he reportedly stammered as a child, Beecher possessed a rich, versatile, and melodious voice; often spoke extemporaneously, disregarding rhetorical structure or symmetry; and sympathetically responded to the needs of his audience. He thrived on his power of persuasion, referring to the orator's voice as "the bell of the soul, or the iron and crashing of the anvil. It is a magician's wand, full of incantation and witchery; or it is a scepter in a king's hand, and sways men with imperial authority."[63] Beecher effectively introduced elements of humor and illustrations from contemporary life to reinforce his message, deliberately reflecting back the values and concerns of his audience:

> If I know my own business—and the presumption is I do—it is to hunt men and to study them. Do you suppose I study old, musty books when I want to preach? *I study you!*... When I want to know what is right and what is wrong, I see how *you* do; and I have abundant illustration on every side.[64]

In sympathy with his congregation's interests, Beecher garnered respect from middle-class followers for his social activism, which included "slave auctions" to buy the freedom of escaped slaves and rifles ("Beecher's Bibles"), which were sent to Kansas to support the abolitionist cause. Beecher became a powerful spokesman for religious liberalization, moral and social reform (including women's rights and temperance), Victorian values, nationalism, and abolition. Detractors, however, found him self-serving and continually overstepping his bounds—criticisms suggesting a performance that was not wholly effective and that was unable to persuade audiences outside the reach of his church. This limitation could also suggest that his power of persuasion rested more on personal charisma than on the language employed.

A large presence ("a physique that filled the eye"), Beecher worked outdoors on his farm and exuded even temper, confidence, and "robust health."[65] In *The American Pulpit* (1856), Henry Fowler describes how Beecher capitalized on his "natural" gifts and magnetic power:

> Here gather, twice on every Sabbath of the year... about twenty-five hundred people, and the audience sometimes numbers three thousand. It is not unusual for the capacious body of the church, the broad galleries, the second elevated gallery, the several aisles, and all vacancies about pulpit and doors to be occupied by eager listeners, and sometimes hundreds turn away, unable to find footing within the audience-room. Its persistence imparts to it the dignity of a moral phenomenon. It is unprecedented in the history of audiences, whether religious, literary, political, or artistical... from two to three thousand people

centre to an unchanged attraction. No dramatic genius, no melodious voice, no popular eloquence has ever done so much as that. Neither Macready, Garrick, nor Jenny Lind, nor Rachel, nor Gough, nor Clay, nor Choate has done it. The theatre must change its "Star" monthly, the singer must migrate often, the orator must make "angel visits" to concentrate three thousand people.[66]

Imagine Fowler's amazement if he had known that this passionate following would continued unabated for another 30 years. Melding dramatic genius, melodious voice, and popular eloquence—not to mention humble economic beginnings and a nonthreatening Gospel of Love—created a seductive masculine attraction. Comparing Beecher's "star power," not only to the principal speakers of his time but also to the greatest actors, acknowledges his overpowering charisma in (and as) performance. Beecher's congregation enjoyed the dual thrill of moral uplift and theatrical titillation, minus the taint inevitably linked with the playhouse. Beecher consciously manipulated the design of Plymouth Church in Brooklyn (1849), where he served for 40 years, to maximize his power over the congregation: "I want the audience to surround me, so that they will come up on every side, and behind me, so that I shall be in the center of the crowd, and have the people surge all about me."[67] In identifying his worshippers as an audience, Beecher suggests an awareness of performance both in the style and the substance of his preaching. Not all people, of course, delighted in Beecher's powers of persuasion and the overtly performative nature of his religious character. Sinclair Lewis posthumously crowned him "a combination of St. Augustine, Barnum, and John Barrymore." Paxton Hibben, a rather critical biographer, suggested Beecher's conscious manipulation of the self: "the dramatization of Henry Ward Beecher, played by Henry Ward Beecher."[68]

The theatricalization and commodification of social improvement suggests a connection to the temperance dramas that were so popular midcentury. Dramatic, moral allegories like William H. Smith's *The Drunkard; or, The Fallen Saved* (1844) and William W. Pratt's *Ten Nights in a Barroom* (1858) presented fallen heroes who had returned to sobriety and social respectability. Smith's hero thanks the saintly temperance philanthropist who rescued him, a man not unlike Beecher: "What gratitude do I not owe this generous, noble-hearted man, who, from the depths of wretchedness and horror, has restored me to the world, to myself, and to religion."[69] In *Melodrama and the Myth of America*, Jeffrey Mason argues that these dramas blamed the dangers of temptation and largely absolved the fallen from responsibility: "To succumb to temptation was to demonstrate weakness and poor guidance rather than malice, and also to provide a model to whom the average reader or listener could easily relate."[70] William H. Smith, who was well publicized as a former drinker, originally played the title role in his drama and provided the impression that he "was playing his own life" and offering his own sin and failings as a model of masculine reformation. Furthering the connection between temperance and the theatre, John Bartholomew Gough, another actor of the Jacksonian period, also quit drinking and became a temperance lecturer.[71] Combining moral reform and capitalistic gain, P. T. Barnum's revival of *The Drunkard* in 1850—presented for a record 100 consecutive performances at his American Museum in New York— brought members of genteel society to the theatre.

Beecher's masculine image, which was calculated to inspire his audience, harmonized with evolving societal expectations. He wept for the plight of the slave, embraced the power of women (Beecher campaigned for suffrage), and openly expressed, rather than concealed, his emotions. An adultery scandal involving his friend's wife, Elizabeth Tilton, at least temporarily clouded his reputation in the 1870s. A public trial reached no verdict, but he was exonerated twice by his Plymouth Church, and he continued to enjoy a positive national reputation. If anything, the scandal added to perceptions of his already admired virility—Beecher had ten children with his loyal wife.[72] More overtly and self-consciously than did men of politics, Beecher, in concert with his congregation, both embodied the ideal and guided the behavior of middle-class men.

Although it never disappears, the elevated intellectual ideal of John Quincy Adams, which was rejected by voters in favor of Jackson's manly model, slowly returned to prominence by midcentury. Guided and validated by their audiences, the Great Triumvirate, Lincoln, and Beecher all contributed refinements to Adams's model—adding passion, humility, and sensitivity, while also incorporating elements of Jackson's "folksiness," accessibility, and pragmatic action—creating a complex, fully formed masculine ideal to rival Jackson's. America's classical actors underwent a similar journey and, in the years approaching the Civil War, Edwin Booth most successfully incorporated these disparate, sometimes contradictory elements into a consciously theatrical persona. These political, religious, and dramatic performers worked with constituents, parishioners, and audiences to construct masculine images that were in harmony with middle-class expectations.

Figure 1.5 John Quincy Adams. The Library Company of Philadelphia.

Figure 1.6 Judge Robert T. Conrad—dramatist of Edwin Forrest vehicle *Jack Cade* and Whig mayor of Philadelphia. The Library Company of Philadelphia.

Figure 1.7 "Abraham Lincoln, President of the United States, Signing the Emancipation Proclamation" (1864), engraved by John Serz after a painting by W. E. Winner. The Library Company of Philadelphia.

Figure 1.8 Henry Ward Beecher. The Library Company of Philadelphia.

Seated or reclined at a table with books, the relaxed (almost casual) ease of each masculine figure exudes a soft, cerebral refinement. While these men may also have been portrayed in portraits that were similar to those of Jackson, Forrest, Douglass, and Grant (figures 1.1–1.4), the reverse was rarely true. Refined men could tweak or strengthen their manly image by assuming an aspect of forceful command, but Jacksonian leaders were typically stuck with a single, dominant and dominating ideal. The representation of Edwin Booth as Hamlet seems to draw on a similar, although less casual, pose of intellectual repose (figure 4.2).

TEACHING MANHOOD THROUGH NINETEENTH-CENTURY ADVICE LITERATURE

I have suggested that male role models could be found both in politics and in the pulpit—but neither of those realms offered realistic guides for day-to-day conduct. Middle-class men popularized advice literature that codified parameters of manly behavior and served as manuals of social performance. America's victory in the War of 1812 brought a unifying sense of nationalism, but a changing political, economic, and geographic climate eroded social stability. With increased immigration and a rural workforce relocating to cities, urbanization reconfigured the national landscape and brought new groups of men into contact with one another. In *Melodramatic Formations,* Bruce McConachie outlines this transformation:

> Overall, the urban population of the United States increased from 7.2 percent in 1820 to 19.8 percent in 1860, with the cities of the Northeast increasing by almost twice that rate. In New York, for example—the fastest-growing city in the country—the population increased by more than half again as much during each decade from 1790 to 1860, rising from a mere 30,000 to over 800,000 by the Civil War.[73]

The young, urban male, often separated from the stability of the patriarchal home environment and no longer benefitting from the instruction of the apprenticeship system, lacked traditional masculine guidance. Biography and portraiture presented elevated, idealized masculine images, but the popularity of etiquette manuals, conduct books, and advice literature responded to a middle-class need for practical guidance.[74] Advances in printing and transportation allowed for faster and cheaper dissemination of conduct literature. On an average, over three per year were published from the late 1820s until the Civil War.[75] These guidelines for social advancement and rules of decorum served as ideological manuals of performance, providing guidance to an ambitious, uncertain, and predominantly middle-class readership. The advice proved remarkably consistent through the end of the nineteenth century, dictating similar social rules and providing a unified view of civilized behavior. Because a vast majority of nineteenth-century advice literature was gender oriented, authors of conduct manuals consciously defined American manliness and codes of behavior.[76]

Because it ostensibly lacked a hierarchy of manners, a respect for social deference, and "appropriate" models of behavior, the nation stood vulnerable to the charge, in *The American Gentleman's Guide to Politeness and Fashion* (1857), that Americans saw "Rudeness and Republicanism as synonymous terms."[77] Foreign condemnations of American behavior further fed fears of behavioral inadequacy and inferiority. Fanny Kemble's *American Journal* (1835) and Frances Trollope's *Domestic Manners of the Americans* (1832), among others, attacked Americans' lack of decorum and preposterous attempts at gentility:

> To doubt that talent and mental power of every kind, exist in America would be absurd; why should it not? But in taste and learning they are woefully deficient; and it this which renders them incapable of graduating a scale by which to measure themselves. Hence arises that overweening complacency and self-esteem, both national and individual, which at once renders them so extremely obnoxious to ridicule, and so peculiarly restive under it.[78]

Trollope's attack could well have been directed at then-President Jackson. His inaugural celebration was dominated by a mob that showed complete disregard both for the White House and for the president. This outburst revealed the potential dangers of egalitarian government and validated foreign criticisms of American manners, but it also suggested divergent masculine expectations. The public display of coarse excesses embarrassed middle-class and elite men, who were powerless to restrain or to dictate moderation to the working class. The community of men comprising Jackson's "mob" neither read nor followed the behavioral precepts of the conduct manuals, instead finding manly inspiration in popular melodrama, dime novels, and story papers.[79] The fight for dominance between these contrasting and incompatible masculinities would contribute to the tensions fueling the Astor Place Riot.

American men remained suspicious of and resistant to all forms of codified behavior and formal etiquette that seemed to advocate class separation and prejudice. *Atlantic Monthly*'s (July 1870) review of the *Bazar Book of Decorum* pragmatically articulated everything that an American man should need for success:

> All the wisdom needed for the career of the ordinary republican aspirant can be condensed into three rules which he may write down on his reversible paper cuff: 1. Keep out of fine society; 2. Be cleanly, simple, and honest; 3. Never be ashamed of a blunder. Everything beyond this is vanity.[80]

Yet the popularity of conduct manuals suggested the necessity, even if reluctantly recognized, of transforming manners and speech for social and economic success. *The Art of Good Behavior* (1846) treads carefully over issues of privilege to avoid charges of snobbery: "In this free land, there are no political distinctions, and the only social ones depend on character and manners. We have no privileged classes, no titled nobility, and everyone has the right, and should have the ambition to be a gentleman."[81] One year before this publication, the aptly named Trueman of Anna Cora Mowatt's *Fashion; or, Life in New York* (1845) similarly responded to a claim that America had no nobility:

> Stop there! I object to your use of that word. When justice is found only among lawyers—health among physicians—and patriotism among politicians, *then* may you say that there is no *nobility* where there are no titles! But we *have* kings, princes, and nobles in abundance—of *Nature's stamp,* if not of *Fashion's,*—we have honest men, warm-hearted and brave, and we have women—gentle, fair, and true, to whom no *title* could add *nobility.*

Fashion showed the etiquette book in action; advice literature and domestic melodrama used indistinguishable language to preach an identical message. In her preface to the London edition, Mowatt exposed the potential hypocrisy that was inherent in social climbing:

> The Comedy of *Fashion* was intended as a good-natured satire upon some of the follies incident to a new country, where foreign dress sometimes passes for gold, where the vanities rather than the virtues of other lands are too often imitated, and where the stamp of *fashion* gives currency even to the coinage of vice.[82]

Mowatt's play presents Americans as aware of their own social inadequacies but as simultaneously mistrustful of the maxim that manners alone make the man.

Cautioned to exhibit open, honest, republican behavior, young men were instructed to prize reputation above all else. Henry Ward Beecher cautioned, "[Y]ou should be doing a much more important thing [than the pursuit of wealth], namely, you should be gaining an inward integrity; training yourself to be a man of upright dealing, establishing a character for the strictest rectitude." However, proper behavior, far from being an end in itself, promised financial gain and social position, as *A Gentleman* (1893) reminded, "[P]oliteness is power, and...for the ambitious man there is no surer road to the highest places...than through good manners."[83] *The Young Man's Guide to True Greatness* (1858) advocated single-minded commitment to action and hard work, directly linking diligence to financial gain and elevated social position: "[W]hile idleness leads to poverty, wretchedness, and, generally to a life of immorality and licentiousness, industry leads to a rich and ample harvest, to wealth, and to an honorable and desirable position in the best classes of society."[84] *The Young Man: Hints Addressed to the Young Men of the United States* (1845) held the young man responsible not only for his own success and the unstained integrity of his character but also for the reputation and progress of the burgeoning nation:

> [Y]ou are coming forward to live and act in a nation unharnessed and free,—where the whole machinery is planned with a view to have men make their own rulers,—to make every man a lord in the sphere which he occupies.... Hence it is, that our young men are coming on the *stage of action,* in circumstances which compel them not only to look to themselves for all that they are to be... but they have to share the responsibility of the mighty destiny of at least a continent.[85]

The idea of a young man stepping onto a stage as he engages in social interactions consciously frames etiquette as a genteel performance. This common metaphor encouraged the frequent use of theatrical vocabulary to describe the preparation, setting, and presentation of proper decorum.

The Illustrated Manners Book (1855) made self-government essential to success: "The man who is liable to fits of passion; who cannot control his temper, but is subject to ungovernable excitements of any kind, is always in danger. The first element of gentlemanly dignity is self-control."[86] In addition to emotional restraint, *How to Be a Man* (1847) encouraged men to pursue physical fitness in order to "discipline the body to obey the will."[87] Advice literature called for absolute self-command and warned against the temptations and dissipations of frivolous city living, including the theatre, alcohol, and gambling. Channeling Jonathan Edwards's "Sinners in the Hands of an Angry God", even the normally forgiving Beecher impressed these desperate stakes upon his readers: "Your feet stand on slippery places, whence in due time they shall slide, if you refuse the warnings which I raise.... Too late you shall look back upon life as a MIGHTY GAME, in which you were the stake and Satan the winner."[88] Reflecting middle-class values, moral reform melodramas such as *The Drunkard* provided object lessons warning of the emasculating dangers of excess:

> Is this to be the issue of my life? Oh, must I ever yield to the fell tempter, and bending like a weak bulrush to the blast, still bow my manhood lower than the brute? Why, surely I have eyes to see, hands to work with, feet to walk, and brain

to think, yet the best gifts of Heaven I abuse, lay aside her bounties, and with my own hand, willingly put out the light of reason.... Rum! Eternal curses on you! Had it not been for your infernal poison..., I had been still a man.[89]

With the future of his country, the welfare of his family, the maintenance of his character (if not the security of his immortal soul) at stake, the middle-class man faced enormous pressure to conform and to succeed. Confined by social laws and shackled by a demand for rigid self-discipline, these high stakes exacerbated the irresolvable internal conflict between ambitious capitalism and placid egalitarianism.

Advice literature writers, such as Samuel Robert Wells in *How to Behave: A Pocket Manual of Republican Etiquette* (1856), created a system of social behavior that reflected the country's democratic equality as well as its ambition: "True republicanism requires that every man shall have an equal chance—that every man shall be free to become as unequal as he can."[90] This uneasy contradiction, this *freedom to become unequal*, reflected a democracy that supported social leveling while it simultaneously encouraged the emulation of specific masculine ideals to achieve greatness. Karen Halttunen argues that American men, who were simultaneously trapped and liberated by the republican nature of democracy, fiercely defended their rights of equality to other men while resenting the confines of identification as a member of the common rank: "Because he lived suspended between the facts of his present social condition and the promise of his future, because he held a vertical vision of life in an allegedly fluid and boundless social system, he was plagued with anxiety concerning his social identity."[91] This contrast between men's subjective experience and the pervasive ideologies surrounding them created crises of masculinity. Jackson's political triumph promised potential success for the self-made man; however, as Tocqueville recognized, America's democratic system, which provided "general equality of condition among the people," never could guarantee equality of success:

> [W]hen men are nearly alike and all follow the same track, it is very difficult for any one individual to walk quickly and cleave a way through the dense throng that surrounds and presses on him.... They can never attain as much as they desire. It perpetually retires from before them, yet without hiding itself from their sight, and in retiring draws them on. At every moment they think they are about to grasp it; it escapes at every moment from their hold.[92]

The dangling carrot of success demanded a desperate, unending race on a treadmill, and the writers of conduct literature promised success to those who followed their precepts.

While condemning the pretensions, privileges, and perceived insincerities of a European inherited aristocracy, *Hints on Etiquette and the Usages of Society* (1844) reinforced class hierarchies built on a society that necessarily excluded the unsuccessful:

> Etiquette is the barrier which society draws around itself as a protection against offenses the 'law' can not touch—it is a shield against the intrusion of the impertinent, the improper, and the vulgar—a guard against those obtuse persons who, having neither talent nor delicacy, would be continually thrusting themselves into the society of men to whom their presence might (from the difference of feeling and habit) be offensive, and even insupportable.[93]

The brutal honesty of this social stratification plainly labeled an inferior class of people. *Social Etiquette of New York* (1887) similarly proffered proper behavior as protection from the unworthy: "It is like a wall built up around us to protect us from disagreeable, underbred people who refuse to take the trouble to be civil."[94] Equal access to proper social behavior represented both an advantage and a drawback to advice manuals. Any man could transform behavior to better himself, but conduct literature also educated those for whom gentlemanly behavior was not a natural gift, revealing coded language that allowed strangers into the inner circle. The genteel performance of model behavior could easily be counterfeited, and motivations of men, mostly strangers, in the impersonal metropolis were indecipherable.

Fashion's Trueman stated, "When you open your lips let your heart speak. Never tell a lie! Let your face be the looking-glass of your soul—your heart its clock—while your tongue rings the hours!"[95] Conduct manuals, however, sought an acceptable balance between transparent, natural, and sincere behavior and a self-conscious, Chesterfieldian series of specific, yet arbitrary, social conventions. Defending their precepts as natural and scientific, authors of works such as *The Illustrated Manners Book* instilled a fear of social and moral ostracism if the principles of conduct were violated: "[E]very genuine and valuable rule of behavior may be referred to some principle of natural law; so the observance of what may seem at first glance a matter of trifling etiquette, may be a moral duty; and a breach of decorum a crime."[96] *American Gentleman's Guide* encouraged cultivated behavior with "no stage effect."[97] But while "stage effect" was to be avoided at all costs, no one denied that the performance was taking place. A man just could not be caught acting. The ideal performance of gentility and masculinity became the "invisible" one, performed so seamlessly that audiences remained unaware that they observed (and interacted with) an actor, rather than a genuine human being. Consciously cultivating the appearance of natural spontaneity remained the goal of masculine performance on both sides of the curtain. The self-conscious theatricalization of an American male—and the ways in which he performed and perceived the inextricable nature of his nationality and gender—establishes a context in which to understand the performance of masculinity on the American stage. The following chapters examine male identity in the plays performed, the nation's principal actors, and manly performances in both the public and private sphere. The popularity of these actors with various audiences reflected mutual constructions of manhood, ultimately revealing a further splintering of American manliness and the ways in which men of the theatre navigated these treacherous masculine shoals.

2. "A Glorious Image of Unperverted Manhood": Edwin Forrest as Masculine Ideal

> *In the four quarters of the globe, who reads an American book? Or goes to an American play?.... [Where are] their Siddonses, Kembles, Keans, or O'Neills?*[1]
>
> Sidney Smith, 1820

In response to Sydney Smith's oft-quoted attack on American culture, when Edwin Forrest debuted in Boston seven years later, the *New England Galaxy* enthused, "[C]ertainly the gentleman, whose name appears at the head of this article [E. Forrest], gives glorious promise of a splendid career, and justifies the hope of saying—Here! when asked, 'Where is our Kemble?'"[2] In this chapter I examine the fulfillment of that promise, as well as Forrest's carefully constructed masculine image. Forrest literally and figuratively dominated the antebellum American stage. Although criticized for lack of subtlety and emotional dimension, no actor matched his physical stature, vocal power, and muscular passion. As an embodiment of self-made manhood, he inspired working-class male audiences, providing a theatrical equivalent of the Jacksonian model. Stigmatized by his role in the tensions leading up to the Astor Place Riot, as well as by a high-profile divorce, Forrest repelled the image-conscious middle class and elite. In his playwriting competitions, Forrest found dramatic vehicles that celebrated and propagated his masculine image. A close examination of the changes that he dictated in Robert T. Conrad's *Jack Cade* suggests Forrest's conscious construction and performance of manliness.

Born in Philadelphia, the birthplace of American democracy, just 30 years after the Declaration of Independence, Edwin Forrest represented the public, theatrical fulfillment of self-made manhood. Son to a Scotch immigrant father and second-generation American mother of German descent, Edwin Forrest came from an urban, working-class home. His father worked as a street peddler but after marriage took a subordinate position in a bank. While not impoverished, the family struggled financially. His father's ongoing illness and eventual death from consumption, coupled with an economic depression, forced Edwin to end his formal schooling at the age of 13 to help support his family. Before fully committing to his destiny as an actor, Forrest took his first job as a print shop apprentice for the *Aurora,* one of Philadelphia's leading anti-Federalist periodicals, which may have inspired his political passion for the Jacksonian Democrats. In later years, papers such as Boston's *Daily Bee* (1856) exaggerated and romanticized Forrest's poverty (even more than his idol Andrew Jackson's): "From the humblest beginnings, and through more of discouragement and opposition than most men have been called to encounter, he has steadily climbed to the highest pinnacle of histrionic distinction and excellence."[3] The *Dayton Journal* (1865) presented Forrest's triumph over humble beginnings as an inspiration, which provided a role model for the similarly disadvantaged: "His success is indeed an incentive to the young men of the country who are struggling with adverse circumstances—and is typical of our free, go-ahead and 'universal Yankee nation.'"[4] The reassurance and inspiration that Jackson provided from a political platform, Forrest offered from a theatrical one. As articulated by Forrest's hand-picked biographer, "He [Forrest] loved to stand out in some commanding form of virtue, heroism, or struggle, battling with trials that would appall common souls, setting a good example, and evoking enthusiasm."[5] Published five years after Forrest's death in 1872, his authorized biography, initially credited solely to Unitarian Reverend William Rounseville Alger, was actually cowritten with his younger cousin, Horatio. Horatio Alger, Jr. most famously penned boys' stories such as *Ragged Dick; or, Street Life in New York with the Boot Blacks* (1867), which featured rags-to-riches accounts of impoverished young men who, through hard work and determination, rise to respectability.[6] Because of the overwhelming popularity of dime novel fiction and biographies, Forrest's chroniclers (and Forrest himself) constructed a similar narrative.

An early biography, published when the actor was only 31, prioritized wealth over artistry in describing Forrest's early theatrical pursuits: "His early days of adversity taught him the value of money, and his first ambition, after gaining an honorable name, was to acquire wealth."[7] Whether fact, fiction, or something in between, Forrest performed a legacy of a poor boy achieving greatness and affluence through a singular force of will: "That great artist ... was once a poor boy—a very poor and unknown boy—with scarcely a friend to say 'God speed you.' But he knew that industry and perseverance would help him onward to wealth and fame."[8] The speaker, supposedly a worker on Forrest's Fonthill Castle, praised the tragedian at the "roofing ceremony." Forrest's valorization of simple yeoman virtues contrasted visibly with his consuming drive for public acclaim, monetary gain, and social prestige. Like Jackson, Forrest pursued and embodied both democratic and aristocratic ideals. Normally clothed in a plain black frock coat, Forrest cultivated and consciously performed an image of austere, accessible simplicity, which was praised in John Carboy's biographical sketch: "He was of the people, and with the people. The arrangement of his carelessly tied neck-tie, the broad collar, and wide black ribbon to which his watch was attached, were democratic—plain and indicative of the man's disposition. He was in no sense of the word a 'society' man."[9] This costume ill-suited a man capable of "extravagant narcissism," in the words of biographer Richard Moody, in paying $10,000 for a statue of himself as Coriolanus.[10] The eleven-foot, three-ton marble statue by Thomas Ball, completed in 1867, stood for many years in the lobby of the Forrest Home for "decayed" actors and currently looms over the lobby of the Walnut Street Theatre in Philadelphia. Although he condemned the oppressive greed of aristocratic excess, Forrest built Fonthill Castle, named after the gothic Fonthill Abbey of eccentric novelist William Beckford (reportedly the richest commoner in England), on the banks of the Hudson for his bride.[11] Forrest claimed, "In erecting this edifice I am impelled by no vain desire to occupy a grand mansion for the gratification of self love." He intended, after his death, "that a certain number of decayed or superannuated actors and actresses of American birth (all foreigners to be strictly excluded) may inhabit the mansion."[12] The Forrests never actually lived in the castle, separating before its completion, though Forrest did stay briefly in the gardener's cottage.

The Edwin Forrest-Catherine Sinclair divorce case, still the longest case to have been tried before the New York State Supreme Court, was one of the most sensational and scandalous events in the country, with each estranged partner accusing the other of repeated adultery.[13] Likely exacerbated by the tensions between Forrest and Englishman William Charles Macready that culminated in the Astor Place Riot, Forrest's reserved and reclusive manner became incompatible with the social ambitions and vivacity of the Englishwoman, Catherine Norton Sinclair, who held moderately progressive views on a woman's role in marriage. Forrest caned an ill N. P. Willis, noted journalist and accused lover of his estranged wife, for writing a series of articles that criticized Forrest for the marital problems and accused him of social pretension in marrying Catherine Sinclair.

Charles O'Conor, who would go on to defend Jefferson Davis following the Civil War, represented Sinclair. Forrest was represented by John Van Buren, former attorney general of New York and son of President Martin Van Buren. Forrest lost the case but appealed at various levels for the next 18 years before finally conceding defeat. Driven largely by financial necessity, Sinclair became an actress and a theatre manager, helping start the career of young Edwin Booth and achieving moderate success primarily due to her cause célèbre. I will explore further hints of Forrest's attitude toward strong women in his adaptation of *Jack Cade*. Ironically, the castle that Forrest built to house his princess became a haven for the cultivation of women. Subsequently sold to the Sisters of Charity of New York as a convent (which likely appealed to Forrest's expectations of proper female education), the sisters eventually made Fonthill part of the College of Mount Saint Vincent, a school for women, where today it houses the offices of admissions and financial aid.

Forrest amassed enormous wealth but loudly maintained a persistent distrust and contempt for high society throughout his nearly 50-year career. In his obituary, *Forney's Weekly Press* (1872) praised his lifelong loyalty to his working-class roots: "[He] never courted popularity; he never flattered power. Importuned a thousand times to enter society, he rather avoided it."[14] Shortly after his less-than-successful final theatrical tour of London, *The United States Magazine and Democratic Review* (1846) framed Forrest's return to America as an act of triumph rather than as one of defeat: "Mr. Forrest would at any time be more flattered by the honest yell of a 'Bowery b'hoy,' than the approving smirk of England's proudest duke."[15] His vociferous, public condemnation of privileged society endeared him to young, white, working-class male audiences. Forrest's dislike of cultured crowds at least partially resulted from his insecurity and unease in their presence and his thinly masked jealousy of, and desire to be embraced by, the elite. Biographer Montrose Moses, who was born six years after Forrest died, saw the actor's brusque confidence as a mask: "He was always posing, always striking attitudes, always trying his powers...always storing away bits of knowledge in the belief they would give him the culture and refinement he never quite grasped or made his own."[16] Reflecting the anxiety that American men experienced in searching for reassuring masculine models, Forrest doggedly attached himself to a clearly defined, albeit illusory and self-constructed, American manhood.

Forrest's stoic image was enhanced by his overpowering size and the strength of his voice and body (similar to the dominating presences of Daniel Webster and Henry Ward Beecher), which provided Forrest's most striking qualities as an actor and a man. In *Lippincott's Magazine,* John Foster Kirk presents Forrest's stature as if it were an unfair advantage: "[I]t would have seemed ridiculous that he should be cast for any parts except the greatest: the other actors, even those who were taller, looked insignificant beside him, and their voices, when strongest, seemed thin, and...juiceless, in the comparison."[17] The dancer Fanny Elssler described Forrest as "a fit representative of those classic heroes of antiquity, whose splendid *physique* throws the more effeminate figure of our day into ludicrous contrast."[18] Just as the flowery speech of foppish aristocrats was condemned in the political world of plain-spoken Jacksonian democracy, so also physical appearance acted as a gauge of masculine worth. Reportedly a thin and sickly child, Forrest refashioned his physique through physical training and a strict health regimen. The well-publicized image of self-disciplined and self-made manhood showed Forrest literally constructing his body as well as figuratively building a successful career from humble beginnings. His vocal power matched his physical presence. Although condemned by detractors such as journalist Charles Congdon as a "bovine bellower," Philadelphia's *The Age* applauded Forrest's (like Beecher's) great vocal range and expression:

> His voice is full, round and sonorous, and capable of expressing all the tones by which the passions and emotions of the heart and mind are shown to the world. It can hurl defiance at the tyrant and wrong-doer, plead in tones of tenderness for the weak and erring, and pour into the ear of beauty those dulcet strains which make earth a paradise and bring back Eden times to a cold, heartless world.[19]

Although he may indeed have possessed this range, in her brief biographical article, Lisle Lester (whom Mark Twain called "probably the worst writer in the world") correctly identifies Forrest's fame and popularity as stemming from far less subtle use of his instrument: "[H]e was making the wings tremble and shaking the dust from the flies overhead."[20]

According to New York's *Sunday Times* (1860), Forrest's almost inhuman power made him the perfect personification of the conquering barbarian rebel, while his grand and tragic stature matched the Founding Fathers' desire to recreate classical ideals:

> Standing before them in his colossal strength of form, his chiseled and massive features the indices of an iron will, he seems the type of that American man before whose indomitable energy the wilderness of the New World has receded, and from whom have come a race of giants always rushing forward to

conquests over the physical and moral world. The moment the eye rests on him the mind accepts him, by instinct, as embodying visibly those ideas of strength and grandeur out of which the fables of antiquity shaped the stories of Theseus or of Hercules, and which inspired the Grecian chisel to express in the poetry of marble the form of demi-god and hero.[21]

This mythic image, which simultaneously presented Forrest as unbridled frontier conqueror and exalted god, may explain his *initial* appeal across class lines, as a range of urban audience members perceived their respective ideals in Forrest's stature and strength. Whereas this description explains an audience's admiration for and emulation of Forrest, it also presents an unattainable model—a man destined not to be one of the democratic crowd but to lead it. Forrest's awesome physical presence and the overpowering dynamism of his stage persona combined to create an idealized model of American masculinity:

> [W]hat a glorious image of unperverted manhood, of personified health and strength and beauty, he presented!....As he stepped upon the stage in his naked fighting-trim, his muscular coating unified all over him and quivering with vital power, his skin polished by exercise and friction to a smooth and marble hardness, conscious of his enormous potency, fearless of anything on the earth, proudly aware of the impression he knew his mere appearance, backed by his fame, would make on the audience who impatiently awaited him,—he used to stand and receive the long, tumultuous cheering that greeted him, as immovable as a planted statue of Hercules. In the rank and state of his physical organism and its feelings he had the superiority of a god over common men.[22]

Alger's sensual language, which bordered on the pornographic, suggested that Forrest added an overtly physical and sexual component to the Jacksonian masculine model that was conspicuously absent from previously discussed manly examples, and this potential for unbridled sexuality may have been a part of what scared away (at least on a subliminal level) some members of Forrest's upper-class audience.

The *New York World* (1862) suggested that his combination of power and passion achieved a superhuman level of emotional expression: "His are the rage, the grief, the despair of an Hercules or an Achilles."[23] As Forrest gave free rein to passionate impulses on stage, so in life he appeared ungovernable, incapable of self-restraint, and unable to forgive or forget a perceived slight and demanded public vindication. In the eyes of middle-class viewers and the etiquette books they read, Forrest's inability to control his temper amounted to a masculine flaw. In his youth he had trained in the "manly art" of boxing, and he remained a fighter in every aspect of his life. He sued for divorce, lost, and continued (vocally and legally) to contest the decision for 18 years; he publicly beat a man for criticizing him in the newspaper; he sued a newspaper for defamation of artistic character; he aggressively protected his questionable legal ownership of his contest plays; and he (at least indirectly) caused the biggest theatrical riot in the country's history. Biographer Richard Moody described Forrest's iron resolve as "a pathological inability to accept defeat."[24] At least by middle-class standards, Forrest's masculine performance went too far and so ultimately proved less effective or less *manly* that it originally might have appeared. A range of audiences applauded Forrest's fighting spirit on stage through the 1830s and 40s, but by the time of his public battles in the 1850s and 60s, much of the country's middle-class population embraced a more genteel societal norm and began searching for less violent, more sensitive models.

Forrest's biographies and a vast majority of his favorable contemporary press lionize him and describe him in remarkably similar terms. Such an overwhelming amount of rhetoric about Forrest's manliness exists that it is easy to take this trait for granted without interrogating *why* it was so important for his contemporaries to distinguish him in that way. His masculine performance onstage and offstage, which was clearly inspired by Andrew Jackson's ethos, suggests a static, codependent relationship with working-class male audiences. As urban theatres began to cater to this clientele, Forrest introduced an ideal that departed from the elevated British model—an ideal at once seemingly accessible and tantalizing unattainable. These audiences valorized his muscular simplicity, making it unnecessary and undesirable for him to refine his craft and persona.

"THE HEART OF THE MASSES": A MUSCULAR PERFORMER AS WORKING-CLASS CHAMPION

Even in his earliest amateur performances, Colonel John Swift (later the mayor of Philadelphia) recognized in the 11-year-old Forrest "the germ of tragic greatness."[25] The promise of this "germ," which was fulfilled in Forrest's eventual stage dominance, also ushered in a uniquely American performance aesthetic that built on existing, dominant acting styles. The *New York Mirror* (1826) immediately recognized Forrest's successful debut—one that exhibited "rapid advancement...towards professional eminence" as an Othello who was "superior to any in this country except Kean's"—as a future hallmark of American acting.[26] Charles Durang, who witnessed this debut, enthused, "Forrest came upon us with all the *genius*—the *spirit* and *power* of the great Edmund Kean. He *came*—we *saw*—and he *conquered!*"[27] While certainly not the first American actor to be compared favorably to a British star, an early biographer saw Forrest's meteoric rise to stardom as legitimizing American theatre:

> Before Mr. Forrest's success, the poor American who dared attempt to tread the boards, was pressed down as an object of pity and contempt, by the haughty English manager, and insolent player, who dreaded a rival talent. But Forrest came like a blazing meteor, and proved to the United States, that genius was as powerful here, as on the other side of the Atlantic.[28]

The fortuitous timing of his emergence as the "first" great American actor followed the War of 1812, when the nation had once and for all shaken off the British yoke. Although the effusion likely was overblown, and his acting style may not have been the original creation that it was often held to be, Forrest did present a grand and tragic figure to rival his European counterparts.

Although often credited as the founder of an original American acting school, Forrest's acting (like that of many of his contemporaries) largely relied on direct observation of the great actors of his time. The two primary acting approaches of the period, which were embodied in the stately elocution and intellectualism of John Philip Kemble (1757–1823) and the unpredictable and fiery passion of Edmund Kean (1787–1833), influenced Forrest's performance. Inspired early in his career by Kemble disciple Thomas Abthorpe Cooper (1776–1849), Forrest maintained elements of the intelligence, dignity, and clarity of the "classical" school throughout his career. Ultimately, however, Forrest shared the stage with Kean and more fully embraced the sensationalism, unpredictability, and wild extremes of the "romantic" school. Although not a perfect correlation, the differences and tensions between these two approaches to acting in many ways mirrored the disparity of masculine images represented by John Quincy Adams and Andrew Jackson in the political world.

Whereas Forrest was the most acclaimed and successful American proponent of the heroic and fiery romantic school, he was not alone. Many muscular rivals and imitators similarly relied on passionate outbursts and moments of dramatic inspiration. Not coincidentally, these actors predominantly played to popular audiences in working-class theatres. Embodying the extremes of romantic expression, the lives and careers of several successful adherents of Forrest's passionate acting school (including Augustus A. Addams, David Ingersoll, Charles Eaton, J. Hudson Kirby, and, most infamously, John Wilkes Booth) ended at moments of peak popularity before the age of 30. Unable to modulate the intensity of their offstage lives, or drunk on the fervent worship of their supporters, these young men ultimately destroyed themselves. Their figurative immolation illustrated the danger, if not the impossibility, of realizing Forrest's unattainable ideal. These actors exuded a Byronic image of romanticism, melancholy, and melodramatic energy—presenting troubling masculine images that were in many ways similar to the self-destructive, romantic British stars who dominated the first half of the century: George Frederick Cooke, Edmund Kean, and Junius Brutus Booth. Theatres and audiences in antebellum America tended to attract a certain type of rowdy young man in desperate need of adulation. These American performers lived an extreme life and died young, embodying the lessons that Beecher and the etiquette manuals warned would lead to despair and degradation. They provided quintessentially American examples of the young man squandering his considerable gifts and represented the ultimate fear of the young republic—that it would have one or two glorious moments, then self-destruct. Forrest provided a complex and often contradictory masculine image. In life, he consciously cultivated an image of simple austerity that was jarringly marred by tantrums. His onstage acting style similarly married a sentimental majesty with a raging passion that astounded audiences, at least in part, because of its incongruity.

Forrest's theatrical training was eclectic, lacking a lengthy or extensive apprenticeship, and unlike many famous actors of the period, he did not come from a theatrical family. Early appearances on stage seem prompted by a desire to be noticed, and this need for attention followed Forrest throughout his career. Forrest did receive some formal training in elocution from Lemuel G. White, provided by his father, and he continued training himself in this area for many years.[29] Forrest's father died when Edwin was 13, and the family (6 children in all) was frequently described as financially insolvent. Either the family made significant sacrifice to provide Edwin with this experience, or their poverty was exaggerated.[30] Similar to Beecher's impulse to study his audience and to base his performances on observations of their behaviors, Forrest also incorporated observations from life into his acting. A teenage Forrest reportedly spent several months with the Choctaw Indian tribe during a period of depression, theatrical frustration, and financial need, developing a friendship with Chief Push-ma-ta-ha. He later supposedly used his experiences on stage in *Metamora* to great effect. His lifelong obsession with *King Lear* led him to asylums to study the mentally ill, and his portrayal of the character proved to be one of his most effective.[31]

Forrest's first significant performance experience was in the theatres of the West, where strong gesture and bold interpretation held the attention of comparatively less experienced and sophisticated audiences. James Murdoch (1811–1893), a prominent acting contemporary, idealized Forrest's rustic artistic beginnings: "The acting of Forrest was natural, impulsive and ardent, because he was not so well trained as his English rivals in what may be termed a false refinement."[32] Forrest's comparative lack of training and etiquette, considered a virtue by another fellow actor, Joe Cowell, drew attention to his "natural" talents and abilities: "He possessed a fine, untaught face, and good, manly figure, and, though unpolished in his deportment, his manners were frank and honest, and his uncultivated taste, speaking the language of truth and Nature, could be readily understood."[33] The natural quality Forrest brought to his stage speech and performance emerged from, or at least coevolved with, changing styles of public speaking and performances of masculinity, as the relatively detached intellectualism of John Quincy Adams gave way to the less polished and more impassioned exhortations of Henry Ward Beecher. Devotees—such as actor-friend Gabriel Harrison, who claimed to have watched Forrest over 400 times—praised his acting as startlingly lifelike and passionately defended the magnitude and power of Forrest's dramatic incarnations against charges of melodramatic excess:

> Are the wonderful figures of Michael Angelo [sic] melodramatic because they are so strongly outlined? Is Niagara unnatural and full of trick because it is mighty and thunders so in its fall?.... Whenever I saw him act I used to feel with exultation how perfectly grand God had made him. How grand a form! how grand a mind! how grand a heart! how grand a voice! how grand a flood of passion, sweeping all these to their mark in perfect unison![34]

New York's *Albion* (1848) praised Forrest as a larger-than-life masculine ideal and a shining example of the vigorous republic:

> The *masses are with him;* and if acting, as an art, is supposed to be an exponent of nature, Mr. Forrest, in thus conciliating the suffrages of the million, must have touched the chords which vibrate in the breasts of men as a body, or he could not obtain that supremacy over the feelings of his auditors he has so long and so triumphantly exercised.[35]

Figure 2.1 Edwin Forrest as Spartacus in *The Gladiator*. The Library Company of Philadelphia.

Figure 2.2 Cartoon of Edwin Forrest as Spartacus in *The Gladiator*. Image courtesy of the author.

Differing images of Forrest as Spartacus reveal a radical contrast in perception. Figure 2.1 grants the virile Forrest a muscular dignity, whereas figure 2.2 ridicules his oversized physicality and emotional expression

Whereas Forrest possibly represented something natural, it was a grand and supreme nature—elevated far above the admiring masses. Lisle Lester, looking back on his career, claimed, "Edwin Forrest possessed more animal magnetism than has ever been seen or utilized before or since upon the American stage."[36] While the level of magnetism Forrest exuded compared to Beecher's, the minister's was spiritual rather than animalistic.

No one denied the grandness of the scale, but detractors of Forrest's muscular and bombastic style, of course, saw little of nature or originality in his work:

> The sum of criticism upon it [Forrest's performance] seems to be that the acting is a boundless exaggeration of all the traditional conventions of the stage.... You have seen and heard exactly the same thing a hundred times, with more or less excellence.... The life of "the stage" was never more adequately depicted. It is the sock-and-buskin view of nature and emotion. And it has a palpable physical effect.

The *Harper's* editor, catering to the genteel, middle-class reader, wrote in 1863—admittedly well after Forrest's professional zenith and long past the time when Forrest's artistic "innovations" had been institutionalized: "To criticise it as acting is...useless.... That human beings, under any conceivable circumstances, should ever talk or act as they are represented in the Forrest drama...is beyond belief."[37] Near the height of the tensions with William Charles Macready that would soon culminate in the Astor Place Riot, New York's *Courier and Enquirer* (1847), an anti-Democratic paper that criticized Forrest throughout his career, castigated "his whole style rough, unrefined, heavy, and laborious. His gentlemen are not such as Shakespeare drew; they are great roaring boys that cry like fat babies, and puff and blow like sledge men."[38] But even relatively early in his career, the *Knickerbocker Magazine* (1837), appealing to intellectual elite, attacked Forrest's attempts at Shakespearean originality, mocked his intellectual justifications for a non-traditionally jocular Richard III, and dismissed his performance as "a sort of artificial thunder, without the lightning."[39] Even Alger, the most positive of Forrest's biographers, acknowledged two major faults in Forrest's acting: an "excess...of physical and spiritual force in the expression of...destructive passion" and a "lack of *souplesse*, physical and spiritual mobility." Alger however staunchly defended "the honest massiveness and glow of his delineations...by a studious and manly art unmarred with any insincere trickery."[40]

Forrest quickly earned his theatrical reputation by enacting the major, serious Shakespearean roles (Othello, Macbeth, Richard III, Lear, Hamlet, Coriolanus) and the heroes of a handful of contemporary English dramas

(Richelieu, Virginius, Damon, William Tell) that served as the standard test for any young actor of the period. Forrest never played lovers or comic roles, consciously and exclusively seeking tragic characters that reflected his strength and stature. While many actors after the era of Edmund Kean prided themselves on their ability to lose themselves within a role, Forrest was always unmistakably visible as Forrest. He maintained what Philadelphia's *The Age* (1872) called a "vitalized individuality" that no character or costume could hide or diminish.[41] Lawrence Barrett, one of the most famous classical actors of the mid-nineteenth century, condemned Forrest's inability or unwillingness to submerge himself into a character: "He [Forrest] was in all things marked and distinctive. His obtrusive personality often destroyed the harmony of the portrait he was painting."[42] John Foster Kirk, another acting contemporary, suggested that Forrest unsuccessfully sought identification in his characters: "[N]ot only did he not seem to lose his own individuality, but he did not seem to find it in that of any personage that he represented."[43] In his recognizability, Forrest very much resembled great orators of the day, such as Beecher and Webster. People often came to hear them talk because of who they were, how they spoke, and what they represented, regardless of the topic. Although Forrest primarily appealed to lower-class audiences, his stature and performance characteristics resembled those of Webster and Beecher, which suggested that similar masculine models existed on the stage, on the political platform, and in the pulpit. While impossible to determine who was borrowing from whom, these similarities suggest a consistency in how certain behaviors and characteristics engendered an ideal form of masculinity, even if they differed in the medium and context of their articulation.

Throughout his career, Forrest exerted substantial political influence over predominantly working-class audiences and provided a theatrical template of the ideal Jacksonian male. A friend and fan of Andrew Jackson, Forrest actively campaigned for him and others of his party throughout his life. Forrest spoke at a national convention for Jackson's successor, Martin Van Buren, and even received an offer from the New York Democratic Republican Nominating Committee to run for state representative. Although flattered by the offer, Forrest confined his leadership to the less overtly political realm of the American stage. As late as 1860, after one of several retirement announcements, he was mentioned as a viable presidential candidate.[44] Forrest's political views echoed Jackson's, and he championed a system that provided freedom of opportunity, which allowed him to prosper. Forrest posited a survival of the fittest in his "Oration Delivered at the Democratic Republican Celebration, Fourth of July, 1838," a speech likely written by friend William Leggett: "[S]trength must ever have an advantage over weakness." Forrest went on to identify his most important guiding political watchword, simplicity, as "the invariable characteristic of truth.... The grand elementary principles of whatever is most valuable to man are distinguished by simplicity."[45] Echoing the uncomplicated nature of Jackson's oratory, simplicity also guided Forrest's acting style, flattening emotional dimension within some roles in pursuit of strong, clear, unwavering interpretations. Although critics attacked this approach as reductive and unsophisticated, Forrest's vigor and passion balanced the simplicity of his portrayals, which may explain why imitators so often failed.

Forrest's image, onstage and offstage, often collided with the restrained and regulated ideals of genteel masculinity that were suggested by advice literature, and elite critics rejected Forrest as an inappropriate masculine model as early as the 1830s. Increasingly conservative and genteel middle-class audiences, according to Alger, deplored Forrest's vulgar display of muscularity: "[B]y the standards of a squeamish politeness it [the superlative development of physical beauty] is considered something low and coarse."[46] Guided by conduct manuals, the emerging middle classes placed an increasing premium on social anonymity (as *The Young Lady's Friend* [1837] cautioned, "singularity is to be avoided"), and Forrest's massive, thunderous stage presence offended delicate sensibilities.[47] Although Forrest harbored a desire for widespread social acceptance and celebrity, the very nature of his success in personal and professional life depended on glittering personality and passionate, emotional, uninhibited expression. The mutual attraction between Forrest and his working-class audience hinged on the actor's temperament and acting style, and the stronger this attraction, the more elevated audiences kept at a distance.

According to New York's *Albion* (1848), Forrest's emotional connection to, and identification with, working-class Americans earned their vociferous adulation:

> [H]e stands forth as the very embodiment... of *the masses* of American character. Hence his peculiarities. Hence his amazing success. And further, Mr. Forrest in his acting is not merely the embodiment of national character, but he is the beau ideal of a peculiar phase of that character—its *democratic idiosyncrasies*.... Mr. Forrest has got the heart, nay, the "very heart of hearts," of *the masses*, however he may have failed to conciliate the full approbation of the strictly critical and the fastidious.[48]

Extending beyond personal identification, Boston's *Daily Bee* (1856) lauded Forrest as a fearless champion and representative of his nation: "As an American by birth and sympathy, trained in an exclusively American school, we are proud of Mr. Forrest as an index of American progress, and an illustration of what American genius may accomplish in one of the highest, purest, and noblest fields of art."[49] Forrest passionately defended his country and himself, which, in the minds of Forrest and his fans, were often interchangeable. As the *United States Magazine and Democratic Review* (1845) noted, "We take interest in Mr. Forrest because we see in him, elemental qualities, characteristic of the country; and we feel therefore any slight put upon him, is in its essence, a wound directed at the country itself."[50] The passion of this connection, combined with the class divisions that generally separated Forrest's supporters from his detractors, eventually contributed to the tragedy of the Astor Place Riot. Forrest especially dominated and inspired his audience in the prize-winning plays that championed Jacksonian rebellion and freedoms, in which the *Philadelphia Press* (1861) claimed, "[H]e uttered a frenzied defiance that made the hearts of half the audience stand still."[51] This frenzy, however, too often hardened the hearts of the other half.

"CREATING NEW MODELS FOR OTHERS TO COPY": FORREST AS FATHER OF AMERICAN DRAMA

Capitalizing on the democratic fervor and hearty nationalistic sentiment that elected Jackson to his first term, Forrest announced his first American drama competition in 1828: "To the author of the best Tragedy, in five acts, of which the hero or principal character shall be an aboriginal of this country, the sum of five hundred dollars, and half of the proceeds of the third representation, with my own gratuitous services on that occasion."[52] Responding to this announcement, the *New York Mirror* (1828) praised Forrest as an exemplar of American enterprise and potential: "[T]he naturally energetic man possesses the prerogative of breaking from the trammels of common regulation and of creating new laws for others to obey, new models for others to copy."[53] Forrest held 9 contests spread over 22 years, eventually raising the prize to a thousand dollars and lifting the restriction in subject matter.[54] His ambition and shrewd foresight prove all the more extraordinary for a 22-year-old actor only 2 years removed from his New York debut. In a letter to Jacksonian journalist and friend

William Leggett in November of 1828, Forrest outlined the need for his proposed playwriting competition:

> Feeling extremely desirous that dramatic letters should be more cultivated in my native country, and believing that the dearth of writers in that department is rather the result of a want of the proper incentive than of any deficiency of the requisite talents, I should feel greatly obliged to you if you would communicate to the public, in the next number of the 'Critic,' the following offer.[55]

Although no one doubted Forrest's patriotism, the actor was fully aware of the potential for personal gain. Even though satirically denounced by the *New York Mirror* (1834), the patriotic appeal of drama with a strong nationalistic flavor promised almost limitless profit: "Say that your play is American, talk of the 'new school,' 'native talent,' 'patriotic attachments,' 'intelligent people,' etc., and deprecate any criticism as cruel, and having a tendency to crush the 'rising drama of America.'"[56] Forrest likely earned over half of his fortune from the contest-winning plays, and a brief examination of his three most popular works (*Metamora*, *The Gladiator*, and *Jack Cade*) provides insight into Forrest's deliberate construction of masculine image.[57]

Robert Montgomery Bird, who penned four of the nine contest winners, alleged that Forrest promised $3000 for each of Bird's last three prize-winning plays. This claim of a verbal contract seems at least plausible, because Bird and Forrest established something of a partnership in the first half of the 1830s, although no formal agreement existed. Known for a frugality that bordered on avarice, Forrest has been condemned (during his lifetime and frequently since) for financially cheating his award-winning playwrights. The $500–1000 that was promised to winning dramatists in the 1820s and 30s roughly equals 10,000–20,000 in today's dollars. Forrest admittedly earned the modern equivalent of at least hundreds of thousands of dollars from the plays, but no effective copyright laws existed at the time. Dramatic authors earned far more from Forrest than theatrical managers who could use proven foreign scripts at no cost whatsoever. While meager by contemporary standards, the financial incentive he offered finally attracted worthy American writers to try their hand at drama. While Forrest could, and perhaps should, have shared more of the proceeds, he was in no way obligated beyond his promise in the contest announcement. Disputes over money eventually dissolved the partnership and friendship of Bird and Forrest.

Edwin Forrest awarded prizes to nine plays, which are listed with the dates of first production: *Metamora; or, The Last of the Wampanoags* by John Augustus Stone (December 15, 1829); *Caius Marius* by Richard Penn

"A Glorious Image of Unperverted Manhood" 69

Smith (January 12, 1831); *Pelopidas; or, The Fall of the Polemarchs* by Robert Montgomery Bird (accepted but never produced by Forrest); *The Gladiator* by Bird (September 26, 1831); *Oralloossa* by Bird (October 10, 1832); *The Ancient Briton* by John Augustus Stone (March 27, 1833); *The Broker of Bogota* by Bird (February 12, 1834); *Jack Cade* by Robert T. Conrad—first produced by another actor in 1835 under the title *Aylmere* and later by Forrest under its more famous title (May 24, 1841); *Mohammed, The Arabian Prophet* by G. H. Miles (first performed on October 27, 1851, but never by Forrest). *Metamora, The Gladiator,* and *Jack Cade* enjoyed unprecedented success for American dramas, and Forrest retained them in his standard repertory for the rest of his career. Forrest performed these three contest-winning plays literally thousands of times, and they likely were viewed by more than 3 million people in total.[58] The remaining six plays either failed to catch the public's imagination or were deemed by Forrest as not meeting expectations.[59] The values espoused and the hero portrayed

Figure 2.3 "Downfall of Mother Bank" (1833), by Henry R. Robinson. The Library Company of Philadelphia.

The cartoon of Andrew Jackson defeating the corrupt Second Bank of the United States reveals an inherent and overt theatricality. Bruce McConachie clearly recognizes Andrew Jackson's actions, and his constituents' perception of them, as a performance: "When President Jackson slew 'the Monster' in 1832, fellow Democrats applauded him like a stage hero in a melodrama" ("Theatre of Edwin Forrest," 5). The presidential struggle was mirrored in Forrest's onstage struggle to free the slaves in *The Gladiator*, to free the bondmen in *Jack Cade*, or to free his homeland from the cruel tyranny of the British in *Metamora*.

in these six "lesser" plays do not closely match the striking similarities of his three triumphs, which suggests that his audiences communicated clear and consistent expectations of the stories he should tell and the heroes he should embody. Forrest demanded roles that exhibited him as a symbol of American nationalism, even though, amazingly, he never played a white American on stage. A young Walt Whitman praised Forrest for making "the hearts of the masses swell responsively to all those nobler manlier aspirations in behalf of mortal freedom."[60] Forrest's onstage persona consistently featured a rebellious republican hero fighting against the oppression of a callous aristocracy for the good of exploited commons—not unlike his political idol, Jackson. *Metamora, The Gladiator,* and *Jack Cade,* written by fellow Philadelphians, provided models of ideal masculinity while simultaneously guiding the behavior of comparatively common men.

Whereas many Native American characters succeeded on the American stage—most notably in James Nelson Barker's *The Indian Princess* (1808) and Mordecai Noah's *She Would Be a Soldier* (1819)—none matched the popularity of *Metamora,* which was based on the life of Indian chief Metacomet (also known as King Philip), who led the Wampanoags against New England colonists in the 1670s. Revealing America's conflicting views on the Indian issue, the theatrical embodiment of Metamora fulfilled white notions of savage nobility while simultaneously revealing the "barbarous red devil's" utter disregard for life.[61] It also exposed the culpability, greed, and bloodlust of the British and suggested the impossibility of reconciling the desires and the ideals of the Indian and the English. Forrest's character demonstrated that bravery and honesty were somehow indigenous to the land: "Firmly he stood upon the jutting height, as if a sculptor's hand had carved him there. With awe I gazed as on the cliff he turned—the grandest model of a might man." He fights for his freedom, property, and religion against the British: "Our lands! Our nation's freedom! Or the grave!"[62] Even when falsely accused of a murder that ostensibly justifies the white settlers taking his land, Metamora consistently maintains his honor and wisdom. In between heroic battles, he saves a young white woman from the rage of his own people and from marriage to an aristocratic Englishman, whom he kills to protect the young woman's honor. His tribe is destroyed, his infant son is killed, and he himself stabs his wife before dying in a hail of musket fire.

In *The Gladiator,* imperial Rome provided a backdrop for an exploration of slavery, freedom, and the potential power and dignity of a natural man. The enslaved Spartacus, a simple shepherd, refuses to fight in the gladiatorial contests until it is presented as an opportunity to save his wife and child. After killing one man in the gladiatorial ring, he discovers that the next opponent is his long-lost brother. They refuse to fight, and Spartacus leads an uprising of the slave population against the tyranny of Roman oppression. His brother and other followers want to lay siege to Rome, but Spartacus wants simply to return to his native Thrace. When not consumed by battle and self-preservation, he saves the captured niece of his enemy, praetor Crassus. Spartacus's brother, wife, and son are killed in their escape attempt, and Spartacus dies in an enraged and ultimately futile attempt against the Romans:

> Let me beside the praetor. Mark, no prisoners;
> Kill, kill, kill all! There's nothing now but blood
> Can give me joy.[63]

Before the action of *Jack Cade,* Cade's father (a bondman) is tortured and killed after striking the evil Lord Say. Young Cade strikes Lord Say in retaliation and flees to Italy. The plot begins ten years later with Cade's return to Kent and his vow to free the cruelly oppressed bondmen. Cade's mother is killed by Say; Cade's son starves to death when the family is forced to hide in the forest; and Cade's wife goes mad and is imprisoned after killing an aristocratic would-be rapist. Cade reluctantly becomes a leader,

> but only
> Until our chains are molten in the glow
> Of kindled spirits; for I seek not power,
> I know no glory,—save the godlike joy of making
> The bondman free.[64]

Cade takes the rebel forces into London, demanding the surrender of Lord Say and a signed charter to free the bondmen. Cade kills Say, but not before being struck by Say's poisoned dagger. Cade's mad wife dies in his arms and, as the sealed charter is delivered, he dies: "Free! free! The bondman is avenged, and England free!"[65] In Forrest's revision of the script, the final three words read "my country free!" The passion of Forrest's patriotism is both possessive and as American as possible.

Like Forrest, the three heroes spring from humble beginnings. Spartacus was a simple shepherd, and Jack Cade was a bondsman/peasant. And although Metamora is a chief, he exudes frontier simplicity: "[E]arth seems conscious of her proudest son."[66] Each irresistibly charismatic hero longs to return to a utopian nature and live simply off the land. All three, however, possess innate nobility that naturally elevates them above the common existence of slave/serf/savage that providence requires them to lead, and all three were selected by the hand of a higher power to enact vengeance and to lead their people to freedom. Also, like Forrest, all three demonstrate great physical strength, uncommon bravery, and extraordinary force of will. Each hero not only faces insurmountable odds in his fight against the callous tyranny of aristocratic foes but also stands firm against the weakness, fear, greed, ambition, and invariably poor judgment of the fellow commoners whom he leads. Metamora must combat the bloodlust and savagery of his braves one moment and chastise their weakness and cowardice the next:

> [T]he palefaces come toward your dwellings and no warrior's hatchet is raised for vengeance. The war whoop is hush in the camp and we hear no more the triumph of battle... for you have fallen from the high path of your fathers, and Metamora must alone avenge the Wampanoag's wrongs.[67]

Spartacus must weather the greedy, rash ambition of the tens of thousands at his command, including his own long-lost brother, who is responsible for the deaths of those thousands, and is later responsible for the death of Spartacus's own wife and child:

> Couldst thou not die with those thou led'st to death,
> That men, who after should have called thee madman?
> ....Most wretched man,
> Thou has murder'd fifty thousand men, destroyed
> Thy brother and thy country, and all hope
> Of the earth's disenthralment.[68]

Jack Cade prevents his followers from committing rape and plunder:

> be it proclaimed throughout our host,
> The commons rise for right—a holy right—
> And not for lawless license. Whoso robs
> Or doth a wrong unto the citizens,
> Shall, in the king's name suffer death.

And when Cade's men encourage him to continue their conquest beyond earning their freedom, he preaches restraint:

> Alas, you know not what you crave.
> It is a pearl fished up from seas of blood;
> A feather ye would sluice your veins to win,
> That it may flaunt upon your tyrant's brow,
> Making him more your tyrant.[69]

While the plays are full of external action and physical battle, the internals of the Forrest hero remains static. Although the machinations of aristocratic villains may prod him into rage, vengeance or action, his compass never wavers. No one can improve or teach him, and his perfection simultaneously isolates and elevates him. He has no true friends, and his family seems to exist primarily for villains to destroy. Emotional bonds represent crutches to be stripped away and drive the hero to self-sacrifice. Although he fights for the freedom of the masses, with surprising frequency, the fight proves a solitary one. The hero must die alone—both alone in battle and stripped of the love of his family—a martyr to the cause. Christ-like, he pays the ultimate sacrifice for the weakness of the people he is destined to lead. While many romantic melodramas of this period present a hero who stands alone in his fight, most British heroes (following an Aristotelian model) are destroyed because of some tragic flaw—they are ultimately responsible for their own failure.[70] A Forrest hero, however, holds no responsibility for his inevitable downfall. He either succumbs to the numeric superiority of the evil villain, or (more significantly) the common people he leads fall short of the physical, intellectual, and moral superiority of their hero.

The reductive morality and literary simplicity of Forrest's prize-winning works often prompted attacks from elevated critics. The *Boston Daily Atlas* (1833) derided Forrest's dramas and the audiences who patronized them: "The Public Taste!—On Tuesday evening, Forrest played LEAR to a beggarly account of empty boxes;—Metamora, last night, drew an overflowing house.—Such is the critical discernment of the Literary Metropolis!"[71] A rival newspaper, the *New England Galaxy* (1833), immediately defended the audience and placed the blame on the actor, suggesting that less demanding native products better suited Forrest's temperament and abilities: "Perhaps the true solution of the wonder is that nobody supposes Forrest is capable of performing the character of Lear, with propriety or discrimination—and he is known to play the Indian Chief to the life."[72] Elite and educated audiences equated and confined Forrest's masculine capabilities to the intellectual and emotional limitations of the plays he championed. Forrest defended an American's right and ability to write for the stage: "In a country like ours, where all men are free and equal, no aristocracy should be tolerated, save that aristocracy of superior mind, before which none need be ashamed to bow."[73] And it was the perceived inferior minds writing, performing, and viewing these works that limited Forrest's appeal.

The *New England Galaxy* (1831) praised Bird's efforts on *The Gladiator* as an enormous step forward for native drama:

> [A]fter the numerous shocking abortions to which our playwrights have within a year or two called the public attention, we cannot but hail with peculiar satisfaction the appearance of a regular, well-constructed, well-written, five-act play, which is fairly entitled to notice in the dramatic annals of the day, and forms an era in the literature of our country.[74]

Bird connected Forrest emotionally to his natural audience, granting a dignity and respect to working-class patrons that was previously reserved solely for the elite. The dramatic efforts of Bird, Stone, and Conrad represented an improvement over the native "abortions" then on stage, but these plays still largely relied on melodrama and rant and contained characters that lacked subtlety and dimension. Bird, embittered by his struggles with Forrest and the lack of sophistication offered in the theatre, condemned both the state of contemporary American drama and the audiences who patronized it:

> Our theatres are in a lamentable condition and not at all fashionable. To write for and be admired by the groundlings! Villains that will clap when you are most nonsensical and applaud you most heartily when you are most vulgar; that will call you 'A genius, by G–' when you can make the judicious grieve and 'a witty devil' when you force a woman to blush.[75]

These shortcomings, however, cannot fairly be blamed on Forrest or his playwrights, who are guilty of no worse crime than theatrical pragmatism and expediency. As prominent nineteenth-century drama critic William Winter accurately assessed, all too often American drama was crafted "to dominate a multitude that had never heard anything short of thunder and never felt anything till it was hit with a club."[76]

MAKING A REAL MAN OUT OF CADE: CREATING AN AMERICAN HERO

Shortly after Forrest's premiere in the play, Edgar Allan Poe praised Robert T. Conrad's *Jack Cade:* "In its new dress, this drama has been one of the most successful ever written by an American, not only attracting crowded houses, but extorting the good word of our best critics."[77] For contemporary theatergoers, mention of the Jack Cade Rebellion likely recalls only the famous line from Shakespeare's *Henry VI,* Part 2, "The first thing we do, let's kill all the lawyers." Shakespeare presents Cade (in what is actually a combination of the most sensational elements of the Peasant Rebellion of 1450, led by Jack Cade, and Wat Tyler's Peasants' Rebellion of 1381) as a rustic buffoon and ridiculous pretender to the throne—a pawn and thug, who is desperate to destroy the monarchy. Comprising most of the fourth act, the Cade subplot initially serves as comic relief before darkening to illustrate the dangers of ambition, disorder, and anarchy. Robert T. Conrad's *Jack Cade* garners what little notice it has received through its connection to Edwin Forrest. According to Alger, Forrest's depiction of the title character profoundly moved urban working-class male audiences:

> The Jack Cade of Forrest stirred the great passions in the bosom of the people, swept the chords of their elementary sympathies with tempestuous and irresistible power.... Jack Cade was his incarnate tribuneship of the people... inflamed by personal wrongs and inspired with a... desperate love of liberty. In it he was a sort of dramatic Demosthenes, rousing the cowardly and slumberous hosts of mankind to redeem themselves with their own right hands.[78]

Forrest's performances of *Jack Cade* represented more than one-fourth of his total appearances on Philadelphia stages from 1841 to 1855 (69 out of 263). In fact, performances of this role surpassed the combined total of *Metamora* and *The Gladiator* during that period (30 and 36, respectively).[79] *Jack Cade,* the only prize-winning play produced prior to Forrest's involvement, won the award in 1841 after an at least moderately successful initial run in Philadelphia. Conrad originally wrote the role for Forrest's rival, the brilliant but self-destructive Augustus A. Addams, who was too drunk to perform in its 1835 opening, although he briefly and unsuccessfully played the role in 1836.[80] Conrad dutifully adapted the play under Forrest's careful guidance.

Though a textual treatment of this play may seem tangential to the performance of masculinity, such an analysis demonstrates the degree of craft and calculation that is required in every aspect of creating a male persona on the nineteenth-century stage. Contextualizing changes that were implemented from the play's composition (1835) to Forrest's triumph in it (1841) provides valuable insights into the essence of Forrest's self-constructed manhood as well as national struggles to promulgate masculine identities. Between the 1835 and 1841 productions, Forrest transformed a Whig-inspired drama that reflected a strong gothic influence to a comparatively simplistic ode to Jacksonian manhood. Edwin Forrest and Robert T. Conrad theatrically manipulated history to further conflicting artistic, political, and masculine agendas within this complex period. The United States underwent significant political, economic, and social changes from 1835 to 1841. The 1830s featured a strong surge of American nationalism. The working class idolized Andrew Jackson, but 1837 brought the end of Jackson's second term as president and terminated his reign as "King Andrew the First." The presidency of Martin Van Buren (Jackson's vice president and successor) faced the Panic of 1837, the most severe economic depression in the country's young history. Through the 1830s, Richard Hofstadter argues that Whigs were stigmatized as "a type that kept the manners and aspirations and prejudices of an aristocratic class without being able to retain its authority."[81] The election of 1840 found the Whig party, which had previously been unable to create an acceptable alternative model of masculinity, desperate to drop the stigma of aristocracy. Thus they borrowed a page from the Democrats and presented their candidate, the Indian-fighting William Henry Harrison, as the embodiment of all rustic and rural virtues. The Whigs reincarnated themselves as the self-appointed champions of democracy, vowing to combat the evils of Van Buren's privileged aristocracy.

The figure of Jack Cade captured American attention on December 18, 1834. An article in the conservative Whig *Morning Courier and New-York Enquirer* condemned rival newspaper editor William Leggett (1801–1839), whose strong antibank and antimonopoly views revealed him to be a staunch Jacksonian, as "the Jack Cade of the *Evening Post*." Later that day, Leggett launched a spirited counterattack in his own paper, turning the insult into a compliment:

> It then ill becomes republicans, enjoying the freedom which they [those who fought for the liberty of the United States] achieved, admiring...their conduct, and revering their memory, to use the name of one who sacrificed his life in an ill-starred effort in defence of the same glorious and universal principles of equal liberty, as a by-word and term of mockery and reproach.

Leggett severely criticized Shakespeare's representation of Cade, which was inspired by the "prejudice, bigotry and servility" of the chroniclers, and praised the leader of the rebellion as an inspiring champion of liberty who was fighting against a "rapacious monarch...and licentious and factious nobles."[82] Leggett reclaimed Cade as the quintessential republican American hero. Robert T. Conrad's adaptation of the rebellion closely follows Leggett's outline, even though Conrad claimed not to have read Leggett's defense of Cade until after his play was already in production.[83]

Robert T. Conrad (1810–1858), popularly known as Judge Conrad, trained for a legal career but maintained a lifelong interest both in journalism and in literature. He edited the *Daily Commercial Intelligencer,* which later merged with the *Philadelphia Gazette*—both respected and influential Whig periodicals. Following the success of his first play, *Conrad, King of Naples* (1832)—which according to Edgar Allan Poe "elicited applause from the more judicious"—and the overwhelming response to *Jack Cade,* in 1845, Conrad became an editor of the *North American,* a Philadelphia daily newspaper that became a leading Whig journal. In 1848, he became coeditor of *Graham's Magazine,* which provided opportunities for the development of American literature, and which, as historian Ellis Paxson Oberholzer claims, "sought to find a mean between the uninteresting and severe literature that only Tories read and the namby-pambyism which was the ruling note of the age."[84] His most popular play and his various poems were published in 1852 as *Aylmere, or The Bondman of Kent; and Other Poems.* Judge Conrad became the first elected mayor of the newly consolidated Philadelphia in 1854, running as a candidate for the combined Whig and American parties, and strongly supporting the nationalistic policies of the Know-Nothing Party, which required the policemen of the city to be native-born Americans. Although he encountered resistance to his strict administration of law, Conrad received praise for his administrative and organizational skills in coordinating and unifying Philadelphia's disparate boroughs into a cohesive city. Edgar Allan Poe placed Conrad in "the first place among our Philadelphia *literati,*" exposing his connection with a privileged audience.[85] Poe also praised the efficacy of his literary efforts: "They are full of a rapid earnestness and energy that *compel* the reader to acquiesce in the sentiment urged."[86] This combination of sincerity and persuasion ultimately drew the attention of the nation's greatest tragedian.

Forrest initially asked his friend William Leggett to dramatize the story of Jack Cade in 1837, but Leggett refused, ostensibly to avoid unfavorable comparison to Shakespeare. Three months after Leggett's death in 1838, Forrest requested a copy of Conrad's adaptation. After correspondence, negotiations, and preparations, Forrest presented the revised work at New York's Park Theatre on May 24, 1841. Forrest initially performed the play under Conrad's title, *Aylmere; or, The Bondman of Kent,* to mediocre reception. At the encouragement of theatre manager Francis Courtney Wemyss, it was rechristened *Jack Cade; or, The Noble Yeoman*, and under that name the play achieved its significant national popularity.[87]

Differentiating changes—made purely to streamline the play for production—from additions, deletions, or alterations of a text that was at odds with the Jacksonian message (or violating the parameters of Forrest's masculine image) presents significant challenges. Nearly all alterations in the dramatic text were cuts, many of which significantly mar the meter of the verse, disrupting the flow of the poetic line and giving the language a stop-and-start feel, almost as if awkwardly winding up a music box.[88] Not only was Conrad's play written in the blank verse of Shakespeare, but it also sought a Shakespearean tone in mixing comic and serious elements throughout. Forrest generally eliminates lighter moments, providing a more consistently elevated tragic tone, although these adjustments also limit character dimension and flatten dramatic situations. Few additions to *Jack Cade* appear significant, with only one insertion over a single line. Act III of *Aylmere* ends with Cade's capture, and he learns of his son's death as the curtain comes down. *Jack Cade* adds a short exchange between Cade and the villainous Say, in which Cade begs once more to kiss his lifeless child: "A poor, a sinless child, whom thou hast driven / To famine and to death." Say refuses, and Cade vows revenge for the death of his father, mother, and child as he is dragged offstage to end the act.[89] This relatively minor concession,which was specifically requested by Forrest, allowed him to show paternal strength and passion, as he did in *The Gladiator* and other productions.

The aesthetics and the politics of Conrad and Forrest differed radically, yet no definitive evidence documents the emotional tenor of their collaboration. Edgar Allan Poe, writing anonymously in *Graham's Magazine*, hints at potential challenges:

> [I]n its [*Jack Cade*'s] composition, the dramatist had to contend with the great perplexity of moulding his principal character to the mental and physical conformation of the actor for whom it was expressly designed. The actor was Mr. Forrest. We mean no depreciation of his histrionic abilities—but we wish to suggest that had these abilities been even greater, the difficulty in question would have been none the less. The genius of an author—and very especially of the dramatic author—should be left *totally* untrammeled. Even the semblance of a restriction—even a purely imaginary restraint—is all-potent to damp the true ardor of the poet. It is the encasing of his wings in lead. The play-wright who constructs a really good play under such circumstances as those to which we allude, demonstrates a very unusual degree of talent indeed.[90]

Although careful not to impugn Forrest, Poe suggests difficulties in working around the tragedian's dramatic demands and performance limitations. Poe appears more impressed with Conrad's diplomacy than with the play itself: "The fierce, bold, vengeful, yet noble nature of the hero [Cade] is drawn with exceeding force and truth, and when we regard it as drawn for the peculiar acting of Mr. Forrest, we cannot help regarding it as altogether a masterpiece."[91] Even though "peculiar" here almost certainly means particular or unique, Poe still implies that the ability to make Forrest look noble and truthful deserved the highest possible praise. In his introduction to the published version of the play, Conrad publicly thanks Forrest for his guidance in preparing the work for performance:

> The tragedy, as originally written and now presented to the reader, comprises much that was not designed for, and is not adapted to, the stage.... To the judgment and taste of Mr. Forrest he is indebted for the suggestions which prepared "Aylmere" for the stage; and to the eminent genius of that unrivalled tragedian and liberal patron of dramatic literature, its flattering success at home and abroad may be justly ascribed.[92]

No evidence suggests *Aylmere* was written for any forum other than the stage. In fact, the play had already enjoyed moderate theatrical success. Conrad, however, did not adopt any of Forrest's suggestions for the published form, presumably feeling that the complete, unedited version could stand on its own. By 1852, the play's success under its more popular title, *Jack Cade*, would have made Conrad's work far more marketable. Conrad deliberately separated his work as a dramatist from Forrest's stage production. Conrad's published play and poems catered to a more educated and elite clientele than the one that frequented Forrest.

While both plots are similar, the second scene of *Aylmere* begins comically with a young, soon-to-be-married couple in mock argument. The tone quickly darkens as the bondmen discuss Lord Say's attempt to stop the wedding, and Friar Lacy (sympathetic to the bondmen's cause) forces the village men to acknowledge the hopelessness of their submissive situation:

> The curse is on us all. What though you be
> A yeoman born? Go to, you are not free.
> You may nor toil nor rest, nor love nor hate,
> Nor joy nor grieve, without your baron's leave.
> Free quotha! Ay, free as the falcon is
> That flies on high, but may be caged again.[93]

This impotent call to action requires a rallying point to unite the hearts and wills of the common men, and the disguised Cade will soon appear. Forrest's version of *Jack Cade* cuts the entire scene, and at least three possible explanations justify its removal. First, from a practical standpoint, the scene delays the entrance of the title character. Second, the lighter elements of the scene, which ends with Lacy giving the prospective bridegroom marriage advice, mar Forrest's purely tragic quality. Finally, the impassioned call for freedom, even though not fully heeded, was not articulated by the title character. Friar Lacy, who is in many ways reminiscent of *Romeo and Juliet*'s Friar Laurence, plays a forceful role in *Aylmere* that is decidedly diminished in *Jack Cade*. Also, the common bondmen in *Aylmere*'s second scene show a more obvious discontent and a stronger willingness to take action than they do in the first scene of the play, in which they appear truly helpless. *Aylmere*'s men need a catalyst more than they need a leader. A later scene, also cut by Forrest, shows the bondmen (led by a weapon-wielding Friar Lacy) bonding together and planning to rescue the captured Cade. Again, the commoners' willingness and ability to act without leadership possibly motivates the scene's omission. Conrad's version of the story asserted the *community* as hero, rather than relying on a solitary Napoleonic figure—ultimately encouraging a more truly egalitarian world. Conrad's play anticipated the Whig strategy in the 1840 election, creating a central masculine figure who is one of the people, rather than one who will reach down to them.

Forrest limited passages that mocked the commons too harshly and moderated the outrage of the hero and his followers. Lord Say, a villain with no redeeming qualities, attacks the gullible and fickle character of the bondmen:

> They but ask fair words—fair words.
> Hail them as gods, and you as worms may crush them,
> Knead them with the spurning heel into the dunghill:
> But when they bow before some fungous idol.
> Or rush, like worried herds o'er some dread cliff,
> Into a certain ruin,—seek to save them—
> Speak, strive, strike, struggle, die for them—and they –
> While your spent heart gasps out its latest drops,
> For them—*for them*—will trample on it![94]

Forrest may have feared offending his audience. Because of the passionate adoration he engendered, he may also not have wished audiences to think too critically about the idol before which they bowed. *Jack Cade* never presents the plight of the masses as completely hopeless. The entire story reveals their oppression, but a tangible devil awaits battle. In Conrad's *Aylmere,* the poor feebly rage against an invisible and all-powerful foe:

> Knows the poor wretch a joy? they find it out!
> A pride? they crush it! Doth he sweat to win
> Some comfort for his cot? their curse falls on it!
> Yearneth he o'er some holy sympathy
> For wife or child? they tear the golden thread
> From out the rugged texture of his fate,
> And leave his desolate.[95]

For Forrest, this sentiment proves too bleak. The poor, weary, and oppressed must have some refuge. Helplessly watching his son die of starvation in the forest, Conrad's Aylmere questions what he has done to merit his harsh desserts:

> I am not thwart in form, nor is my soul
> Distempered; shame sits not upon my brow,
> Nor has wrong soiled my hand; why, Heaven, am I
> Spurned from the general feast thou has provided?[96]

Hopeless despair or immediate, violent action provides the only possible recourse. Fear of bitter questions and discontent may well explain why Forrest tempers the bondmen's complaints. Forrest de-emphasizes Cade's willingness to steal to save his son from starvation, in opposition to Aylmere's bitter justification in Conrad's original:

> I'll buy it with blood!
> Why should the perfumed lordling roll in gold,
> And thou, wan child of sorrow, die for that
> Which he throws careless to his cringing lacquey?
> Each laced and lisping fool is rich; whilst I—
> Oh, shame on justice!—watch my infant starving!—
> No, 'tis no crime—no crime![97]

Forrest's elimination of this passage not only replaces the vulnerable humanity of the hero with unwavering idealism, but also could suggest fear of popular uprisings.

Conrad's hero demanded nothing less than armed rebellion against the tyranny of aristocratic oppressors:

>   Think not she's [Liberty's] won
> With gentle smiles, and yielding blandishments:
> She spurns your dainty wooer;
> And turns to sinewy arms and hearts of steel.
> The war-cloud is her couch; her matin hymn
> The battle-shout of freemen.[98]

Jack Cade's hero encouraged a softer, less desperate defiance. Once the Aylmere-led rebellion takes London, the bondmen in *Aylmere* call for his coronation, the march of their army onto France, and further glories. This section, also eliminated from *Jack Cade,* reveals the danger of common men realizing their power:

>   'Tis a flame,
> That like the glorious torch of the volcano,
> Lights the pale land, and leaves it desolate![99]

Ironically, only eight years after the successful opening of *Jack Cade,* Forrest's goading of his followers, which capitalized on a growing class rivalry and desperate nationalistic fears, contributed significantly to the Astor Place riot.

FINDING THE MANLY VOICE BY SILENCING THE FEMALE

Forrest's manipulations of the play suggest a deliberate decision to guide masculine behavior. The differences between the 1835 and 1841 texts also provide intriguing insights into the construction and treatment of women, as the diminution of the feminine presence and voice further illuminates Forrest's masculine ideal. Conrad constantly uses the suffering and dishonor of women as catalysts for male action. The martyred death of the Widow Cade incites Cade into active rebellion against the aristocracy. The attempted rape of Kate Worthy sparks the first murder of an aristocrat at the hands of a bondman and spurs the village men to action. The attempted rape, subsequent madness, and eventual death of Mariamne serve to strengthen Cade's resolve, justifying what might otherwise be considered harsh or unjust behavior. Cade even goads a reluctant and peaceful bondman with the memory of his recently deceased wife to force him into joining the fight: "I could weep for thee, / And thy wife murdered, save that tears kill not." The response? "The tears shed for her shall be red and heart-drawn!"[100] The treatment of Mariamne and Kate, both of whom face would-be rapists with courage and defiance in Conrad's original script, and both of whom are comparatively silenced by Forrest, reflects the triumph of aggressive Jacksonian masculinity over submissive women who require protection and domination. The concept of rape held different, yet vital, symbolic meanings for Forrest and Conrad. For Conrad, attempted rapes of these strong and virtuous women serve as catalysts to inspire rebellion against the tyranny of aristocratic rule. In Forrest's *Jack Cade*, on the other hand, women are reduced to ciphers and the rapes to symbolic efforts to emasculate the Jacksonian hero—victimizing and destroying his sexual property. Kate is a child of the villein class, citizens of the feudal system who were essentially slaves to their landowners or lords but were considered free and equal to everyone else. Mariamne, although socially elevated, is disguised as a woman of the village. Perceived class distinctions between these women and their seducers underscore the injustice of the social and political system and parallel the domination of the lords over the bondmen.

The wedding of Kate Worthy, daughter of a blacksmith, and Will Mowbray, a young yeoman, provides an important subplot. Forrest's 1841 version cuts the scene that introduces Kate—a light and comic prenuptial celebration, reminiscent in tone of the pastoral shepherd scenes in Shakespeare's *A Winter's Tale*, which presents Kate as a less educated, but more spirited, personification of Perdita. Her impish teasing of the prospective bridegroom ("I must ever have my way!"), in which she interprets the marriage contract as free license to disruptive behavior, playfully parallels the bondsmen's demands for their rights under the charter:

> Will, remember!
> 'Tis i' the contract that I shall be shrewish.
> If there be murmuring, thou shalt be so spur-galled!
> I'll beat thee, Will, i' faith![101]

Eliminating this introduction, her single protest against marriage to Will in the following scene, without the context of her earlier comic objections, vaguely disconcerts, suggesting that the marriage is truly against her will and presenting the bride as a victim of the village villeins as well as of the aristocratic villains. Lord Say's steward, Courtnay, who also woos Kate, threatens their happy nuptials and convinces Say to forbid the wedding:

> I'd force this blacksmith knave give up his daughter,
> If but to teach him that he is my thrall,
> Even yeoman though he be.[102]

The yeoman title reflected the real or imagined Arcadian values of Jeffersonian republicanism, and Say's blatant exercise of power for power's sake rankled audience expectations of democratic entitlement. As the village defiantly continues with its wedding plans, a drunken Courtnay attempts to rape Kate, but her father beats Courtnay to death with his blacksmith hammer. This attack on Kate galvanizes the bondmen, sparking the revolt. When Say and Courtnay interrupt the marriage festival, Forrest curbs her most forceful efforts to restrain her father and bridegroom from a seemingly suicidal rebellion in her defense "Thou'lt not deny me now. I know thou wilt not."[103] Kate is reduced to a damsel in distress. Courtnay's attempted rape and brutal murder stuns Kate into silence. In Conrad's *Aylmere*, the killing of the carefree, vital spirit within the "merry madcap" is tragic. This death of hope and happiness makes an armed rebellion against the aristocracy a moral imperative, and men of the village will fight to the death to avenge this desecration. In Forrest's *Jack Cade*, the violence silences a voice that has already been muted. Rather than driving the bondmen into vengeful action, the attack on the purity of their silent daughter fills them with impotent rage. Forrest's refashioning of the rape reveals the necessity of a great Jacksonian commander to remove the oppressive yoke from the passionate but powerless bondmen and lead them to freedom. Forrest transformed the play into the struggle of one man against insurmountable odds, rather than the outrage of a united community suggested by Conrad.

While not silenced to the same extent as Kate Worthy, Forrest similarly diminishes the strength and significance of Cade's wife. Conrad introduces Mariamne in private discussion with Cade, expressing concern for his safety against the armies of the aristocracy: "In the wild war, / Thou and thy friends are kindling." Conrad's Mariamne fights to overcome Cade's stubborn resolve, appealing to the husband and father of her son who brought her into this strange land, and she foretells of the dangers to come:

> Trifle not with my fears. I am alone,
> Nor kith, nor country have I, hope nor stay,
> Save thee, my husband. Ponder not so wildly
> On these stern doings![104]

Conrad presents the marriage as a partnership, but Forrest eliminates these arguments and warnings. Mariamne's submission to his decision—identical in both versions—without the passion of her earlier resolve to rescue her husband and family, makes the surrender of Forrest's heroine sound vapid and inane:

> 'Twere delight to share
> A peaceful lot with thee; but if fate wills
> The storm should gather o'er thee,—be it so,
> By thy dear side I'll think it sunshine, Aylmere![105]

Because she does not provide a substantial obstacle to his single-minded quest for freedom, Forrest's Cade demonstrates unquestioned command over both family and countrymen.

Forrest's renegotiation of Cade's marriage, which unquestionably places husband in control of happily submissive wife, provides potential insight into the dynamics of his own contentious marriage. Departing from traditional feminine ideals that are presented in the conduct manuals, Forrest's wife, Englishwoman Catherine Sinclair, represented the New Woman (during this era also known as an advanced woman or a bluestocking), who would emerge fully formed in the late nineteenth century—especially modeled in the plays of Henrik Ibsen.[106] The women's movement progressed slowly through the nineteenth century, but several published efforts and publicized travails drew attention to a woman's role in society and marriage. Mary Wollstonecraft's *A Vindication of the Rights of Woman* (1792) laid important philosophical groundwork.[107] On the legal front, the scandalous marital separation of the Honorable George Chapple Norton from Caroline Norton, and the British courts' failure to protect her rights as wife or mother, led her into political activism in the 1830s and 40s. Scotswoman Marion Reid wrote the influential *A Plea for Women* (1843), which advocated women's equal place in society and was published multiple times in the United States in the five years leading up to the infamous Forrest-Sinclair divorce.[108] Explicit in this trial was the acceptable behavior of a married woman. Whereas the socially adept and vivacious Sinclair did not advocate equality, she did expect a certain level of autonomy and viewed marriage as a partnership and articulated in a letter to a male friend "that for man to attain the high position for which he is by nature fitted, woman must keep pace with him. . . . [W]oman has as high a mission to perform in this world as man has." Forrest maintained rather strict and conservative views on women that were incompatible with his wife's liberalism, and the growing tension between them possibly colored his view of Cade and Mariamne.[109] On stage at least, Forrest would be the unquestioned master of his own domain.

When first accosted by Clifford, her aristocratic would-be rapist, Mariamne betrays her privileged station:

> Pass on in thy base hunt!
> Here thou'lt find pride even prouder than thine own,
> And scorn to which thy scorn is lowliness![110]

Forrest's removal of this passage reduces Mariamne's self-defense to a fruitless appeal for gentleman-like behavior and respect for womanhood: "that name entitled to / Each true man's courtesy."[111] This melodramatic plea, which was inevitably ignored by the callous aristocrat, reinforces the image of women as helpless victims. Clifford initially sees Mariamne as little more than a rustic conquest, but his ardor only grows at the prospect of seducing a woman of his own class under the safe guise of sport with a country wench: "If in thy cloud I thought thee bright, forgive me, / That now, thou shin'st undimmed—I worship thee." As he prepares to accost Mariamne in prison, Conrad gives Clifford a moment of pause: "Will not my name / Rot in the foulness of this villain deed?"[112] Forrest's elimination of this passage diminishes the significance and atrocity of the rape while strengthening the class-based view of women as inconsequential and submissive victims. During the antebellum period, legal, societal, and literary responses to rape and seduction depended largely on the status and reputation of the victim, with the assumption articulated by Patricia Cline Cohen that "a seduced rich girl suffers more damage."[113] Women of the upper classes rarely testified in rape cases, keeping their reputations intact, while women of the lower classes risked humiliation and loss of reputation with little hope of legal redress. The era's seduction novels, which condemned male's animal lust and valorized female's innocence and "passionlessness," featured women of the upper classes who died or were driven mad after being defiled by lustful men.[114] Seduction invariably became a crime against both woman and family, if not the entire community. In fact the first American novel, *The Power of Sympathy* (1789), although advocating for the moral education of women, ultimately illustrated the dangers to both the individual and society of seduction and giving into one's passions.[115]

When the lustful Clifford attempts seduction by force, Mariamne kills him with her husband's knife. Conrad's Aylmere gives her the knife to fight off potential danger in his absence: "Be it, what I cannot be—thy protector!"[116] Forrest literally rewrites the speech, and his hero presents the knife as an instrument to free her from dishonor by turning it on *herself*: "In peril's hour, be it thy refuge!"[117] Conrad's Aylmere places Mariamne's safety above all; Forrest's Cade requires death before dishonor. *Her* death before *his* dishonor. In *Aylmere,* Mariamne plunges the knife into her would-be rapist shouting, "This for Aylmere!.... For mine honour, this— and this!"[118] Forrest discards the second half of her outcry; and in the final line of the scene, as the last words she utters before descending into madness, Forrest adds, "'Twas for thy [Aylmere's] honour, I did strike the blow."[119] By refocusing the anguish of the experience, rape becomes an assault on Cade's honor. Conrad intimates that a women's honor rests within and is her own to defend, whereas Forrest assumes a masculine proprietorship of female virtue, suggesting marriage relinquishes a woman's right not only to her virtue but also to her ability and right to defend it. Conrad created complex female characters who were empowered through struggles against aristocratic foes. Forrest's adaptation reduces them to a commodity—a source of male honor and a key to male domination. Reconfigured to conform both to Forrest's interpretation of Jacksonian masculinity and the era's shifting notions of female virtue, *Jack Cade* "spoke" to a working-class male audience. This unique masculine voice emerged, however, after silencing the women who inhabited its world.

Jack Cade was a historical figure who was co-opted both by the Whigs and the Democrats between 1834 and 1841, used as a pejorative condemnation by Whig journalists, rebranded by newspaper editor William Leggett as a Jacksonian hero who championed republican freedom, given still another identity as a working-class-supportive Whig through Conrad's theatrical manipulation, and restored as Leggett's charismatic Jacksonian at Forrest's insistence. Forrest's performance (of this story and others) created very clear binaries between good and evil, man and woman, leader and follower. Forrest's carefully constructed interpretation of *Jack Cade* preached a safe, controlled rebellion—a passive patriotism. Although political or theatrical audiences may enthusiastically applaud the power and will of their champion, connect with their hero's supposed humble beginnings, and enjoy a vicarious thrill in their leader's triumphs, audiences (like the commoners in Forrest's play) are actually encouraged to await leadership. Forrest and Jackson are the exemplars of exalted masculine behavior, but the ideals they represent, like all ideals, are unattainable. In the early 1830s, Tocqueville recognized this lack of strong individual expression in the general character of American manhood:

> I found very few men who displayed that manly candor and masculine independence of opinion which frequently distinguished the Americans in former times, and which constitutes the leading feature in distinguished characters wheresoever they may be found. It seems, at first sight, as if all the minds of the Americans were formed upon one model, so accurately do they follow the same route.[120]

Jackson and Forrest represent this model. The comparatively elite manhood that was performed in the early years of the Republic may actually have demonstrated America's quintessential frontier spirit better than the passive hero worship of the Jacksonian era.

Forrest creates a world in which the strong, regardless of wealth or status, inevitably rise to power, leading the weak and abolishing tyranny. However, only one hero reaches the top. Encouraging a dual manhood—a *communal manhood* of self-restraint and self-sacrifice that supports a *self-made manhood* rewarding the strong—Forrest modeled an ideal while validating and intensifying this communal sense of purpose.[121] These distinct masculine models operated in tandem, implying a natural meritocracy of masculinity. Forrest's greatest success may have been in creating an ideological market for "myth consumers" and in then feeding them exactly what they thought they wanted.[122] His audience did not have to be *like* him; they could live *through* him. Forrest created the most conspicuous and the least complicated manly image on America's antebellum stage. The simplicity and strength of this dominant model reassured audiences and inspired emulation, but its inflexibility also limited its duration and appeal. The following chapters explore actors' and audiences' mutual search for and construction of alternate masculinities. But like the political figures who situated themselves (attracted or repelled) in relation to Andrew Jackson, Forrest represents the overpowering image that most influences other theatrical possibilities.

3. A Masculine Identity Worth Dying For: The Astor Place Riot

> *It is really singular that, deriving all, or nearly all, the acting plays from England, applauding and constantly in association with the best English actors, there should exist, behind the scenes of the American theatres, such an inveterate hatred to the foreign artist, that every little word uttered should be construed into an intentional national insult.*
>
> Francis Wemyss, 1847[1]

The violence of a single day in 1849 captivated the country. A contest of manly wills on American soil pitted a younger native (a massive physical presence) against a more experienced foreigner, a dozen years his senior, who earned his reputation as the best in the world. Each man exhibited a successful, yet entirely different, style of artistry. Both acted as surrogates for nationalistic tensions, and their competition dramatized larger social conflicts. The grudge between the two, one that was personal as well as professional, publicly escalated, with each publishing "cards" in the papers. For months, newspapers throughout the country intentionally built up the anticipation and animosity of this rivalry, capitalizing on patriotism and xenophobia. Despite the best efforts of authorities, the contest ended in bloodshed. In the sixteenth round, American Tom Hyer defeated Irishman Yankee Sullivan in the fight of the century—February 7, 1849. The *Spirit of the Times* (1860) captured the national hysteria surrounding the fight:

> Thus ended a contest which had excited more interest than any other pugilistic encounter that ever took place in this country; but which, though it engaged thousands of minds for a period of six long months, was done up, when once

begun, in seventeen minutes and eighteen seconds.... There never was, perhaps, a battle in which there was so much fighting in so short a space of time; none, certainly, in which more resolute punishment was given and taken, without flinching on either side."[2]

Three months and three days later, with a comparable absence of flinching, the culmination of another battle resulted in greater punishment.

The personal and professional feud between Edwin Forrest and British touring star William Charles Macready triggered the Astor Place Riot (May 10, 1849). Aggravated by anti-elite sentiments of the working-class Bowery, their increasing sense of economic insecurity, and their belligerent nationalism, this conflict crystallized what had been a growing separation between classes. Escalating anxieties between North and South over slavery, exploding urbanization, the dehumanization of industrialism, and the ruthless competition of capitalism all undermined the security of both the individual and the nation. The valorization (and denigration) of competing visions of American masculinity—differing in class, politics, education, and social behavior—revealed divergent values and radically contrasting means of expression and persuasion. Urban working-class males often demanded recognition and respect through intimidation and popular sovereignty, whereas the middle and upper classes displayed power and exerted dominance primarily through legal means. The riot offered men of all classes the opportunity of "reconstructed manhood," to borrow a phrase from Henry Ward Beecher, a chance to solidify or redefine "how people ought to live and what they ought to be."[3]

Whereas Edwin Forrest represented an ideal of unattainable romantic heroism for working-class audiences, the Yankee character (introduced in Royall Tyler's *The Contrast*) provided these men with an accessible, real-life model, revealing a contrast of shrewdness and naiveté mixed with fierce independence. David Humphreys' *The Yankey in England* (1815) provided a detailed description of the dichotomies inherent in the stage Yankee:

> Inquisitive from natural and excessive curiosity, confirmed by habit; credulous, from inexperience and want of knowledge of the world; believing himself to be perfectly acquainted with whatever he partially knows; tenacious of prejudices; docile, when rightly managed; when otherwise treated, independent to obstinacy; easily betrayed into ridiculous mistakes; incapable of being overawed by external circumstances; suspicious, vigilant and quick of perception, he is ever ready to parry or repel the attacks of raillery, by retorts of rustic and sarcastic, if not of original and refined wit and humor.[4]

This description provides intriguing parallels to the mob that was manipulated into the tragedy at Astor Place. This Yankee model stepped out from his position as a secondary character (from Jonathan in *The Contrast* to Will Dowton in *The Drunkard*) to become a hero in his own right, mirroring the aspirations and growing influence of the urban working class, which enjoyed the opportunity to mold, or at least affirm, public manifestations of its own image. Manhood in the playhouse emerged directly from observations of men on the street, and that same theatrical performance served as a practical model of behavior that was taken out the theatre doors—suggesting a mutual negotiation of masculine synergism within the imagined community of the theatre.

Mose, the fire-fighting Bowery B'hoy, who was popularized by Francis S. Chanfrau (1824–1884), urbanized the low-comedy Yankee. Mose first appeared in Benjamin A. Baker's *A Glance at New York* (1848), which was based on Pierce Egan's British comedy *Tom and Jerry; or, Life in London* (1821)[5] Born on the Bowery, the Jewish Chanfrau (who did impressions of Forrest in his early career) subsumed his own ethnic identity into Mose, who was generally identified with the Irish and other white immigrants. Francis Wemyss identified Chanfrau's Mose as an immediately ubiquitous figure in the circular imitation of urban masculinity: "He at once became the dramatic 'lion' of the town; his likeness pervaded every window, and his sayings were uttered by every urchin in the city, as well as by a very good portion of the older part of the male community."[6] Charles Gayler, who wrote *Our American Cousin at Home* (1860) for Chanfrau, argues the dangerous amiability of the Bowery tough:

> [T]he New York firemen and runners, with the various 'machines,' as the old-fashioned fire-engines were called, formed a distinct class.... They were a rough, uncouth, roystering [*sic*] lot, sudden and quick in quarrel when the merits of the machine to which they were attached were brought in question, or when they imagined their natural rights were infringed upon; but they were brave, generous and warm-hearted.[7]

Growing out of the stage Yankee tradition, but within the enforced limitations of his social position, Mose more readily used violence to solve problems. The strength of working-class audiences who patronized Chanfrau and Forrest grew unchecked through the 1830s and 40s—their sovereignty unquestioned so long as they remained in their own sphere. Rioting, a working-class expression of egalitarian freedom, also provided an emotional outlet for frustrations and established a sense of community through ritualized acts of defiance, destroying symbols of aristocratic pretense and oppression.[8] Working-class men saw their participation in the events leading up to the riot as an opportunity to live the dream promised to them in Forrest's dramas.

THE ASTOR PLACE RIOT; A DRAMA IN FIVE ACTS

The Astor Place Riot represents both a political and a theatrical spectacle.[9] Framing the riot as a melodrama suggests the ultimate "acting out" of nineteenth-century masculinity. The exposition of the early acts reveals how the history and behavior of each main character inevitably leads to conflict. In each act, stakes escalate, building up to the tragic climax. Each of the drama's principal players (Forrest and Macready) represented hero and villain because the perspective of the individual viewer or participant completely determined valor or villainy. Fighting the effeminacy and privilege embodied in Macready and Astor Place, rioters cast themselves as featured players in a Forrestian drama of oppression, with the firm intention of realizing the republican myth. The outcome of the riot, however, revealed the lie behind this myth.

DRAMATIS PERSONAE: EDWIN FORREST AND WILLIAM CHARLES MACREADY

Each actor's contribution to the actual riot was largely symbolic—important for what he represented, but equally important for what he did *not* represent. Urban working-class men who appropriated Forrest's active, heroic role defined character as being at sharp variance with the pretentious sophistication of the intellectual elite and the stifling decorum of the middle classes. As a theatrical audience, they demonstrated sovereignty by shouting down perceived insults and demanding the capitulation of all actors, especially foreign (and particularly British) ones. Macready provided an irresistible target, as argued by the *Account of the Terrific and Fatal Riot at the New-York Astor Place Opera House, on the Night of May 10th, 1849:*

> Macready was a subordinate personage, and he was to be put down less on his own account, than to spite his aristocratic supporters. The question became not only a national, but a social one. It was the rich against the poor—the aristocracy against the people; and this hatred of wealth and privilege is increasing over the world, and ready to burst out whenever there is the slightest occasion. The rich and well-bred are too apt to despise the poor and ignorant, and they must not think it strange if they are hated in return.[10]

Macready's fine shadings of character, appreciated by middle-class and elite viewers, failed to connect with the working class, who criticized Macready's performance as overly subtle, pretentious, and ultimately inaccessible: "We cannot comprehend the meaning of some of his extraordinary sinkings and transitions of voice. They may be very fine and very sublime; but we confess that the refinements are much too sublimated for the grosser atmosphere of our 'groundling' taste."[11] The upper classes framed working-class dislike for Macready as an inability to appreciate his masculine or theatrical nuances. Speaking for an elite audience, Walt Whitman equally disassociated from the obvious muscularity of Forrest:

> [A]ll persons of thought will confess to no great fondness for acting which particularly seeks to 'tickle the ears of the groundlings.' We allude to the loud mouthed ranting style—the tearing of every thing to shivers—which is so much the ambition of some of our players.... To men of taste, all this is exceedingly ridiculous.[12]

This fundamental difference in the mode of expression between "groundling taste" and "men of taste" suggests different and untranslatable languages of masculinity. The polarity of these two groups, which lacks any common ground of reference and identification, made communication impossible.

To elevate his status, Macready raised the social position of the actor and purposely cultivated the acquaintance and patronage of the finest minds and noblest manners both in England and in America. Famous for a fiery temper, and often described as petty and jealous, Macready (like Forrest) made few friends within his own profession. Macready disliked the world of the theatre and most of the people who worked in it, rejecting fellow actors as unworthy of respect or deference, just as he was excluded by the inner circle of elite masculinity. Author Henry James praised and defended his separation from theatrical peers:

> Compared with most members of the theatrical profession, he [Macready] was an accomplished scholar; he was zealous, conscientious, rigidly dutiful, decorous, conservative in his personal tastes and habits. He was never popular, we believe, with the members of his own profession, who thought him arrogant and unsociable, and for whom he fixed the standard, in every way, uncomfortably high.[13]

The only American actors to share Macready's intellectualism, and at least partial social acceptance, were comic performers like James Henry Hackett and William E. Burton.

Macready and Forrest, who were professional friends until at least a couple of years before the riot, shared a number of interesting traits. Each felt the isolation and responsibility of being his country's greatest actor as well as the frustration of only partial social acceptance. In their acting styles, whereas Macready favored the classical school and Forrest the romantic, both combined these methods effectively. More important, however, their respective audiences read these two hardworking, ambitious, egocentric, fiery-tempered social climbers in totally different ways. Whereas Forrest provided a rallying point for the heroism of the urban working class, to this group, Macready personified both the arrogance of the British as well as the aristocratic pretension of the upper class. Twelve days before the riot the *New York Herald* (1849) argued, "For ourselves as Americans, we prefer the unsophisticated energy of the daring child of nature to the more glossy polish of the artificial European civilian...Some prefer the toga, some prefer the tomahawk."[14] "Toga" and "tomahawk" referred to roles that were often associated with the two actors (Brutus, or possibly Virginius, for Macready and Metamora for Forrest). The toga symbolized

Figure 3.1 William Charles Macready. The Library Company of Philadelphia.

All surviving images of the mature Macready present the "eminent tragedian" similarly—as a dignified, humorless, somewhat forbidding presence.

Old World values and European dramatic traditions, whereas the tomahawk celebrated a purely native aesthetic. The toga additionally suggested classical learning and intellectual debate, whereas the tomahawk signified brutal violence.[15]

THE SETTING—ASTOR PLACE OPERA HOUSE

A growing audience fragmentation, which was accelerated by industrialization and the country's subsequent urbanization—not to mention drastically reduced admission prices in the 1820s—led to a concentration of working-class males in urban centers that were fully able to sustain a growing number of theatres dedicated to entertaining this audience.[16] The opening of New York's Bowery Theatre in 1826, the year of Forrest and Macready's New York debuts, challenged the supremacy of the Park Theatre, which largely catered to the city's elite audiences. The Bowery's fashionable location suggested an intention to play to the upper classes, but insufficient patronage led manager Thomas S. Hamblin to lower admission prices to draw another audience. Philadelphia's Arch Street Theatre (1831) and Walnut Street Theatre (1834) and Boston's Tremont Theatre (originally built for the upper class in the 1830s) followed the Bowery's lead, catering to working-class audiences in admission charged, entertainment offered, and stars featured. The Bowery Theatre, renamed the American Theatre in 1830, capitalized on the boisterous nationalism of its primary audience and specialized in well-known tragic heroes and patriotic melodrama, which featured romantic actors who were noted for their physical and passionate performances. Ironically, both the classical and the romantic acting schools shared the same dramatic repertoire and artistic proving ground. Shakespeare remained the standard by which all legitimate actors were judged, with a smattering of other proven theatrical warhorses (mostly British), although a limited number of new American works premiered and, encouraged by popular actors such as Forrest or James H. Hackett, gradually proved their viability.[17] Audiences and actors typically frequented and validated the same texts, but the masculine behavior on the stage and in the audience could hardly have been more dissimilar.

Beginning in the 1820s, working-class audiences reveled in their sovereign control over urban playhouses. The New York *Mirror* (1833), often serving as an arbiter of social behavior, reported on the problems that were caused as this audience interacted with "respectable" patrons:

> A great want of order and respectability [exists] in the conduct of the pit audience.... A dirty-looking fellow a few nights since, taking it into his head that the pit was hardly comfortable enough for him, coolly stepped into the dress-circle, and there seated himself very much to the discomfort of some well-dressed females in the same box... while his comrades in the pit, seeing that he was not to be moved, gave him three cheers.[18]

Working-class male audiences would not be ruled or confined, physically or behaviorally, and their unbridled exuberance violated the refinement and safety of "proper" women and the upper classes—further necessitating separate theatres divided by social behavior. As described by the *Spirit of the Times* (1846), performers and theatre managers acceded to the demands and whims of working-class audiences:

> We determine to have the worth of our money when we go to the theatre; we made Blangy dance her best dances twice; we made Mrs. Sequin repeat 'Marble Halls',... and tonight we are going to encore Mrs. Kean's 'I don't believe it' in The Gamester. We hope she'll prove agreeable and disbelieve it twice for our sakes. Perhaps we'll flatter Mr. Kean by making him take poison twice.[19]

The theatre provided a forum to hear, affirm, and empower lower-class voices. Of course, no one class or social group during this (or any) period was entirely homogenous, nor did they operate in concert. This lack of cohesion especially held true for the lower classes, where the constant infusion of new immigrants changed the demographics throughout the century. Although this *Spirit of the Times* (1846) account exaggerated and parodied working-class power, it also demonstrated that the rowdy element could not be ignored.

The following year, a group of 150 wealthy New Yorkers financed by subscription the 1800-seat Astor Place Opera House, which was named after John Jacob Astor. The naming of the Astor Place Opera House, which was used both for theatrical and operatic performances, suggested a preference for the exclusionary connotations of opera, not to mention association with the enormous wealth of the Astor family.[20] A prominent symbol of elite masculinity that violated working-class visions of manhood, Astor Place enforced a strict dress code and charged an admission fee that was typically 25 cents higher than the fee being charged by competing theatres. The upper classes made proper decorum a priority in social gatherings. Segregation from the working class removed any impediment to the carefully constructed refuge of refinement, and the *Spirit of the Times* (1847) lauded the exclusive opulence: "[A]n atmosphere of elegance and refinement makes itself palpable to the sense. There is a feeling of repose, of security from rude and impertinent interruption, a languor of voluptuous enjoyment."[21] Astor Place provided a safe and decorous enclave for what George Foster described as the "exclusively aristocratic Upper Ten Thousand." Foster, a reporter for Horace Greeley's *New York Tribune*, sensationalized the seamy urban underbelly in *New York by Gaslight* (1850), permitting elites to indulge a morbid fascination with the lives of the abject poor and further emphasizing an emotional separation between the classes.[22] Elite audiences reveled in the luxury of discrimination, but apparently failed to provide adequate patronage, given that the *New York Herald* (1848) reported that the first complete season ended with "a dead loss of $20,000."[23]

The Astor Place audience did not seek a model of behavior in the actor, whom they typically viewed as a creature of inferior social position, but rather went to the theatre to enjoy a communal performance of genteel masculinity. As an anonymous author going by the name of the "American Citizen" argued, the exclusive quality of an actor like Macready provided a token of status: "In Macready, they beheld the pet of princes and nobles."[24] Although Macready moved freely within the social sphere of the elite and comported himself as if he belonged in their company, once offstage, he became an object of cultural fascination rather than a model of manhood.

ACT ONE: EMINENCE IN YANKEELAND; OR, MACREADY'S FIRST AMERICAN TOUR (1826–1827)

Macready, "the eminent tragedian," made his American debut at New York's elite Park Theatre in 1826, the same year in which Forrest made his triumphant New York debut at the working-class Bowery. Macready and Forrest did not meet at this time, although they did compete for New York's theatrical audience in the fall of that year. Forrest, a 20-year old who was making 40 dollars a week, enjoyed his first significant theatrical success, and Macready, who was 13 years his senior, was widely hailed as England's greatest living actor. The *New York Times* (1826) praised Macready, both the actor and the man, as having "talents of uncommon eminence, [and] an unspotted private character."[25] The *New York Mirror* (1826) praised Macready for bringing nobility to the stage and for a unity of performance that became his trademark: "His acting is not a point, a flash, a flat-scene, and then another point, and flash, and flat again. It is like a finished picture, that does not lay claim to praise on any detached or peculiar merit, but on the general excellence of the execution."[26] While hardly a passionate endorsement, the idea of observing a "finished picture" suggests elevating acting to a higher art form. Roughly 30 years later, Edwin Booth drew similar comments. Audiences and critics treated Macready with warmth and respect, but his performance rarely elicited the passionate adoration that Booth would enjoy.

Macready was accused of anti-American sentiments on this first tour. His harsh chastisement of a negligent property man in a Philadelphia performance of *William Tell* was interpreted as an affront to America itself. Local newspaper attacks forced Macready to apologize to the company, and the uproar remained local and quickly faded. Oddly, no mention of the incident appeared in the days surrounding the Astor Place Riot over 20 years later, although most of Macready's other past "abuses" of Americans resurfaced. Wemyss claimed that if penny presses had been more powerfully active during Macready's first tour, his American career likely would have been over. The fact that Macready criticized a man of the theatre backstage, rather than indulging in a more public display directed at "legitimate" citizens, likely prevented him from suffering the severity of Edmund Kean's fate.[27]

There is no evidence which proves that Forrest viewed Macready's performance on his first American tour, although Forrest studied most prominent British actors in his young career. Macready observed Forrest as Marc Antony and William Tell and admired his "natural requisites"— figure, voice, and unschooled intelligence—while noting that his "performance was marked by vehemence and rude force." Macready found Forrest capable of greatness with "severe study of his art" but thought that prospect unlikely: "The injudicious and ignorant flattery, and the factious applause of his supporters in low-priced theatres, would fill his purse, would blind him to his deficiency in taste and judgment, and satisfy his vanity, confirming his self-opinion of attained perfection."[28] Macready did not begin his diary until 1827, so his initial impressions of Forrest may have been colored by their future conflict. But a New York critique from 1828 similarly encouraged "unwearied perseverance" in the young Forrest: "Nature has done much for him, but nature cannot do all. He has climbed above the multitude—but there are heights yet above him, on which his eyes should be fixed."[29] Macready, perhaps with the benefit of hindsight, placed a heavy burden on American audiences, essentially absolving Forrest of responsibility for deficiencies and recognizing his masculine character, both onstage and offstage, as the popular construction of an uneducated mob: "[T]he state of society here and the condition of the fine arts are in themselves evidences of the improbability of an artist being formed by them.... The masses, rich and poor, are essentially, ignorant and vulgar—utterly deficient in taste and without the modesty to distrust themselves."[30] These comments, attacking Forrest's audience and Macready's own, came during later tours of the United States in 1843 and 1848. Although rumors persisted that Macready publicly expressed disdain for American audiences, there seems to be no evidence that supports these claims, and Macready's diary was published posthumously. Macready managed to survive his lucrative first American tour with temper largely in check, potentially offensive opinions kept to himself, purse full, and reputation intact. Emerging issues of national identity (Macready's attack on the property man) and class (Macready's public acceptance by the social and intellectual elite, as well as Macready's private condemnations of the "masses"), however, warned of trouble on the horizon.

ACT TWO: SAVAGE INVASION; OR, FORREST'S FIRST TOUR OF ENGLAND (1836–1837)

After a two-year European tour that was free from performing, Forrest decided to spread America's glory onto the English stage, and the British press and people largely responded with enthusiasm, praising his booming voice, emotional abandon ("he threw his whole power of body and soul into the whirlwind," according to an 1836 *Morning Advertiser*), and massive presence:

> His figure is cast in the proportions of the Farnese Hercules. The development of the muscles, indeed, rather exceeds the ideal of strength, and, in its excess, the beauty of symmetrical power is in some degree sacrificed.... His features are boldly marked, full of energy and expression, and, although not capable of much variety, they possess a remarkable tone of *mental* vigor.[31]

Although the *London Atlas* (1836) may have felt Forrest's massive body exceeded British taste, the *London Sun* (1836) suggested that his form and energy matched England's expectations of the manly Yankee spirit: "America may well feel proud of him; for though he is not strictly speaking, what is called a classical actor, yet he has all the energy, all the indomitable love of freedom that characterizes the transatlantic world."[32] By excluding Forrest from the classical actor category—a classification that Macready definitively embodied—British critics placed the American in the pantheon of theatrical masculinity without threatening the exalted station of their comparatively subdued, intellectual, and eminent tragedian. No London critics made significant comparisons between Forrest and Macready in Forrest's first visit to England. Instead, Forrest often drew comparison to the thrilling memory of Edmund Kean, whom many said he emulated. Macready, however, represented an entirely different species of actor and man. Forrest was not, in fact, the first American actor to perform in England. In 1833, British playgoers enjoyed James H. Hackett's performance in William Bayle Bernard's *The Kentuckian; or, A Trip to New York* (sometimes also called *A Kentuckian's Trip to New York*) as Colonel Nimrod Wildfire, a plain-talking, coonskin-wearing Kentucky Congressman, who was humorously based on Davy Crockett. Hackett, however, represented a refined and intellectual presence offstage and placed lower forms of American manhood on humorous display.[33]

The fulsome, if sometimes qualified, praise that was directed at Forrest often categorized him as something quite outside the theatrical experience of the London stage and distinctly separate from the English acting model: "His very figure and voice were in his favor, the one being strongly muscular, the other replete with a rough music befitting one who in his youth has dwelt, a free barbarian, among the mountains."[34] The *London Sun*'s identification of Forrest as an ideal representation of mountain-dwelling, muscular barbarity strongly implied a style of manhood well beneath the expectations of an English gentleman, suggesting that at least a portion of Forrest's appeal may have resembled the curiosity of a circus exhibit. John Forster of the *London Examiner*, a close friend of Macready's, consistently and vociferously attacked Forrest: "Will and passion are the sole characteristics of the performance.... [He] looked like a savage newly caught from out of the American backwoods."[35] Forster's detailed criticisms of Forrest from October 1836 to March 1837, although mean-spirited, actually provide one of the most thorough contemporary pictures of Forrest's performance style. Forster accused him of a literalism in performance that indicated a lack of intellectual understanding, a focus on making points calculated to appeal to the audience's basest instincts, and a lack of unity and logical dramatic progression in his character development.

Forrest, however, embraced the overall tenor of critical response: "The London press, as you probably have noticed, has been divided concerning my professional merits; though as a good republican I ought to be satisfied, seeing I had an overwhelming majority on my side."[36] Forrest's triumphant homecoming, which validated manly and nationalistic confidence, presaged (by weeks) Ralph Waldo Emerson's "The American Scholar" speech, which Oliver Wendell Holmes, Sr. declared America's "Intellectual Declaration of Independence." Every facet of the nation's manhood sought autonomy from British domination. Although his diary revealed bitterness and jealousy, Macready outwardly remained cordial to Forrest and invited the American to his home, introducing him to many of the English elite. Forrest, feted by the Garrick Club and toasted by Macready, glowingly wrote to William Leggett: "[Macready] has behaved in the handsomest manner to me.... [H]e has extended to me many delicate courtesies and attentions, all showing the native kindness of his heart, and great refinement and good breeding."[37] Macready even introduced Forrest to the Sinclairs, the family of his soon-to-be bride.

ACT THREE: DEMOCRACY VS. ARISTOCRACY; OR, MACREADY'S SECOND TRIP TO AMERICA (1843–1844)

Tension increased between England and the United States. British resentment of "Pennsylvania Repudiators," who were responsible for the default of that state and its businesses of money that were owed to England, created both social and political problems between the two countries. Border disputes in Maine (1838–1839) as well as in the Oregon country and the annexation of Texas in the 1840s further eroded this fragile relationship. English writers such as Mrs. Trollope, Captain Basil Hall, and Charles Dickens, who happened to be a close friend of Macready, mocked and deplored nearly every aspect of American life. Defensive Americans sought every opportunity to exact revenge. After Macready's artistically successful but financially disappointing years as manager of Drury Lane (1841–1843), he returned to the United States with an eye toward retiring in "dear Yankeeland."[38] In addition to the major eastern cities, Macready lucratively expanded his tour to include the South and the West. Direct comparisons between Forrest and Macready became more frequent, with most, such as the *St. Louis Republican* (1844), siding with Forrest: "Those who see a superiority in Macready over our own great actor, must be blinded by prejudice."[39] Newspaper comparisons, such as in the *American Advocate* (1844), took on an increasingly nationalistic tone: "Native Americanism vs. Foreignism. Which of the two to choose? Why Forrest, of course."[40]

Forrest deliberately sought opportunities for head-to-head competition, which Macready considered "ungentlemanly conduct":

> [S]ince my appearance, they have announced him in *American* letters, as 'Mr. E. Forrest, *The National Tragedian!*'—and put him up in my parts the nights after I have played them—It would (except that he is not estimated highly by the *leading* people) do him disservice with the intelligent and better sort, but I believe it has an effect of making a sort of factious rush to the Theatre—as his houses were very *bad* before this device was practiced.[41]

Forrest reaped significant benefit in money and reputation through this "factious rush" of patriotic chauvinism, capitalizing on nationalistic sentiments. He used the feud with Macready to fuel a career that was flagging at home and abroad, essentially transplanting his masculine persona from the stage to the real world to invigorate it. Interest in Forrest's playwriting competitions had evaporated (*Jack Cade* was his only new vehicle in the last 10 years), and the market for talented native actors had expanded considerably since (and because of) his debut. While not suffering at the box office, America's national tragedian had given essentially the same performance for over 15 years, and audiences craved novelty and sensation. Biographer Richard Moody notes that Forrest often lost on his home soil in head-to-head competition with the Englishman:

> In Mobile Macready averaged $455 nightly against $397 for Forrest, and in St. Louis Macready also held the edge, $422 to $269.... He [Macready] was overjoyed... to learn that Forrest had drawn a measly $200 house at a performance at the Walnut Street Theatre in Philadelphia. 'If it be so, he is justly punished for his ungentlemanly conduct.'[42]

Forrest used his challenge of Macready to rekindle working-class interest, linking himself even more directly with issues of American masculinity and honor in the hope that they (his audience and the issues) would sustain him.

Forrest's desire for direct confrontation with Macready was in sympathy with his working-class code of honor. Forrest's actions offended Macready's audience as being tactless and unworthy of a gentleman. Macready never considered Forrest to be in his class (theatrically or otherwise) and found the more frequent critical comparisons and Forrest's attempts at competition to be an insult: "*He is not an artist.* Let him be an American actor—and a great American actor—but keep on this side of the Atlantic, and no one will gainsay his comparative excellence."[43] Assuming the high aesthetic and moral ground, Macready's refusal to engage Forrest drew the sympathy of his elite audience as surely as did Forrest's gathering of working-class support. Forrest's direct challenge of Macready, which the Englishman's supporters saw as coarse presumption, and Macready's refusal to acknowledge, which Forrest's audience saw as effeminate cowardice, allowed both men to win, because each played an entirely different game—and, more importantly, played it in front of different referees with different rulebooks.

Macready remained outwardly friendly toward Forrest and privately praised him on occasion ("I like all I see of Forrest very much. He appears a clear-headed, honest, kind man; what can be better?") but became increasingly critical of his lack of artistry:

> I had a very high opinion of his powers of mind when I saw him sixteen years ago; I said then, if he would cultivate those powers and really study... he would make one of the very first actors of this or any day. But I thought he would not do so, as his countrymen were, by their extravagant applause, possessing him with the idea... that it was unnecessary.... He has great physical power. But I could discern no imagination, no original thought, no poetry at all in his acting.... [H]e has not enriched, refined, elevated, and enlarged his mind; it is very much where it was, in the matter of poetry and art, when I last saw him.... He had all the qualification, all the material out of which to build up a great artist, an actor for all the world. He is now only an actor for the less intelligent of the Americans.[44]

This diatribe toward Forrest the actor concluded with praise of the man ("But he is something better—an upright and well-intentioned man."), suggesting that Macready struggled not to make the professional tensions a personal matter. This extreme emotional shift also suggests a fight for gentlemanly self-control.

While likely fueled by jealousy, Macready's critique of Forrest's artistry holds some truth when compared to other contemporary accounts and suggests why Forrest needed competition with Macready to reinvigorate his career. Macready's condemnation of Forrest's lack of thought, imagination, and taste ultimately relegated Forrest to a subservient, if not debased, level of masculinity. Forrest's perceived disinterest in study, lack of self-discipline and discernment, and unwillingness to elevate both art and audience, limited him forever to association with his democratic supporters. Macready placed much of the onus for Forrest's artistic, intellectual, and masculine shortcomings on an audience inability to appreciate anything but the muscular, coarse, and bombastic: "From what I can learn the audiences of the

United States have been accustomed to exaggeration in all its forms, and have applauded what has been most extravagant; it is not therefore surprising, that they should bestow such little applause on me, not having their accustomed cues."[45] Whereas Macready's snobbish dismissal could be attributed to disappointment over his own reception, the appreciation of subtlety and refinement that marked his gentlemanly code, and which guided his social and intellectual peers, truly was anathema to Forrest's audience. Macready actually felt encouraged by his progress in refining the palate of more discerning audiences: "[T]he audience were much more decorous, attentive, and appreciative than I have heretofore found them. I suppose they begin to understand me."[46] Macready and his audience developed a common language of communication and arrived at a mutual understanding of theatrical and masculine expectations. Gradually, however, Forrest's persistence in seeking out theatrical combat eroded Macready's personal good feelings: "He is not a good actor—not at all an artist. He acts Hamlet on Monday in opposition to me, and I hear, made this *engagement to oppose me!* This is not the English generosity of rivalry."[47]

ACT FOUR: MUCH ADO ABOUT A HISS; OR, FORREST'S FINAL TRIP TO LONDON (1845–1846)

Closely following Macready's return to England, Forrest arrived in London eager to continue the rivalry and add further triumphs to his career, only to encounter a series of frustrations and disappointments. The dispute over the Oregon territory, the continued nonpayment of state debts, and the collapse of the Second Bank of the United States made England pointedly unreceptive to all things American. At a time when legitimate drama struggled on the London stage, Forrest's acting, essentially unchanged since his last visit (except perhaps relying even more strongly on bombast), underwhelmed the *London Spectator* (1845): "His passion is a violent effort of physical vehemence.... [H]e spoke like a braggart beating the air with big words, and only seemed in earnest when butchery was to be done."[48] Other London reviews (including the *Times* and the *News*) interestingly found his performances tedious and deliberate, as if compensating for being an overly physical actor. Only in Ireland, where audiences connected with his republican sentiments and muscular performance style, did Forrest enjoy marked success. The *Examiner* (1845) derided Forrest's Macbeth as a "great amusement...our best comic actors do not often excite so great a quantity of mirth."[49] In a letter to her mother, American

Charlotte Cushman, who had been widely praised in her London debut as Lady Macbeth, confirmed the souring of the British public: "Forrest has failed most dreadfully. In *Macbeth* they shouted with laughter and hissed him to death.... The papers cut him all to pieces."⁵⁰ In his London debut performance of *Othello,* Forrest claimed to have been "saluted with a shower of hisses," as part of "a systematic plan arranged in advance under the stimulus of national prejudice and personal interest."⁵¹ No one corroborated this claim, and no newspaper reviews mentioned this treatment.

Forrest announced his intention to play in Paris without previously securing an engagement, believing that the democratic sympathies of the French for their American cousins would assure his success. John Mitchell, who managed all English drama in France, refused Forrest's request. Without proof, Forrest charged Macready, who was currently under Mitchell's management, with negatively influencing Mitchell's decision. To add insult to injury, Edward Bulwer-Lytton, England's most successful playwright, refused Forrest permission to perform *Richelieu* and *the Lady of Lyons.* Forrest requested a nightly performance rate that Bulwer-Lytton did not allow any actor, and the author demanded what Forrest considered an unreasonably large sum for a set number of performances. Again, Forrest blamed Macready for constructing a conspiracy to thwart his success and convincing Bulwer-Lytton and Mitchell to act against him. Both of these men, who were generally respected and admired, publicly denied any undue influence. When the dispute between Forrest and Macready became fodder for American newspapers in the months leading up to the Astor Place Riot, Macready solicited letters from Mitchell and Bulwer-Lytton, as well as from the editor of the *London Examiner,* absolving Macready of responsibility. These and other letters and remarks were printed in 1849: *The Replies from England to Certain Statements Circulated in This Country Respecting Mr. Macready.*

In *A Rejoinder to "The Replies From England, etc. to Certain Statements Circulated in this Country Respecting Mr. Macready." Together with an Impartial History and Review of the Lamentable Occurrences at the Astor Place Opera House, on the 10th of May, 1849. By an American Citizen,* Macready stood accused of colluding with critic friend Forster and poisoning the goodwill of the public and press: "The undisguised hatred of the English for every thing American, and the subsequent conduct of Macready in this country, lead me to believe that Forster only expressed his dislike of Mr. Forrest because he was an American, and obeyed the commands of his 'eminent' friend."⁵² The truth of this charge, about which Forrest never presented any sort of proof, seemed unlikely. Forster, who was often unpleasant to Forrest, passionately championed his friend Macready at every turn, but Macready, likely out of fear that he would appear responsible, pointedly asked Forster to treat Forrest kindly. Also, because of illness, Forster did not review any of Forrest's London performances in his second tour, although biographers of both Forrest and Macready mistakenly attribute criticisms in the *London Examiner* to Forster.[53] By this time, entries in Macready's diary suggest professional jealousy of and personal dislike for his rival, and he toured the provinces when the American performed in London—likely to avoid the embarrassment of head-to-head rivalry. Neither Macready nor Forster ever had the power to directly suborn the judgment of either the press or the public. Although widely considered England's greatest tragedian, Macready's appeal was hardly unanimous. Many critics (mostly those catering to working-class audiences) agreed with Macready's detractors in America and dismissed his performances as cold and formal. And British criticisms of Forrest resembled those that he suffered at the hands of those Americans who were disenchanted with his dramatic excesses. Most importantly, while often abrasive, neither Macready nor Forster was ever accused of dishonesty. Macready, who was seemingly honest and self-critical within the secret confines of his diary, admitted to no overt actions against Forrest; such weakness, deception, and confrontation violated his personal, moral, and masculine code. Whereas social mobility remained easier in America than in aristocratic England, rhetoric that privileged actions over birth similarly began to define British gentlemen and to roughly correspond to the striving aspirations of America's middle-class male.[54]

Forrest, however, relished confrontation. Perhaps operating on the theory that any publicity was good publicity, he flung their dispute into the public sphere. At an Edinburgh performance of Macready's *Hamlet* (March 2, 1846), Forrest hissed Macready. Much was written about this infamous hiss. It followed Hamlet's line, "I must be idle," as the court gathered for the play scene. Macready typically executed a "waving of the handkerchief" and strutted across the stage, later referred to as a "fancy dance" and which Forrest termed the *pas de mouchoir* (dance of the handkerchief). Macready responded to the hiss with proud disdain: "I waved the more, and bowed derisively and contemptuously to the individual."[55] Was Forrest's hiss solitary or one of many? The High Sheriff of Edinburgh and the Manager of the Edinburgh Theatre, as well as *The Scotsman* (Edinburgh), solely accused Forrest. *The Edinburgh Weekly Chronicle* provided the only legitimate voice, public or private, to support Forrest's claim that he did not hiss alone, although they printed nothing about it until 12 days after the event. All responses were passionate but none more so than that of the sheriff (Mr. Gordon): "Not one human being hissed Macready on that night except Forrest. Believe me, there was but one hiss—and one hisser. Forrest was the hisser—Forrest's was the hiss."[56]

Forrest apparently traveled to Edinburgh from Aberdeen, during a break in his performance schedule, specifically to view Macready's performance. None of Forrest's biographers provide a reason for the sudden 120-mile trip. Forrest (fueled by positive responses from Scotch and Irish audiences) may have gone intentionally looking to force competition and create controversy. Nearly three weeks after the incident, Forrest proudly claimed credit, justifying his action as freedom of expression: "That a man may manifest his opinion, after the recognized mode, according to the best of his judgment, when actuated by proper motives and for justifiable ends, is a right which, until now, I never heard questioned, and I contend that that right extends equally to an actor as to any other man."[57] Forrest claimed the hiss as a republican right and a "legitimate mode of evincing...disapprobation in the theatre...a salutary and wholesome corrective of the abuses of the stage; and it was against one of these abuses that *my* dissent was expressed."[58] When the tables were reversed, Forrest never accepted the "wholesome corrective" when he was hissed at and responded with fury. Although still accepted as a popular right, hissing diminished on the legitimate stages of England and America that were patronized by Macready's conservative audiences, who kept a tighter rein on its implementation. As early as 1817, the conservative *American Magazine and Critical Review* counseled moderation and discernment: "There is a tacit convention between the managers and the audience, which an intelligent public knows how to enforce. Custom and common sense regulate the understanding."[59] The Bowery audience that supported Forrest used their power less judiciously and embraced their democratic right to express displeasure, although not toward Forrest. Macready initially rejected the idea of Forrest's culpability, but interviews with eyewitnesses soon convinced him:

> I feel glad that it is not an Englishman—but no Englishman would have done a thing so base; indeed he dared not have done it, and that is one argument in my mind for my belief in Mr. Forrest's guilt. I do not think that such an action has its parallel in all theatrical history! The low-minded ruffian! That man would commit a murder, *if he dared*.[60]

Although Forrest staunchly defended his actions as an audience member and an arbiter of theatrical good taste, the violation that Macready experienced went beyond Forrest's aesthetic judgment. Forrest attacked Macready openly and professionally, venting his personal animosity in a public forum and breaking the rules of gentility. Forrest's code of masculinity demanded a trial of popular opinion and satisfaction through universal condemnation of his rival. Publicly silent, Macready privately vilified Forrest as base and incapable of gentlemanly behavior:

> This seems to me (though, of course, offensive, as anything filthy in the physical or material world would be) to be the seal of his character. Here stands self-confessed this citizen of the United States, to whom the greatest harm that I can do, I will: which is to give him the full benefit of his noble, tasteful, and critical qualities, and 'leave him alone with his glory.'[61]

Again, Macready claimed a higher status and refused to engage Forrest, which only escalated tensions and provoked Forrest into more drastic action. Macready felt a private acknowledgement of the wrong done to a gentleman, accompanied by the debilitating shame of critical self-awareness, to be a more cruel and just treatment than public chastisement.

ACT FIVE: MASCULINE SHOWDOWN; OR, MACREADY'S FINAL TRIP TO AMERICA (1848–1849)

After fearlessly combating the partisan press and the aristocracy of England, Forrest returned to the United States as a conquering hero—hailed by the *Boston Mail* (1848) as the American Tragedian: "[H]e is just entitled to that honor—he has acquired it by his own labors; from a poor boy in a circus he has arisen to be a man of fame and wealth, all of which he has lastingly gained by enterprise and talent, and secured both by economy and temperance."[62] In a curtain speech following a benefit performance, Forrest professed himself a champion of all things American and attacked British arrogance: "that narrow, exclusive, prejudiced, and I may add, anti-American feeling which prescribes geographical limits to the growth of genius and talent." At a jubilee celebration thrown in his honor, even an elite representative such as William Cullen Bryant defended Forrest's actions: "In the intense competition of the stage, Mr. Forrest has obeyed a native instinct in treating his rivals with generosity."[63] Bryant did not elaborate on the exact nature of Forrest's "generosity." In a private letter to his wife, Forrest justified his treatment of Macready, describing it in terms of a physical attack: "Englishmen must be *cuffed* into a proper conduct towards us; a milder treatment would not reach the disease."[64]

Macready returned to America with some trepidation but still considered emigration in retirement, as shown by his lingering admiration for America's republican principles, articulated on Washington's birthday:

> [T]hroughout these free and independent States, the memory of the man who was born this day shall be hallowed by the gratitude and joy of millions of hearts, that will hand down to their children's children the debt of reverence and love which they and mankind owe to him for the benefits his life conferred and his example has left. The birthday of Washington shall be an eternal festival wherever a freeman speaks the English tongue.[65]

On a more practical note, Macready also felt, because of England's comparatively high cost of living, that he could retire to Yankeeland in greater luxury. Newspapers such as the *New York Herald* (1849), which catered to an elite clientele, received Macready warmly and held him blameless in Forrest's troubles abroad:

> The whole opposition to him [Forrest] originated with this little knot of *literatteurs,* inflamed against the United States, on account of the sad treatment of their 'pal' and brother, Master 'Boz' [Charles Dickens]. We have never believed that Mr. Macready originated or stimulated the attacks on Forrest at that time. He is perfectly innocent on that score, notwithstanding Forrest's belief and interminable letters in bad taste to the contrary.[66]

The *Herald* supported Macready as a matter of taste. But democratic newspapers, such as the *Boston Mail,* (1848), continually fueled the debate, casting him as melodramatic villain: "It is... *his* [Macready's] *inhospitality, his crushing influence, his vindictive opposition, and his steadfast determination to ruin the prospects of that gentleman* [Forrest] *in England, that we bring to his door.*"[67]

Framing Macready as an enemy of both the country and of free enterprise, Forrest heightened the feud by following Macready from town to town, often performing identical roles at competing theatres. Capitalizing on the notoriety, New York theatres presented the following burlesques: *Who's Got Macready? or, a Race to Boston* at the Olympic Theatre and *Mr. Macgreedy, or, a Star at the Opera House,* starring Frank Chanfrau (famous as Mose the Fireboy) at the National Theatre.[68] The two men defended themselves in escalating curtain speeches, which culminated in an exchange of "cards" that were published in most of the country's principal newspapers. Forrest derided Macready as a liar and "superannuated driveller," condemning him personally and professionally ("there is nothing in him but self—self—self") and labeling Macready as the master of a vast conspiracy. Forrest also charged him with cowardice: "Mr. Macready...made allusion, I understand, to 'an American actor' who had the temerity on one occasion openly to hiss him! This is true.... But why say 'an American actor?' Why not openly charge me with the act? for I did it, and publicly avowed it."[69] Forrest, again, sought confrontation, figuratively hurling down the gauntlet. Macready formally responded to Forrest's card as "wanting in self-respect so far as to bandy words upon the subject; but as the circulation of such statements is manifestly calculated to prejudice Mr. Macready in the opinion of the American public, and to affect both his professional interests and his estimation in society." Macready claimed that he would, "without delay apply for legal redress."[70] The differing modes of communication—Forrest in a belligerent first person and Macready in a coldly formal third person—suggest the complete incompatibility of their masculine values. Forrest cast himself as hero in a dramatic confrontation, bellowing against perceived injustices. Macready, reluctant publicly to respond in such a "gross" manner, defended his honor and, in threatening legal action, posited a surrogate champion in a comparatively nonviolent forum, the courtroom. Following the riot, the *London Times* (1849) provided a persuasive defense and justification of Macready's reluctance to confront Forrest:

> Among the members of the histrionic profession, it is, we believe, a general rule not to express public disapprobation of each other. Mr. Forrest seems to be highly offended because he is not named, and ambitious for the glory of having been the least courteous actor ever seen in Great Britain, he writes a thing called a 'card,' in which he declares that he is the hero in question. This 'card' is one of the very lowest productions in the English language.... Even the not very delicate stomach of the *New York Herald* cannot put up with such grossness, and honestly declares that it is 'one of the most brutal, ungentlemanly, disgraceful *pronunciamentos* that ever emanated from one theatrical man to another.'[71]

Elite supporters deplored Forrest's behavior, even within the far less exacting realm of theatrical men. However, the anonymous "American Citizen" eagerly championed his native son:

> If his [Forrest's] words are not as dainty as a Chesterfield would use, ... it is only an evidence that he is not schooled in the science that teaches men to deceive by falsehood; if he chooses to call men and things by their right names, it is clear that he is honest, and seeks not the shelter afforded by vague inuendoes [*sic*]

and indirect charges; if his are the bold declarations of honest conviction, he cannot be accused of concealing his opinions, nor as being a man who fears to assume all the responsibility of his acts and expressions.[72]

Forrest's supporters praised him for expressing direct, genuine feelings and deplored Macready's decorous nonconfrontation as an affected, dangerous vision of manhood that only feigned sincerity.

The drama approached its climax when Macready returned to New York—the same day on which Forrest separated from his wife. On May 7, 1849, three competing Macbeths played in New York—Macready at Astor Place, Forrest at the democratic Broadway, and Thomas Hamblin (capitalizing on the publicity) at the Bowery. Fans of Forrest filled the Astor Place, hurling taunts and projectiles at the stage. By the third act, chairs that were thrown from the balcony brought down the curtain. Macready planned to leave the city, but a committee of 47 prominent citizens, including Herman Melville and Washington Irving (45 years after Johnathan Oldstyle mocked animalistic behaviors in working-class audiences), petitioned him to stay. Macready reluctantly complied. The quarrel between the two actors had grown into a social and political question of masculine dominance. In his diary, former New York mayor Philip Hone, a prominent member of the city's elite, presented the issue as a matter of class-based, masculine pride: "The respectable part of our citizens will never consent to be put down by a mob raised to serve the purposes of such a fellow as Forrest."[73] Forrest's audience (enacting the role of dramatic hero that it had been fed for some 20 years in plays like *The Gladiator*) exerted control over a space from which it was excluded, and the elite class drew a proverbial line in the sand beyond which the masses could not pass. The conservative *Morning Express* (1849) supported the lawful suppression of a potentially unruly working-class mob:

> We trust that, taught by the experiences of the past, the municipal authorities will consult at once their own credit and the claims of their constituents to be protected in the enjoyment of their rights, by taking care, beforehand, that no such outrage as that perpetrated at this establishment, last Monday night [May 7], can possibly be repeated.... [T]he lessees of the theatre, at which he [Macready] is engaged—who pay to the city a regular license, and are doubly entitled to its protection, have their rights too, in which they can equitably claim to be maintained by its ordinances.[74]

Similar to Macready's treatment of Forrest, rather than engaging the working-class male on his own level, elite men invoked the law to suppress inappropriate masculine behaviour. Henry James, who recalled the riot from boyhood, condemned the rioters' actions as the "instinctive hostility of barbarism to culture."[75] In Act I, scene vii, Macbeth says to his wife: "I dare do all that may become a man." Yet the radical disparity between interpretations of what "becomes a man" impacted what each side of the Astor Place struggle was willing to dare.

Anticipating trouble, the new Whig mayor of New York (sworn in on May 8) met heads of law enforcement and the managers of the Astor Place Opera House (William Niblo and James H. Hackett, who refused to cancel the performance) to ensure the safety of the audience. There would be 200 policemen stationed inside the theatre, 125 outside it, and approximately 300 members of the National Guard on call. Mayor Caleb Smith Woodhull ordered the removal of a large mound of paving stones at the construction site of a sewer next to Astor Place—for reasons never explained, no one followed this directive. Meanwhile, a Tammany boss (Isaiah Rynders) and the "American Committee" organized and inflamed working-class opposition to Macready:

> WORKINGMEN
> SHALL
> AMERICANS OR ENGLISH RULE
> IN THIS CITY?
> The crew of the English steamer has threatened all Americans who shall dare to express their opinion this night at the English Aristocratic Opera House!!
> We advocate no violence, but a free expression of opinion to all public men!
> WORKINGMEN! FREEMEN!!
> STAND BY YOUR
> LAWFUL RIGHTS.
> *American Committee.*[76]

A "nativist" society (anti-Catholic, anti-immigrant, and especially anti-Irish), the American Committee pledged "America for Americans." Irish immigrants, who actually composed a sizable percentage of the rioters, were united with nativists in their hatred of the British. The committee was headed by E. Z. C. Judson, also known as "Ned Buntline," a dime-novel author of the Buffalo Bill stories and, later, a member of the Know-Nothing Party.[77] The language, although overtly peaceful, resembled the violent cries for freedom uttered by Forrest's Spartacus in *The Gladiator*:

> Death to the Roman fiends, that make their mirth
> Out of the groans of bleeding misery!
> Ho, slaves, arise! it is your hour to kill!
> Kill and spare not—For wrath and liberty! –
> Freedom for bondmen—freedom and revenge![78]

Forrest also provided real-life inspiration for the "free expression of opinion" in his curtain-speech defense of hissing Macready.

The stage was now set for the violent climax. Forrest supporters interrupted Macready's performance. Quickly arrested and held prisoner in the basement of the theatre, they later attempted to set fire to the building. As Macready struggled through *Macbeth,* a mob estimated at anywhere between 10,000 and 24,000 attacked the Opera House, throwing paving stones at the building and the police. Unable to hold the building, the police retreated inside. The National Guard attempted to subdue the crowd but were attacked and ultimately forced to fire on the crowd, killing 31 and injuring nearly 150. Death estimates vary, and the press inflated some contemporary estimates. 22 died on the night of May 10, but an additional 9 died in the following days. The 150 injured included members of the police and the National Guard, who effectively squelched tensions in the following days.

EPILOGUE: CLEARING RUBBLE AND ASSIGNING BLAME

No perceptible change occurred in any of the major New York theatres. Theatrical business continued pretty much as usual, other than the temporary closing of the Astor Place for repairs, although fear of further violence diminished patronage at all playhouses in the days immediately following the riot. A May 11 Shakespearean performance at the Walnut Street Theatre in Philadelphia—the unintentionally ironic *Much Ado About Nothing*—may have comprised the extent of the theatrical response. On the day after the riot, Forrest fully absolved himself of all responsibility for the violence:

> This blood will rest on the heads of the Committee who insisted that Macready should perform despite of the known wishes of the people to the contrary, and on the heads of the public authorities who were requested by many of the citizens to close the house, and thereby prevent any further demonstration.[79]

The Gladiator works on stage, not in the street. Martyred, selfless, intellectual leaders (Spartacus, Metamora, Cade) fueled Forrest's prize-winning dramas. Working-class participants of the riot, however, privileged physical destruction over whatever high ideals inspired it. If the riot had succeeded, halting Macready's performance and forcing him to leave the country forever, Forrest likely would have taken credit for inspiring the victory and thanked the American people for their support. Instead, he finished out the week with his normal repertoire, playing to very small houses, before (unusual for him at that time) taking a short break because of an undisclosed illness—possibly, if not probably, brought on by emotional exhaustion.

Forrest's dominance of the American stage waned. Scandals associated with the riot, which was immediately followed by his divorce, made him even less appealing to the image-conscious middle and upper classes that controlled the nation's legitimate theatre. Health and age forced him to curtail performances in the 1850s and 60s. Although he continued to draw loyal audiences (often in comparatively obscure theatrical outposts), his time had passed. As happens with every generation's actors, his performance style appeared increasingly quaint, and his performances assumed the quality of a nostalgic museum piece. Macready immediately fled to England, never to return to America. He retired from the stage less than two years later. The Opera House, briefly renamed the New York Theatre, never recovered from the stigma of the riot, closing its doors forever in 1852. The building survived as the Clinton Hall Library until 1890.

Newspapers freely assigned blame both to Macready and to Forrest, but many papers, including Boston's *Daily Evening Traveller* (1856), condemned the partisan press for aggravating nationalistic biases characterized by "that intense snobbishness, which refuses to recognize any merit in an American artist because he is an American, and adulates trans-Atlantic talent because it is trans-Atlantic; or that counter-balancing sentiment which patriotically lauds American talent because it is American."[80] Many of Forrest's supporters, including our American Citizen, blamed the Mayor's mishandling of the police and military: "[B]y their [the city authorities'] imprudence, imbecility, and want of courage, and innate contempt for those whom they are pleased to call the 'lower classes,' they have disgraced the city that honored them, and written at least one page of its history with the blood of innocence."[81] Elite patrons of Macready felt that the actions of the military justified and supported the Mayor's resolve: "THE PEACE OF THE CITY MUST AND SHALL BE MAINTAINED."[82]

Philadelphia's *Public Ledger* (1849) somewhat disingenuously evinced surprise that the riot exposed a previously unknown class prejudice: "There is a bitterness and rancor remaining behind...a feeling that there is now in our country, in New York City, what every good patriot hitherto has considered its duty to deny—a *high* and a *low* class."[83] The *Home Journal*

(1849) diminished the significance of the petty quarrel between two actors in light of the "new" awareness of social inequality:

> [T]he 'White and Red Roses of York and Lancaster' were never more distinctly divided into antagonistic parties, than the 'B'hoys' of New York and the 'Upper Ten.'... Macready's real offence, in the eyes of those who drove him from the stage, is in being rather rancidly superfine in his personal manners, and in being dined out continually by the uptowners.[84]

Class concerns joined sectional tensions that lead up to the Civil War, distracting and dividing the nation's thoughts. Fueled by class and race, in the Draft Riots of 1863—caused by northern resistance to laws (favoring the rich) passed to fill Union army shortages—lower-class men targeted both the wealthy and the African Americans, whom they blamed as the cause of the war.[85]

The Astor Place Riot provided a proving ground for proper behavior both within a personal and a group dynamic, which comprised the struggle between Forrest and Macready as well as the audiences who supported them. The opposing sides of this war of masculinity employed markedly different tactics. The battle plan of the working class—in the words of the *United States Magazine and Democratic Review* (1845), "an uncombed, heady, self-cultured mass of strength and energy"—relied on the previously reliable formula of deviant behavior and sovereign rule to enforce submission. The elite, reflecting a changing code of honor and interpolating an alternate level of masculine authority, engaged in intellectual debate through newspapers and employed the police and military as a surrogate masculine force. New York City's police force was professionalized in 1845, and urban centers throughout the country began implementing law enforcement as part of a social responsibility to control unruly elements.[86] The *New York Tribune* (1849) argued for the enforcement of proper decorum in the theatre as a matter of common sense and human courtesy:

> To suppose that, because a man has paid a dollar at the door, he is therefore entitled to annoy and alarm his fellow visitors, to put a stop to the performance, destroy the furniture and endanger the limbs of the performers, is to evince an intensity of stupidity and ruffianism which even 'Mose' should be ashamed of.[87]

This condescending condemnation of working-class behavior, printed the day before the riot, foreshadowed by hours the deathly wages of these social sins.

The men of the urban working class assumed coexisting and equally viable models of masculinity, priding themselves on a coarser performance of manhood that was completely separate from middle-class aspirations of decorum. The violence of the Astor Place Riot validated upper-class enforcement of a single, genteel masculine image and served as a warning of harsh patriarchal discipline. The proper social behavior of a gentleman became legally, as well as socially, enforceable. Elites and the aspiring middle class now freely condemned working-class men, not for political beliefs or economic prejudices, but for social behavior alone. The Astor Place Riot figureheads reflected this same contrast in masculine expression between the reserved introspection of the middle class and the overt physicality of the working class. Macready kept a diary that detailed his feelings, whereas Forrest pronounced his thoughts publicly. Although outwardly stoic, Macready privately proved introspective and remarkably self-critical. Macready's self-awareness provides valuable insight into the essence of his character, revealing his secrets and fears. Forrest lacked, and perhaps felt he did not need, that emotional outlet, because his idealistic view of masculine behavior suggested that inner thought and outer action should be identical. He spoke forcefully and acted decisively without the comfort, or cowardice, of private reflection. Forrest instructed that his private papers be destroyed after his death, so aside from a handful of letters, only Forrest's public persona and his absolute confidence in himself as a man remain.

Forrest encouraged an acting duel of sorts, adjusting his schedule and repertory to match Macready's, thus forcing competition and comparison—as close to a personal, physical confrontation as was practical in the theatrical world. Throwing down the heavy gauntlet of American masculinity, Forrest engaged the darling of the elite in mortal combat, commanded the spotlight, and flexed his muscles against the perceived abuses of aristocratic foes. The personal and professional struggles of Forrest and Macready, each enacting the masculine behavior of their respective audience, fueled the feud and revealed the incompatibility of their manly models. Neither Macready nor Forrest could have acted differently and, therefore, have affected the events that lead up to the riot. By 1849, masculine identities had become so firmly entrenched that no further room for compromise remained—providing a striking parallel to the nation's positions on slavery and the Union.

4. Decorum and Delicacy: The Feminized Manliness of Edwin Booth

> *The transition from Forrest to Edwin Booth marked the most important phase of its [the American stage's] development. Forrest, although he had a spark of genius, was intrinsically and essentially animal. Booth was intellectual and spiritual.... The epoch that accepted Booth as the amplest exponent of taste and feeling in dramatic art was one of intellect and refinement.*[1]
>
> William Winter, 1893

This assessment by Booth's close friend and contemporary, which was published in the year of Booth's death, trumpeted the cultural triumph of the genteel middle classes. Dismissing Forrest and, by association, the working-class male, as a soulless animal a half century after Forrest's theatrical prime suggests a continuing need to champion the validity and primacy of bourgeois masculine values at the expense of alternate manly visions. In this chapter I examine Edwin Booth both as a "feminine" and a "masculine" figure—the latter becoming more and more inflected by the former as his strengths and limitations coalesced into an ideal that was mutually constructed with his middle-class audience. The literal and figurative feminine influence on the American stage brought genteel, middle-class values to both sides of the curtain. Booth's conception of Hamlet represented the ideals and behaviors of a mid-nineteenth-century gentleman, even as his successful portrayal of stage villains complicated his manly image. Booth's restrained endurance of personal tragedies reflected Hamlet's suffering and drew parallels to Abraham Lincoln and the nation in the throes of Civil War. The shift from Forrest to Booth implies a cyclical return to the eighteenth-century mode of masculinity described in chapter 1—built on refinement, repression, and sentiment—but these qualities became more fully assimilated into a distinctly American vision of manhood.

The December 1863 issue of *Harper's New Monthly Magazine* featured the "Easy Chair" editor (George William Curtis) escorting a rustic friend to see Forrest at Niblo's Garden and Booth at the Winter Garden on a single evening. They stopped first at Niblo's:

> It was crammed with people!....And yet it was the thirty or forty *some*thingth night of the engagement...And people are grandfathers now who used to see him play in their youths....[The audience] delights in the representation, and shouts at it, and cries for more, and hastens and squeezes the next night to enjoy it all over again....And it has a palpable physical effect. There were a great many young women around us crying in the tender passages....They were not refined nor intellectual women. They were, perhaps, rather coarse. But they cried good hearty tears....The popular enjoyment arising from this acting is undeniable.[2]

Few contemporaries note an appreciable number of women in Forrest's audience; although by 1863, factory girls like Mose's companion, "Lize," may have accompanied working-class beaux. Curtis likely exaggerated his experience at Niblo's, and on all legs of his journey, to give the impression that Forrest enjoyed a base of appeal that went beyond working-class men. On the next leg of the journey, Curtis took his companion to the Winter Garden where Booth played Iago:

> The difference of the spectacle was striking. The house was comfortably full, not crowded. The air of the audience was that of refined attention rather than of eager interest. Plainly it was a more cultivated and intellectual audience....Yet there was a certain chilliness in the audience which must have affected the actor. It was the attitude of an audience appreciative and expectant of fine points, but not irresistibly swept away.[3]

The writer laments the loss of an unfettered audience response, such as that which greeted Forrest, that might well die with the elder tragedian. Curtis suggests a shift from active engagement to thoughtful watchfulness and emotional detachment.

In the first leg of this three-pronged journey, they had "squeezed into the mass of men" at a Union ratification meeting at the Cooper Institute and listened to a speech by General John Cochrane, which was "greeted with hearty cheers." The editorial visitors admired the democratic throng: "This before us was the government of the country." They praised the great, and uniquely American, power of public speech: "It is by talk, by argument, by comparison, by enlightenment, by every means incessantly brought to bear upon public opinion, that we are governed." As the pair left the Cooper Institute, the editor's rustic but learned friend concluded:

> Statesmanship in modern nations consists in the sagacity with which the national desire is apprehended by official leaders.... Mr. Lincoln is the most successful and excellent of Presidents, because he has an instinctive perception, not of the whims and gusts of the rabble, but of the honest national desire.[4]

By 1860, although passionate oratorical pyrotechnics remained a component of political persuasion (just as the thrill of theatrical bombast and spectacle proved an inescapable part of the playhouse), Curtis suggests a growing need to appeal to intellect and sentiment.

By the middle of the nineteenth century, the composition and decorum of middle-class audiences was transforming. Within this changing audience dynamic, the *New York Tribune* (1855) suggests that Forrest's demeanor and muscular style ill-suited the restrained gentility and delicate sensibility of the image-conscious middle class: "He may have drawn many a responsive cheer from man, but has never drawn a sympathetic tear from woman."[5] Despite the "Easy Chair" claims, Forrest's failure to connect with women (or at least refined women), the arbiters of middle-class taste, diminished his potential, limited the scope of his social and theatrical success, and placed limitations on his viability as a masculine model with appeal across class boundaries. In *The Feminization of American Culture*, Ann Douglas argues that the role of women in shaping the genteel behavior of the middle classes dramatically increased, as "a genuine redemptive mission in their society: to propagate the potentially matriarchal virtues of nurture, generosity, and acceptance; to create the 'culture of the feelings.'"[6] Women held an important role as representatives and enforcers of a code of behavior that was built upon refinement, respectability, and self-restraint, which Lawrence Levine identifies as reframing the social role of theatre: "[A]udiences were to approach the masters and their works with proper respect and proper seriousness, for aesthetic and spiritual elevation rather than mere entertainment was the goal."[7]

Respectable women rarely frequented the theatres of the early nineteenth century; but, beginning in the 1840s and gaining momentum during the nineteenth century, theatres like the Chestnut Street Theatre in Philadelphia appealed to this new and enormously lucrative market:

> It is the desire of the Manager to establish a Series of Elegant FAMILY MATINEES...such as those which have obtained immense popularity in Boston.... It may be well to add that respectable ladies may, with the greatest propriety, should they desire, attend these entertainments without escort, as they are devised mainly for their patronage and amusement.[8]

Theatres sanitized behavior in the auditorium to attract female audiences and to ensure the safety of the family:

> To render the Arch St. Theatre in every way worthy a liberal support, the Third Tier Nuisance [prostitution] will be abolished; improper characters will be prevented from obtaining admission to any part of the house; and the sale of alcohol, in any shape, will be discontinued in the saloons. In sacrificing the large profits attending these usual practices of all other theatres, now attempted for the first time in the United States, [Manager] W.E. Burton looks for a compensation in the more frequent attendance of families, who may depend upon experiencing at the Arch St. Theatre a wholesome entertainment of the highest character, without the possibility of witnessing an impropriety either on or off the stage.[9]

In addition, the changing atmosphere and physical configuration of the auditorium reflected new social priorities, and the *Spirit of the Times* (1861) suggests a shift in audience control from working-class men to middle-class families:

> Even the New Bowery, strange as it may seem, is going to surrender to the demand for change...[T]he shirt-sleeved and peanut pocketed Democracy are to be removed to the upper tiers.... Respectability wants room—wants to take its wife and daughter to the play—and Shilling Democracy must give way.[10]

Harper's Monthly (1870) celebrated this triumph of "respectability," banishing boisterous men to the upper reaches of the theatre and placing the audience power in the women-friendly, family-dominated parquet: "Where the noisy crowd of men were massed, upon hard, backless benches, there is the luminous cloud of lovely toilets mingled with the darker dress of the *jeunesse doree* [rich and fashionable young people]."[11] Such purifications dissuaded Forrest's audience, and indeed, theatres like Sanford's Opera House made it clear that they were not welcome: "It is particularly requested, on behalf of the Ladies, that all whistling, shouting and unnecessary noise, will be avoided."[12] The emphasis on placidity, comfort, and refinement in the "legitimate" theatre redefined the rules of the playhouse as a public space.

Managers of Philadelphia's Chestnut Street Theatre ensured that dramatic fare contributed to the safest, and least objectionable, possible environment: "So smooth, indeed, is the language, so natural and appropriate, that like a perfect *toitette* [sic], it attracts no especial attention. By an afterthought only you recognize its beauty."[13] Sanford's Opera House also championed personal and social benefits of the drama:

> The public are becoming too enlightened to longer listen to the old stories of the demoralizing effects of public amusement, as the body requires medicine, so does the mind require recreation.... Philadelphia has long felt the need of... an establishment... where patrons could bring their children without the fear of corrupting in any way the morals of the young—a place of family resort.[14]

The Walnut Street Theatre fashioned itself as a haven where genteel men and their families could freely respond to sentimental dramas such as *East Lynne* (1863), which "evoked from DENSELY CROWDED AND INTELLIGENT AUDIENCES Manifestations of Hearty Sympathy never before known in a Theatre.... Tears of Unfeigned Sorrow and AUDIBLE SOBS of Grief, Not only from ladies and children but from the sterner sex."[15] *Every Saturday* (1871) chastised middle-class men for submitting to the feminization of the theatre: "What mild creatures we are when sitting at a play! how shy we are of showing our delight when delighted and with what pitiful patience we submit to the long-drawn-out stupidity of thin melodramas."[16] Men who refused to accept this cultural change rebelled by attending entertainments that were associated with rougher working-class spectators. By the 1860s, gentlemen's magazines such as *Spirit of the Times* (1866), which once devoted significant space to the theatre, shifted their entertainment focus to sports and adventure and recognized theatre as a social responsibility and a familial obligation: "the bore of attending dull or even good performances for the sole purpose of escorting their Mary Janes."[17] The leg shows after the war, starting with *The Black Crook* (1866), more actively encouraged male attendance at the theatre, although the legitimate stage (at which alcohol and prostitutes were banned) remained a space that demanded genteel, "feminized" behavior.

Beginning in the mid-1840s and continuing into the early 1870s, three decades of similar announcements, appeals, assurances, and lamentations suggest a continuing and largely consistent journey toward refinement and restraint in auditoriums and on stages that catered to middle-class audiences. Mutually driven by audience aesthetic and theatrical opportunism, this transition from boisterous passion to thoughtful appreciation coincided with Edwin Forrest's increasingly marginalized appeal to theatres and audiences that resisted this gentrification. The social dominance of the middle class, which lead to a desire for theatrical gentility, encouraged the careers of several prominent classical actors and ultimately set the stage for Edwin Booth's development and success.

"DARLING OF MISFORTUNE": TRAGEDY MODERATING LIFE AND ART

Booth's personal journey from rebellion to restraint, which was prompted by personal tragedy and a moderating feminine influence, paralleled the increasingly temperate social behaviors of middle-class men. Whereas the appeal and accessibility of his performance aesthetic marked the pinnacle of the classical style, elevated and dignified British stars such as the Kembles inspired a number of actors and appealed to elite audiences—or to those who aspired to join the elite. English actors Thomas Abthorpe Cooper and William Charles Macready popularized this approach to performing on American stages, and the careers and personas of James E. Murdoch, Edward L. Davenport, and Lawrence Barrett reveal the modifications employed by native actors, as well as the intellectual elevation, moral inspiration, and emotional limitation of this manly model that helped guide Booth on his path to stardom.

James E. Murdoch (1811–1893), whose success peaked in the 1840s, presented refined and idealized characters and also wrote and taught extensively on the art of stage elocution.[18] As the *Spirit of the Times* (1845) noted, Murdoch elevated theatre's position in American society:

> The pervading quality of the performance was grace and propriety of conception and delivery: relieved by electrical flashes on passages of a more elevated character. All our contemporaries concur in acknowledgment of his manly bearing, the beauty of his voice and his admirable reading.[19]

Murdoch's image of "grace," "propriety," and "manly bearing" suggested a less exciting, but more noble, vision of manhood than the Forrestian model that was currently dominating American stages. Actor Joseph Jefferson praised Murdoch's 1853 performance of *School for Scandal*: "There was a manliness about his light comedy that gave it more dignity than the flippant style in which it was usually played. This method elevated the characters exceedingly."[20] Equally noted for playing tragic roles such as Hamlet, Murdoch presented a dignified, moderate, intellectual masculinity. Jefferson praised Murdoch's courage to develop an independent style: "Neither the popularity of Forrest nor the fame of [the elder] Booth could tempt him to an imitation of either of these tragedians, and his comedy was equally free from resembling the style of the Wallacks or that of Charles Kemble."[21] But whereas Murdoch avoided the excess of the romantic tragedians, he also failed to inspire their passionate following.

Anna Cora Mowatt praised the polished and versatile Edward L. Davenport (1815–1877) for "his fine person, manly bearing, and quietly earnest acting."[22] Henry Dickinson Stone complimented his discernment and emotional control, often seemingly in spite of his audience: "In his impersonations, calm judgment controls his impulses; his action and declamation are never measured and gauged by the popular applause, but regulated by his own correct taste."[23] O. A. Roorbach lauded the intelligence of his performance: "A striking quality of Mr. Davenport's acting is its quietness. His best 'points' are made in repose. He is not, however, tame, for it is the energy of the *mind* that is expressed, though not of the body—where the passion is supposed to be of a highly wrought nature."[24] Although he lacked Booth's passion, Davenport's cultured reputation elevated his status. Although he admired him intellectually, critic Adam Badeau questioned the emotional impact of Davenport's restraint: "It never once excited any real emotion in the audience, it never made us feel."[25] Davenport incorporated an odd mixture of high and low in his choice of plays and in elements of his performance style, and, according to critic Henry P. Goddard, Davenport's willingness to fill theatre coffers at any cost ultimately injured his dramatic reputation: "[I]t was this very willingness to play anything and everything that kept him below his true place in the judgment of the careless majority."[26] Davenport faced limitations as a masculine model because he could not find *one role* to embody, which suggested the limited options that were available to men of this period. Often locked into a single, class-determined role for life, men ran the risk of losing their manly status if they attempted to shift their identities—suggesting the absence of masculine fluidity in spite of the promises of social mobility.

The studious, ambitious, and sometimes artificial Lawrence Barrett (1838–1891), another well-known actor of the classical school, successfully played Cassius (*Julius Caesar*), Lanciotto (*Francesca da Rimini*), Hamlet, and Richelieu. A self-educated, self-made man, Barrett's ego and competitive insecurity made him difficult to like, but he proved an effective manager, encouraged new drama, and revived worthy American plays of the past, such as Boker's *Francesca da Rimini*. Now primarily known for reinvigorating Edwin Booth's career in the 1880s (and Austin Brereton's description of Barrett as "lithe and graceful in figure" suggests strong similarities to Booth), Barrett relieved Booth from the responsibility of theatre management (never Booth's forte), allowing him to focus exclusively on acting.[27] Whereas critic Henry P. Phelps praised Barrett as "ambitious, intelligent and painstaking," Alfred Ayres provides a fairly typical accusation of Barrett's pure technicality and lack of warmth:

> Mr. Barrett is generally looked upon as being a brainy man, an earnest man, an ambitious man, and a studious man. He writes well, talks well, and manages well, but in the judgment of the metropolitan connoisseurs he does not play well. His culture and cleverness appear, they say, in everything he does except in his stage personations.[28]

Barrett's flaws as an actor and masculine model also mirrored those that were warned against in the conduct manuals. He attempted to give the appearance of genuineness, but the stage effect was visible.

These intellectual practitioners of the classical school pursued a precisely detailed craft. They elevated the art of acting and theatre's social position, gradually eroding a measure of upper-class prejudice against men of the theatre. William Winter's description of Barrett could serve equally well for all three: "Lawrence Barrett... [showed] himself to be a true artist, a deep student of human nature, a superb executant of dramatic effect...—by the splendid self-control and the refined art with which...he subordinated copious declamation to intense feeling."[29] Murdoch, Davenport, and Barrett (as well as others of the classical school) provided sensitive and intelligent, if often unspectacular, models of genteel masculinity—seeming sometimes to share the problems of refined, intellectual political figures who failed to fully connect with their audiences. While their lack of intensity proved anathema to working-class audiences, their dramatic adaptability appealed to middle-class men who were tentatively finding their way through a complex social landscape. Described as "graceful," "elevated," "intelligent," "well-considered," "tasteful," "earnest," "correct," "calm," "quiet," and exhibiting "manly bearing," they presented safe and ennobling images of American manhood that reflected conservative values of image-conscious elites. However, none of them successfully duplicated the excitement that was felt in Edwin Booth, nor his compelling blend of accessibility and vulnerability.

Born in rural Maryland, Edwin Booth (1833–1893), son of fiery British star Junius Brutus Booth, was named after the elder Booth's friend,

Edwin Forrest. Receiving little formal education, the young Edwin Booth served as companion and pseudo-guardian to his often drunk and mentally unstable father on theatrical tours. The father, encouraging the son to establish an independent theatrical identity, left Edwin to make his own way in California in 1852, but Junius Brutus died on his return trip East. Although their decision to part had been mutual, Edwin still tortured himself for "abandoning" his father. Edwin Booth remained in California, acting with Catherine Sinclair (the former Mrs. Edwin Forrest) in the mid-1850s. Booth served a challenging apprenticeship, playing a wide range of roles for little pay and touring remote outposts in the American West, as well as in Hawaii and Australia.[30] Booth's twenties were marked by profligate behavior—drunkenness, gambling, womanizing, and general irresponsibility—only somewhat moderated by his marriage to Mary Devlin in 1860 but permanently abandoned after her death in 1863. Booth, performing (often drunk) in New York as Mary lay dying in Boston, blamed himself for her death: "[T]he hell within me is intense! My self-reproaches will never cease. [M]y conduct hastened her death; when she heard that I—her all—was lost to all sense of decency and respect for her—her feeble spirit sank."[31]

A similar migration from passionate excess to decorous self-command marked his artistic development. When Booth first performed *Richard III* in New York in 1857, most critics called his performance a pale imitation of his father's, although the *New York Tribune* credited him with "a vigorous truthfulness which startles his audience into wild enthusiasm."[32] Having modeled his youthful acting after his famously passionate father, Booth consciously transformed the nature of his performance style over the following years. He established a respected national reputation by 1860 and even toured England with moderate success in 1861. At the Winter Garden Theatre in New York (November 26, 1864 to March 22, 1865), Booth established himself as the nation's greatest actor by performing his unprecedented 100-night run of *Hamlet*. Three weeks after the close of this theatrical triumph, his younger brother, John Wilkes, assassinated Lincoln. Booth removed himself from the stage for nearly a year (and dissolved his engagement to Blanche Hanel) but returned as Hamlet at the Winter Garden in 1866 to a nearly universal approval. The Winter Garden burned to the ground in 1867, destroying Booth's personal stock of properties, costumes, and scenery. He immediately made plans for Booth's Theatre (1869), a building of sophisticated Victorian design, lavish audience comforts, and revolutionary stage technology. Once completed, its spectacularly mounted productions, which were critical and popular successes, focused primarily on finely detailed "historical recreations" of Shakespeare. Booth managed the theatre until 1874, when he filed for bankruptcy because of mismanagement (his own and others') and a bad economy.[33] With Lawrence Barrett, he embarked on several profitable, popular, and critically acclaimed tours, which were often considered the pinnacle of American Shakespearean acting in the nineteenth century. He published two sets of acting versions of various Shakespearean plays (the first in the late 1860s with actor Henry Hinton, the second with critic William Winter in the late 1870s) that were similar to those published by Charles Kean and Henry Irving, although neither set sold well.[34] In 1888, Booth founded and funded The Players, which was patterned after London's Garrick Club

Figure 4.1 Edwin Booth on the cover of *Harper's Weekly: A Journal of Civilization* (January 13, 1866). The Library Company of Philadelphia.

Harper's Weekly heralded the theatrical return of the melancholy Booth after a nine-month, self-imposed hiatus that followed Lincoln's assassination.

and designed to elevate the social position of actors, to which he donated many of his stage possessions and his personal library, and at which he resided until his death in 1893.

Although burlesques of famous actors proved extremely popular, few satirized Booth, because his acting so closely approached life. George L. Fox's popular burlesque of *Hamlet* focused more on exaggerating production choices than on Booth's performance in the role. Nat Goodwin, "king of burlesque imitators," spoke of his refusal to copy Booth's acting:

> [W]hat's there to hang a caricature on? His art's rounded like a ball. He has no rough knobs sticking out for pegs. In caricature we exaggerate mannerisms. You can't be funny by exaggerating something that is not in the first place a little overdone by the one you burlesque.... No, I won't tackle Booth! I couldn't be funny caricaturing perfection.[35]

The *New York Daily Tribune*'s (1876) amazement at Booth's nearly invisible performance balanced emotional attraction with technical appreciation:

> His execution...was marvelous for concentration of intellect, grace of action, symmetry of molding, growth of emotional experience and condition, thrilling flashes of frenzy, and perfect precision in utterance and method. The processes of art have long since become to him a second nature; and he represents this character [Hamlet] with such consummate ease that only in the retrospect will a critical observer appreciate the splendid poise and firm touch with which all the beautifully complex mechanism of the work has been conducted.[36]

While "natural" represents a relative term based on intrinsically contingent aesthetic criteria, Booth brought acting closer to life than audiences previously had seen on stage. Karen Halttunen finds a similar formalized pursuit of natural ease in the social performance of the middle classes:

> a system of polite conduct that demanded a flawless self-discipline practiced within an apparently easy, natural, sincere manner. At the center of the genteel performance was an important contradiction: the contents of polite social intercourse, as perceived by sentimentalists, were natural and sincere feelings; but the forms of polite conduct, as evidenced in the detailed complexity of the laws of etiquette, were deliberate and restrained.[37]

The dual nature of actor and character requires conscious, minute manipulation of behavior to appear natural, and the success of Booth's comparatively seamless depiction, which hid all traces of its process, resembled the "invisible" social conduct that was advocated in advice literature.

William Winter's praise of Booth, onstage and offstage, suggests a masculine model that is far removed from Edwin Forrest: "So much, in the character and in the acting of Edwin Booth is gentle, delicate, winning, and admirable."[38] Providing another departure from the manly muscularity of Forrest, E. C. Stedman's *Atlantic Monthly* description of Booth's physique, bordering on the hermaphroditic, praised the younger tragedian's "broad shoulders, slender hips, and comely tapering limbs, all supple, and knit together with harmonious grace." Of average height (5'7") and a slight build, Booth was ill-suited for roles of great stature or overpowering presence. Although he initially attempted to follow in the passionate artistic steps of his father, as Stedman suggests, Booth's physical and emotional proclivities demanded roles of emotional complexity and seething, repressed feeling, characters "softened and strengthened by the repose of logical thought, and interfused with that serene spirit which lifts the man of feeling so far above the child of passions unrestrained."[39] Booth's admirers praised the moral superiority of his masculine self-control and derided the weakness of unchecked emotion (even on stage) as unmanly. As early as 1857, the *Boston Traveler* praised Booth's subtlety: "There is no ear-splitting violence. He has the magnetic, sympathizing quality in his tones. They charm you, without telling you the secret of their charm. This quality is the gift of nature. No art can catch it."[40] Booth actually sought a heightened reality that was in no way limited to, in the words of critic and early mentor Adam Badeau, the "cold, debasing realism" of life that would became the goal of actors toward the end of the century. Rather, Booth carefully elevated what was natural to "the poetry of the stage" through careful control of his (and his characters') emotions.[41]

William Winter credited Booth's acting as a model for middle-class audiences: "Edwin Booth's ministrations had developed acuteness of perception, diffused refinement, awakened emotion, imparted spiritual knowledge of a lofty ideal, and provided a high standard of dramatic art."[42] The career of influential drama critic William Winter (1836–1917) grew alongside that of Edwin Booth, who was three years his senior. Winter began writing criticism after moving to New York in 1859. Most theatrical criticism in antebellum America was written anonymously or under a pseudonym and was blatantly partisan in support of (or in opposition to) specific theatres or performers. Like Winter, other prominent drama critics of the Civil War era (including Henry Austin Clapp, Laurence Hutton, and John Rankin Towse), often articulated conservative, middle-class views and applied moral standards to theatrical works and performances. Detailed correspondence between Booth and Winter, covering decades, suggests Winter's impact on Booth's refinement.[43]

As the paradigm of the self-made man dominates Forrest's story, tragedy shapes Booth's. Booth felt guilt and personal responsibility for the deaths of his father and his first wife. The same year that he opened his theatre, Booth married Mary McVicker, who gave birth to a short-lived son in 1870. After the baby's death, McVicker gradually descended into madness. A carriage accident in 1875 severely and permanently injured Booth's left arm and hand. In 1879, an insane Mark Gray shot at Booth as he performed *Richard II* in Chicago. The burning of the Winter Garden and the financial ruin that accompanied Booth's namesake theatre impeded his professional

Figure 4.2 Edwin Booth as Hamlet. Image courtesy of the author.

Although comparatively more intense and tortured, Booth's thoughtful repose suggests a similarity to that of other men of intellectual refinement (figures 1.5–1.8).

advancement. Looming above this entire catalog of disasters, of course, was the stigma attached to his name through the Lincoln assassination. William Winter perceived Booth as profoundly tormented: "[T]hat mood of poetic exaltation, pensive melancholy, and exquisite refinement for which his acting...has long been distinguished, and in that tone of settled spiritual pain—that atmosphere of profound, inexorable grief." Booth's silent suffering in the face of tragedy qualified him for bourgeois gentility but also elevated his admirers by association.[44] Nowhere was the collaborative nature of the relationship between Booth and his audience, which mutually validated values and behaviors, more apparent than in *Hamlet*.

BOOTH'S HAMLET: "A NINETEENTH-CENTURY GENTLEMAN"

The *New York Herald* (1870) lavished praise on Booth's *Hamlet* of the 1860s as the ultimate theatrical synergy: "It was a genuine feast of reason, of beauty, of fashion, and of histrionic intelligence and splendor, both as regards actors, scenery, and audience."[45] Although likely more a hope of what the performance might become than a description of what it was, a San Francisco reviewer's praise of the 19-year-old Booth anticipated increasingly refined perceptions of manhood:

> Melancholy without gloom, contemplative yet without misanthropy, philosophical yet enjoying playfulness in social converse, a man by himself yet with ardent feelings of friendship, a thorough knower of human nature, Hamlet stands as the type of all that is firm, dignified, gentlemanly and to be respected in a man.[46]

While ostensibly discussing the role rather than the man who enacted it, only Booth's interpretation of Hamlet, which was made possible by the audiences and critics who guided and popularized it, revealed this complexity. By 1857, Boston's *Transcript* saw in Booth's Hamlet, "the beau ideal of the sweet, the graceful, the gentlemanly."[47] Nine years later, shortly following his return to the stage after Lincoln's assassination, the *Atlantic Monthly* recognized the appeal of Hamlet's thoughtful melancholy and restraint, which was filtered through the maturity of Booth's performance: "[Hamlet was] the most accomplished gentleman ever drawn...; a gentleman by heart, no less,—full of kindly good-fellowship, brooking no titles with his friends, loving goodness and truth, impatient of fools, scorning affectation; moreover, the glass of fashion and the mould of form, the modern ideal of manly beauty."⁴⁸ Whereas a brooding Hamlet incapable of decisive action may seem an unlikely template for masculine behavior, Booth's understated performance made the Melancholy Dane vital and accessible. Booth's conception and portrayal presented an ideal model of the nineteenth-century gentleman, and through it he systematically sought to elevate his audiences' tastes. Equating Booth's acceptance of personal suffering with the tragedies of the character, middle-class audiences lauded his forbearance and restraint, and their admiration for Booth's self-control extended to his portrayal of villains who hid behind perfectly constructed masks of deception.

Critics like A. C. Wheeler (writing as Nym Crinkle), an opponent of Booth and of his influence on America's theatre and audiences, deplored the limitations that Booth imposed on one of the most popular stage roles:

> Mr. Booth's Hamlet...suppressed passion and elaborated sentiment. It returned to the literary and poetic charms of the play with extraordinary gifts for their declaration, and in doing so it in a measure ignored the dramatic and tragic. Hamlet no longer shattered, it titillated. The divine bolts were left out....Hamlet had become a nineteenth-century gentleman.⁴⁹

This condemnation of nineteenth-century gentlemen, in general, and of Booth in particular, extended beyond the theatrical stage to the social one. Wheeler dismissed Booth (and by association his followers) as "a purely intellectual man," whose acting lacked the instinct and passion which should be a theatrical necessity: "[I]ntelligence sits primly up in front and weighs him by sentences, and gravely acquiesces in his points without a ruffle of emotion or a thrill of enthusiasm."⁵⁰ Wheeler, who always preferred Forrest's passion to Booth's reserve, lamented the deadening refinement of the legitimate stage. Booth's Hamlet simultaneously limited and empowered middle-class men. On the one hand, his "domestication" of Hamlet, which was diminished to bourgeois morality, trivialized the larger issues at stake in the play. On the other, vicarious identification with Hamlet allowed viewers to imagine themselves as men of deep feeling and intellect.

Booth's portrayal of Hamlet acted as a moralizing tool. The brochure for Booth's 1870 production, which was created at his behest, promised that the play would elevate viewers

> from the narrow sphere of our daily lives into a loftier, grander region, whose atmosphere perforce shall purify and exalt our souls...shall infuse some of its own precious metal of nobility, honesty and courage into our own lives, glorifying our too mundane souls with some of its higher, more heavenly attributes!⁵¹

These guidelines for audience response illustrated Booth's deliberate effort to cultivate the gentility of the middle and upper classes and to situate the theatre as an ennobling social necessity. Booth consciously presented Hamlet's universality: "He is the epitome of mankind, not an individual, a sort of magic mirror in which all men and all women see the reflex of themselves."[52] Refusing to subordinate himself, with the power of his stage persona Booth became more than a mere actor: "I have given my life to these great roles. I do not consider myself an entertainer! I am an interpreter. I reveal the soul of masterpieces.... They (the audience) should bow their heads reverently before these poems I reveal to them."[53] Revealing a loftiness, bordering on arrogance, Booth enriched his audience while simultaneously fashioning himself as an elevated model.

William Winter in *The Albion* (1862) proffered Booth as a means to instill cultural appreciation in middle-class audiences: "The sole refuge of this age is art; and that should be kept white, pure, peaceful and beautiful. What we need on stage is what will cheer, comfort, and strengthen."[54] *Harper's New Monthly Magazine*, which was published during the month of Lincoln's assassination, framed Booth's *Hamlet* as high culture:

> His playing throughout has an exquisite tone, like an old picture. The charm of the finest portraits, of Raphael's Julius or Leo, of Titian's Francis I, or Ippolito di Medici, of Vandyck's Charles I, is not the drawing nor even the coloring, so much as the nameless, subtle harmony which is called tone. So in Mr. Booth's Hamlet it is not any particular scene, or passage, or look, or movement that conveys the impression; it is the consistency of every part with every other, the pervasive sense of the mind of a true gentleman sadly strained and jarred.[55]

Booth's performance represented something that only the "true gentleman" could understand, and as an artistic work, it demanded to be studied closely and admired:

> [The manager is] happy in announcing to the many who complain that the Academy [of Music] is too large to enjoy fully the delicately artistic traits of Mr. Edwin Booth's acting.... He will repeat the Character of HAMLET [at the Chestnut St. Theatre], in compliance with the expressed wish of many of the Large and Brilliant Audiences that witnessed...his Unapproachable Performance of that Character.[56]

While this playbill justifies the failure to fill the Academy of Music, it also dismisses theatrical caverns as an inappropriate canvas on which to appreciate Booth's "delicately artistic" work and calls for a more exclusive and intimate temple of worship, suggesting that too much popularity was somehow undesirable. An intriguing potential duality exists in the phrase "Unapproachable Performance"—suggesting that Booth's display was unequaled but also somehow distancing and was placed on a pedestal, beyond the grasp of most.

The *New York World* (1870) posited admiration of his performance as a prerequisite to discernment: "Mr. Booth's *Hamlet* is the perfect expression of the artistic taste of our times. That taste is characterized, and nowhere in so marked a manner as in the drama, by the substitution of finish for feeling, elaborateness for earnestness, accuracy for emotion."[57] While audiences might regret the loss of "feeling," "earnestness," and "emotion," applauding, understanding, and even being disturbed by Booth's Hamlet became a social commodity—a status symbols of bourgeois belonging. The *New York Times* (1870) suggested that Booth's audience must learn to revere an image of decorous moderation rather than one of thrilling dynamism: "If it fails to excite our enthusiasm by the force of unquestionable genius, it commands our respect by its fidelity, its self restraint, its obvious reverence for art, and the admirable influence of its example."[58] True appreciation of Booth in all his complexity required a redefinition of the theatrical experience, as articulated by E. C. Stedman: "[H]e courts rapturous silence rather than clamorous applause."[59]

Although audience response to Booth may well have been quiet, the strength of the emotional connection between the actor and his devotees illustrated Booth's effectiveness. An obsessed young fan, Charles Clarke, composed a 60,000-word description of Booth's 1870 performance, praising "all that Booth has done to drill my mind, and put an edge upon my sensibility; and instruct my emotions, and inform my imagination." Clarke saw that within Booth's quiet resignation, "depths below depths of misery and self-conflict," yet still shone through "some source of mental health and light."[60] Far from being limited to a purely cerebral or spiritual appreciation, Booth elicited a passionate response from audiences. Actress Katherine Goodale, who shared the stage with Booth, enthused: "[Y]ou make them [the audience] crazy! I sit out there and watch them until you make me lose my head over your acting. It's like being whirled around until you're dizzy."[61] Booth, keenly aware of his influence, reveled in his power to manipulate: "I like your picture of my working on my audience. Wouldn't it be better to say *playing* on them, as if they were a pipe?"[62] By 1876, New York's *Daily Tribune* saw Booth's Hamlet striking an especially powerful emotional chord with middle-class men: "[T]he desolate calmness of despairing surrender to bleak and cruel fate... is made so pitiable an object that no man with a heart in his bosom can see him without tears."63 This reaction and sense of identification may have been enhanced by the emotional traumas that so many men directly or indirectly experienced during the Civil War—as the balance of strength and vulnerability of the rebellious James Dean or Marlon Brando who were following World War II, or the counterculture actors after the Vietnam War, struck a chord with many who had lived through the war. Whereas the "Easy Chair" writer of *Harper's* spoke of tears (of coarse women) shed for Forrest, the men responding to Booth revealed a more profound depth of sensitivity and intelligence.

Men who were emotionally overwhelmed by sympathy represented a common thread in the years leading up to the Civil War, which Karen Haltunen identifies as a "cult of mourning" that was propagated by the middle class:

> Mourning, the natural human response to the greatest human affliction, was held sacred by sentimentalists as the purest, the most transparent, and thus the most genteel of all sentiments. In mourning, a middle-class man or woman was believed to establish very clearly the legitimacy of his or her claims to genteel social status.64

In Stowe's *Uncle Tom's Cabin*, after Eliza crosses the ice and seeks shelter with the family of a Northern Senator who supports the Fugitive Slave Act, she asks, "[H]ave you ever lost a child?" She then recounts her pitiful tale:

> The woman [the senator's wife who had recently lost a child] did not sob nor weep. She had gone to a place where tears are dry; but every one around her was, in some way characteristic of themselves, showing signs of hearty sympathy.... Our senator was a statesman, and of course could not be expected to cry, like other mortals; and so he turned his back to the company, and looked out of the window, and seemed particularly busy in clearing his throat and wiping his spectacle-glasses, occasionally blowing his nose in a manner that was calculated to excite suspicion, had any one been in a state to observe critically.65

The quiet emotional expression of manly emotion that was similarly directed toward Booth/Hamlet reflected a sympathetic and empathetic understanding of misery.

The man and the character were inextricably linked in the minds of Booth's audience, as plainly stated by the *Evening Post* (1870): "We of today live in the era of Booth, and Booth, to a majority of us, is Hamlet."66

Even Booth's physical appearance matched expectations in the *New York Times* of the same year:

> His spare and almost attenuated frame, his thoughtful, and, indeed, habitually mournful expression; his hollow, low-pitched voice; his splendid dark eye; his jetty, disheveled locks, and a certain morbidness that is suggested by his whole look and bearing, carry conviction to the mass of beholders that in him they see as near an approach as possible to the Hamlet of Shakespeare.[67]

Critic John Rankin Towse, nostalgically looking back after the death of Booth, imagined the tragedian living Hamlet's suffering on stage rather than acting it: "In his life the sweet and the bitter were mingled in almost equal proportions; and there can be little doubt that his private afflictions, most courageously endured, added to his artistic temperament that touch of grave and tender melancholy so well suited to his Hamlet."[68] Booth's performance blurred the line between life and art, as audiences understood that he (Booth/Hamlet) struggled in the face of overwhelming tragedy, which was not of his making and was beyond his control. The *New York Tribune* (1876) recognized a graceful artistry in Booth's emotional devastation that elicited not merely sympathy but adoration:

> [Booth's] Hamlet possesses the indescribable poetic element which fascinates.... The heart has been broken by grief. The mind has been disordered by a terrible shock. The soul—so predisposed to brooding upon the hollowness of this fragile life and the darkness of futurity...—is full of vast, fantastic shapes, and is swayed by all strange forces of the unknown world.... This is Shakespeare's Hamlet, and this is the nature that Mr. Booth reveals.... This he lives brilliantly, too, knowing that sorrow, howsoever powerful in the element of oppression, cannot fascinate. The Hamlet that is merely sorrowful, though he might arouse pity, would never inspire affection. It is the personality beneath the anguish that makes the anguish so stately, so awful, and so majestic. By itself, the infinite grief of Hamlet would overwhelm with the monotony of gray despair; but, since the nature that shines through it is invested with the mysterious and fascinating glamour of beauty in ruin, the grief becomes an active pathos, and the sufferer is loved as well as pitied.[69]

This suffering of Booth/Hamlet, whose sensitivities and personal tragedies were well publicized, helped assuage the anxieties of middle-class men.

On the national stage, challenges and tragedies that faced Lincoln bore a strong resemblance to those that were experienced by Booth/Hamlet. Lincoln lost one of his sons while in office, and his wife's erratic behavior and instability were well known. Adding to these personal calamities,

Lincoln sent young American men to war against fellow Americans, which resulted in hundreds of thousands of deaths on both sides. This burden of guilt and responsibility weighed on him, yet these desperate times demanded action: "The time is out of joint. O cursed spite, / That ever I was born to set it right."[70] *Atlantic Monthly*'s descriptions of the horrors facing Hamlet reflected not only Booth (and Lincoln) but also the struggles of the nation:

> Upon this noblest youth—so far in advance of his rude and turbulent time—throw a horror that no philosophy, birth, nor training can resist—one of those weights beneath which all humanity bows shuddering; cast over him a stifling dream where only the soul can act, and the limbs refuse their offices; have him pushed along by Fate to the lowering, ruinous catastrophe.[71]

Having just emerged from Fate's "ruinous catastrophe" (the Civil War), audiences viscerally connected to Hamlet's struggle, and the anguish that Booth enacted and experienced applied a cathartic salve to a country that was torn by civil strife. In a brief biographical article in *Harper's Weekly* that appeared days after his return to the stage in 1866, neither his brother (John Wilkes) nor Lincoln are mentioned directly, but the sketch concludes with a call for understanding: "Within the past year he (Booth) has suffered with us all in a common grief, but he has also had, in connection with the very occasion of that grief, a private sorrow which ought to be sacred to us all."[72] Critical emphasis on Booth's suffering, which was exaggerated like Forrest's struggles against youthful deprivation, created an emotional bond with audiences.[73]

William Winter praised the sensitive, ethereal nobility in Booth's artistry: "In all characters that evoke the essential spirit of the man—in all characters, that is, which rest on the basis of spiritualized intellect, or on that of sensibility to fragile loveliness, the joy that is unattainable, the glory that fades, and the beauty that perishes—he is easily peerless."[74] Yet John Rankin Towse identifies a strange contradiction between this perception and many of the roles in which Booth excelled:

> That Booth could give fine expression to the nobler attributes of humanity... he proved abundantly by his Brutus and parts of his Othello and Hamlet, but it is nevertheless a fact that he was most triumphant in characters containing a baser alloy. His alert manner, his flashing eyes, his crisp, somewhat metallic utterance, his capacity for fierce passion, his general suggestion of agile mentality, constituted a most valuable equipment for parts in which the intellectual predominated over the moral or the sentimental.[75]

While primarily remembered for his Hamlet, most of Booth's other successful characters, if not villains, certainly possessed qualities that were contrary to the "spiritualized intellect" and "fragile loveliness" that Winter perceived in his Melancholy Dane. Although considered quite handsome and admired greatly by the fairer sex, Booth had little interest in romantic roles: "This fellow [Benedick in *Much Ado About Nothing*] is a lover.... I loathe the whole pack of them. Always did. Even as a youngster I loved the villains."[76] Part of Booth's attraction to, and possible identification with, devilish characters may have emerged from his self-torture and self-loathing over the death of his first wife: "I can't be good. I'm a fiend! I struggle upward as hard as I can but down I come plump into the sea of evil. I must drown—there's no use struggling."[77]

Of the 12 dramatic characters featured in William Winter's 1872 overview of Booth's career—Hamlet, Richelieu, Othello, Bertuccio (Tom Taylor's *The Fool's Revenge*), Richard III, Brutus (Payne), King Lear, Shylock, Macbeth, Benedick (*Much Ado About Nothing*), Don Caesar de Bazan (Victor Hugo's *Ruy Blas*), and Melnotte (Edward Bulwer-Lytton's *Lady of Lyons*)—the final 3 roles only appeared sporadically in Booth's repertoire. Benedick, one of Shakespeare's most intellectual comic heroes, was never a role for which Booth was primarily known. Melnotte and Don Caesar de Bazan were odd roles to include, because romantic, sentimental melodrama was a genre in which Booth rarely performed and in which he was generally acknowledged to have little ability. Winter did not choose the characters, which were dictated by 12 portraits, and merely provided a brief biographical sketch, which he himself suggested was a bit premature—Booth was not yet 40. Of the remaining 9 roles, Macbeth and Othello enjoyed moderate success at best (although he continued to perform them occasionally), likely because, as Towse points out, the contemporary understanding of these roles required great stature and external passion: "He had a firm intellectual grasp of them, he had imagination and an abundance of nervous energy and intensity, but in the great crises of emotion lacked massiveness and grandeur."[78] In fact, Winter praised Booth's effectiveness as Iago, one of his most celebrated roles, far more than he addressed his shortcomings as Othello. Booth played Othello largely because it was expected by audiences and critics. In many circles, Iago was considered the minor role, especially by Forrest's generation. Forrest only played Iago when he was quite young and was subordinate to a major star. By the time Booth reached the peak of his popularity, it was not unusual for two major actors to alternate in the roles during the run of a show, which Booth did with English star Henry Irving.

So, adding Iago to the seven remaining characters—Hamlet, Richelieu, Bertuccio, Richard III, Brutus, Lear, and Shylock—provides a fairly complete picture of Booth's active and most celebrated repertoire. In Payne's *Brutus; or, The Fall of Tarquin*, the deposed Roman hero (Booth's only traditionally heroic character in the only American-written play) feigns idiocy but ultimately leads his people to victory over the evil, invading Tarquins. At the end, Brutus sentences his son, who is in love with Princess Tarquinia, to death for siding with the enemy. Assayed by many of America's principal actors, including Forrest and Booth, the role provided opportunities for great drama and pathos in Brutus's condemnation of his son. In *Richelieu*, Bulwer-Lytton's melodramatically contrived plot features a duplicitous, witty, and aging Richelieu who is protecting his beloved country and assisting a defenseless orphan. Richelieu proves both a hero and a villain. Lear (in which Booth was criticized for lacking requisite stature), Bertuccio, and Shylock were disappointed fathers who were driven to madness and irrational behavior. In Tom Taylor's *The Fool's Revenge*, which was based on Victor Hugo's *Le Roi s'amuse* (also inspiration for Verdi's *Rigoletto*), Bertuccio's deformed jester avenges his innocent wife's abduction but inadvertently causes his daughter's death. According to Winter, Booth's Shylock contained "moments of pathos, [but was]...chiefly impelled by personal hatred and greed...a fiend-like man, cold and deadly in outward seeming, but fiercely impelled by the pent-up fires of hatred, malice, and cruelty."[79] Richard III, Iago, and Shylock were villains, although Booth's portrayals were dimensional and did elicit pity. The *only* character, in fact, that appeared fully to satisfy Winter's criteria of "spiritualized intellect" and "fragile loveliness" was Hamlet.

The machinations of Booth's evil characters fascinated New York's *Daily Tribune* in their analysis of an 1880 performance:

> In Richard [III], as embodied by him [Booth], the observer recognizes a man consistent with human nature and with himself—false, cruel, wicked, demoniac, yet a human being, with brain, heart, conscience, imagination, and passions, and not merely a stage ruffian....[H]is embodiment of the part shows forth an actual, possible man, whose ambition is intelligible, whose conduct implies rational motive, the workings of whose conscience are visible even in the very pains he takes to avow his dissimilarity from other men, whose remorse treads close on the heels of his fearful crimes, and whose last hours are baleful with terrors and awful with warning. The observer cannot but rejoice over the ruin of such a fiend; but, at the same time, he will deplore, with a grief too deep for tears, the appalling agony, the blank wretchedness, and the eternal doom of such an imperial soul.

Rather than portraying obvious, snarling villains, he presented flawless masks of duplicity: "embodying a man beneath whose calm exterior sleeps a hellish tempest of passion, a smouldering flame of demoniac malignity, a baleful fountain of deadly purpose."[80] According to melodramatic conventions of the day, as well as performances of Shakespeare that were informed by nineteenth-century sensibilities, the villain must repent and be punished, yet Towse recognized the appeal of Booth's skillful hypocrisy: "[F]or parts in which the intellectual predominated over the moral or the sentimental... his duplicity was altogether Machiavellian, exactly adapted to time and circumstance."[81] Booth's adept humanizing of complex stage villains reflected middle-class fears of (and morbid fascination with) the evil within themselves and what might be lurking behind the masks of others. Actor Otis Skinner puzzled over this seeming contrast between the man and the roles he assayed: "With such gentleness as his it was singular that his greatest effects should have been made in parts of sinister and diabolic character."[82] Booth's adaptability and felicity in portraying sensitive hero and malevolent villain, rather than representing incongruity, actually suggests a complicated and nuanced masculine image.

OUT OF THE FORREST AND INTO THE BOOTH: "TWO STARS KEEP NOT THEIR MOTION IN ONE SPHERE"

In contrast to Booth's complexity, Forrest built on clear binaries of good and evil, presenting heroes who were experiencing powerful yet uncomplicated emotions. Lacking internal conflict or self-doubt, these roles provided an ideal showcase for Forrest's masculine excesses. Forrest was unsuited for the roles (or at least the interpretations of the roles) in which Booth excelled, although Hamlet uncomfortably resided in Forrest's repertory. Just before Booth's national success in the role, the *New York Tribune* (1855) described Forrest's Dane as, "a broad-shouldered, athletic, middle-aged man, knit in coarse vigor, who seemed to writhe most uncomfortably under the load of sweet fancies and dreamy philosophic thoughts which thronged upon him."[83] Although Booth performed a few contemporary melodramas, reveling in the passion and pathos of the tragic conclusions, he most often played Shakespearean characters. Forrest's performance of Shakespeare placed the immortal bard within the realm of popular entertainment, whereas Booth's classical delineations

Figure 4.3 Edwin Forrest on the cover of *Vanity Fair* (September 20, 1862). The Library Company of Philadelphia.

Figure 4.4 Edwin Booth on the cover of *Vanity Fair* (November 1, 1862). The Library Company of Philadelphia.

These disparate theatrical images appeared six weeks apart on the covers of *Vanity Fair*. Forrest, in his austere attire (while strangely framed as a brooding Hamlet), is presented as a massive, dignified, and forbidding presence. The caption below his name reads, "The Great Medium Between the Spirit of Shakespeare and the Stage." In short tunic and tights, Booth's costumed Hamlet is seen as a feminized figure with flowing hair and tapering limbs. His caption reads, "*Hamlet.*—'They are Coming to the Play—' "

catered to a comparatively exclusive audience.[84] Forrest and Booth possessed entirely different skills and presented entirely different personas to entirely different audiences with entirely different masculine and theatrical expectations. While Forrest embodied a hypermasculinity, Booth softened and feminized his manly image in accordance with middle-class ideals. Towse recognized the passing of the torch of America's theatrical ideal from Forrest to Booth: "Less virile than the muscular Forrest, whom he [Booth] succeeded, he excelled him in subtlety, brains, grace, and real dramatic fire."[85] Towse's comment, like those of many others Civil War-era critics, reveals the masculine contrast between the two greatest American actors of the nineteenth century, while also exposing a cultural bias that privileged contemporary middle-class values and Booth's corresponding performance aesthetic as "real."

In analyzing Booth's inability to portray immense dramatic figures, critic E. C. Stedman captured the manliness of Forrest, who enjoyed his greatest success in portraying

> towering creatures of action—Othello, Coriolanus, Virginius, Macbeth—somewhat deficient, whether good or evil, in the casuistry of more subtile [sic] dispositions, but giants in emotion, and kingly in repose. They are essentially *masculine*, and we connect their ideals with the stately figure, the deep-chested utterance, the slow, enduring majesty of men.

In Booth, Stedman identified an oppositional characteristic: "The genius of Mr. Booth has that feminine quality which, though allowing him a wider range, and ennabling [sic] him to render even these excepted parts after a tuneful, elaborate, and never ignoble method of his own, might debar him from giving them their highest interpretation."[86] Far from an insult, Stedman's description of Booth as feminine complimented his taste and refinement. Booth privately acknowledged the transformative power of his late wife, elevating her to near sainthood, vowing to live up to her expectations, and crediting her with all that was worthy within himself: "I feel that all my actions have been and are influenced by her whose love is to me the strength and wisdom of my spirit. Whatever I do of serious import, I regard it as a performance of a sacred duty I owe to all that is pure and honest in my nature—a duty to the very region of my heart."[87] Although extreme, Booth embodied changing conceptions of middle-class manhood, glorifying women as paragons of purity and consciously adjusting his performance of masculinity as a duty in service to the feminine ideals of refinement, repression, and sentiment.

Booth, in a letter to William Winter, acknowledged his perception and portrayal of Hamlet as essentially feminine:

> I have always endeavored to make prominent the femininity of Hamlet's character and therein lies the secret of my success—I think. I doubt if ever a robust and masculine treatment of the character will be accepted so generally as the more womanly and refined interpretation. I know that frequently I fall into effeminacy, but we can't always hit the proper key-note.[88]

Booth's consciously created "feminine key-note" ultimately encouraged more complete identification with the tragic figures of both Hamlet and Booth. Booth equated "feminine" with genteel sentiment, whereas "effeminacy" suggested unmanly, womanish behavior and comportment. Booth cultivated the former and feared the latter. Booth expressed self-doubt about the manliness of his self-restraint, echoing middle-class worries about increased feminine influence undermining masculine strength: "Somehow I can't hate longer than it takes to 'cuss' a round oath or two, then I'm serene." Booth went on to deride himself as "unmanly" for not "hating better."[89] As Jackson biographer John William Ward states, "Perhaps the most severe condemnation that can be made of nineteenth-century America is that it equated charity and love with a lack of manhood."[90] Yet forgiveness was an important virtue in a nation that was struggling with the Civil War and Reconstruction, as reflected in Lincoln's second inaugural address:

> With malice toward none; with charity for all; with firmness in the right, as God gives us to see the right, let us strive on to finish the work we are in; to bind up the nation's wounds; to care for him who shall have borne the battle, and for his widow, and his orphan—to do all which may achieve and cherish a just and lasting peace among ourselves, and with all nations.

In "Lincoln and Hamlet," Daniel Kilham Dodge identifies a sensitive gentility in both president and prince: "For in Hamlet there is a marked strain of the feminine, and this same subtle quality is no less marked in the apparently rugged and masculine Lincoln.... In both Hamlet and Lincoln the feminine strain, so often found in men of genius, is associated with their innate purity."[91] Booth's serenity and Lincoln's acceptance sharply contrasted Forrest's egoism, jealousy, and temper: "let me own that I have a religion of Hate—not Revenge—a hatred of oppression in whatever form it may appear—a hatred of hypocrisy, falsehood, and injustice—a hatred of bad and wicked men and women, and a hatred of my enemies."[92] This bitter belligerence could not be further removed from the spirit of Lincoln's address or Beecher's Gospel of Love, which similarly embraced forgiveness and acceptance.

Although representing many of the same qualities as Macready, Booth never experienced the same kind of acrimonious showdown with Forrest, who briefly followed Booth and played some of the same roles. Laurence Hutton recalled simultaneous 1860 Hamlets at New York's Niblo's Garden and Winter Garden theatres: "[T]he contrast between the powerful robustious figure, deep chest tones, and somewhat ponderous action of the elder actor, and the lithe, poetic, romantic, melancholy rendition of the younger, was very marked."[93] But Forrest's health and dwindling audiences and Booth's good-natured placidity prevented significant tension. From the late 1850s, when Booth achieved recognition on the national level, until the early 1870s, however, Booth and Forrest often performed simultaneously in competing theatres, although never together. Forrest's reported refusal to play the Moor to Booth's Iago prevented one of the most potentially significant events on the nineteenth-century American stage. Forrest retained a significant, vocal following among urban working-class males and unsophisticated (or at least uninitiated) audiences in more remote theatrical outposts. The *Daily Missouri Democrat*, responding to an 1866 performance in St. Louis, frankly stated that Forrest "had seen better days, and like [Charles] Kean and others, draws full houses on the strength of his world-wide reputation." The "faded star" had become "disagreeable and exceedingly tedious and tiresome."[94] Because of changing theatrical tastes and behavioral expectations, by the 1860s *Harper's* acknowledged Forrest's acting as an often-ridiculed but enduring American institution: "We may crack our jokes at it. We may call it the muscular school; the brawny art; the biceps aesthetics; the tragic calves; the bovine drama; rant, roar, and rigmarole; but what then?.... For there is the great, the eager, the delighted crowd.... And he moves his world nightly."[95] Forrest continued to appeal; however, it should be noted that he moved only "*his* world," and a separate and ultimately more influential world found masculine models elsewhere.

In 1880, the *New York Daily Tribune* diminished the validity of Forrest's strengths in defending Booth's shortcomings:

> Whenever excessive emotion has induced a strong physical enthusiasm, the natural craving of the spectator is for an overwhelming outburst of physical power. Forrest was usually supreme at such moments.... The fulfillment of them is generally accepted as greatness in acting—whereas, in fact, it is no

more than a 'limb and outward flourish.' Edwin Booth—spiritually a higher actor—frequently fails to fulfil [*sic*] them, simply because he lacks in volume of voice and in brawn."[96]

While Forrest satiated a "natural craving," an appreciation of Booth required a retraining of the audience. Actress Laura Keene, who toured with Booth in the early 1850s, well before his national success, suggested that middle-class audiences demanded a suppression of feeling and an editing of response: "Mr. Booth's style and delivery, in most of his characters, are sedate, temperate, even cold.... He sways his audiences less by the violence of his emotions than by the repression of his feelings."[97] These repressed feelings—seething passions boiling just beneath a placid surface—connected Booth to the restrained behavior of the middle classes, whom John Kasson characterizes as "externally cool and controlled, internally anxious and conflicted."[98] Booth's performance suggested greatness, or at least great feeling, lurked behind the impenetrable mask of the seemingly ordinary.

Booth possessed a wild reputation as a young actor but consciously sanitized his public image by the time he reached national recognition—his earlier behavior being largely forgiven as sowing the proverbial oats. As his second marriage dissolved because of his wife's mental instability, the press sensationalized it, but Booth never commented publicly. Booth consciously submerged his own personality offstage as well as onstage. Unlike the media circus that surrounded Forrest's life, including his much-publicized divorce and frequent litigations, Booth kept personal foibles and tribulations out of the public sphere. This private, self-conscious performance mirrored the careful and conservative behavior of the middle classes in the decade before the Civil War. Whereas Forrest courted confrontation, Booth went to great lengths to avoid it. When British star Henry Irving planned a theatrical tour of America, Booth chose that same time to tour England. Booth wrote to Irving, suggesting an exchange of theatres. Irving ignored the invitation for almost two years, but then proposed (without apology or explanation) just such an arrangement when it benefited him. Suffering such treatment, Forrest might have sparked an international incident. Booth, however, later shared the stage with Irving, and they ultimately developed a mutual respect.

Booth narrowly epitomized the masculine ideal of the genteel middle-class, while simultaneously reflecting a broader definition of American masculinity: "He is thus the ripened product of our eclectic later age, and has this advantage about him, being an American, that he is many-sided, and draws from all foreign schools their distinctive elements to fuse into one new, harmonious whole." By "foreign schools," Stedman refers to Booth's melding of the classical and romantic styles of acting, but this skill in fusing disparate elements extended beyond the theatrical. Forrest (and Jackson) created masculine images in violent opposition to those of European gentlemen, providing the perfect remedy to fears of feminizing influences. Booth (and Beecher and, to a degree, Lincoln) assimilated elements of English gentility, and a refinement that was tempered by the fire of experience, into a distinctly American vision of manhood. Booth theatricalized the cyclical return to the eighteenth-century mode of masculinity that had been rejected in John Quincy Adams. Although still built on articulate intelligence, refinement, and repression, the successful reemergence of this manly model eliminated the most alienating formality, superiority, and aloofness on and off the stage. Booth, Beecher, and Lincoln humanized and democratized intellectual masculinity while incorporating a new component of humility. Like the passionately self-made Forrest and Jackson, these three figures overcame adversity and disadvantages, but their perceived journey to success was built primarily on self-sacrifice and internal resolve, rather than a perpetual fight to dominate and subjugate. Middle-class men responded to values that matched their aspirations: gentility and politeness, rather than coarseness and belligerence. Rather than patriarchal (and sometimes condescending) leadership, these intellectual men compassionately guided and were guided by a community of peers. But, however many-sided Booth's image, he could not possibly reflect the exploding multiplicity of American manhoods. His restrained performance style harmonized almost exclusively with the decorous behavior of his audience and forced all others to seek other models and entertainments.

Although commonly granted a spiritual superiority over the more physically and emotionally demonstrative Forrest, Booth's restrained acting style may have been less a matter of artistic choice than a result of deficiency in physical, vocal, and even emotional resources. Yet Booth's seeming weaknesses became virtues and strengths in a performance that was mutually constructed by actor and viewers. It is doubtful that Booth initially intended to revolutionize acting or to redefine an ideal masculine image, or that he somehow set a personal goal to cultivate the patronage of an emerging middle class that was barely perceptible in his formative years. The right man emerged at a fortuitous time. As outlined by the *Spirit of the Times* (1841), Forrest had been similarly well suited in disposition and abilities to fulfill performance demands and gender expectations of audiences in the unique social and political atmosphere of his own time:

> The class of passions for which his powers are best adapted are consequently those that dwell in the depths of the soul, and demand strong expression—revenge, hate, scorn, indignation. Those that belong to the 'melting pot'—that move to pity and subdue with sorrow lie farther beyond the circle of his genius and resources.[99]

Ability, which was dictated by temperament and molded by circumstance, required the masculine transition from Jackson to Lincoln, and the journey from Forrest to Booth followed a similar path.

5. Impossibly Genial: The Masculine Transformations of John McCullough ∽

> *He [McCullough] left nothing to chance. He observed every detail. He considered and planned every step of the way. He always knew what he wished to accomplish in dramatic art, and he always had in his mind a distinct and practical method by which to accomplish it. He was a direct man in his art because a direct man in his nature.*[1]
>
> William Winter, 1889

The Irish-born "Genial John" McCullough (1832–1885) served as protégé to Edwin Forrest. Although McCullough's imitation of his mentor might have been a pale one, his great physical stature, powerful voice, and genial nature brought him success as an actor and a theatre manager. As audience tastes changed, following the Civil War, McCullough adapted his acting style (with at least moderate success) to embrace the principles of the Delsarte system and the emotional restraint most frequently associated with Edwin Booth, even if he failed to capture Booth's complexity and charismatic vitality. Throughout his life and career, McCullough tirelessly and obsessively sought to improve himself, but, in contrast to the perceived defensive belligerence of Forrest and elevated formality of Booth, McCullough consistently maintained an accessibility that eventually appealed across class lines. Never fully able (or perhaps even willing) to separate himself from association with Forrest, McCullough nevertheless incorporated simplicity, nobility, and moderation into this manly model, especially in his signature role of the noble, tormented father, Virginius. Good luck and good nature helped him avoid potentially damning personal and professional scandals, but near the peak of his popularity and artistry he suffered from a degenerative disease that ended his stage career, which required his commitment to an asylum and led to his death at the age of 52. Although he was considered one of the best actors of his era, his artistic reputation faded fairly quickly after his death. In this chapter I explore McCullough's attempts to navigate the shifting shoals of manly expectations, which provide insights into the challenges facing all men surrounding and following the Civil War.

Unable to write and barely able to read, McCullough joined the massive emigration that was caused by the Irish Potato Famine, settling in Philadelphia in 1847 at the age of 15 . Self-educated, he worked as a chair maker before pursuing a stage career in 1857. The little formal theatre training that he received was under teacher of elocution Lemuel White, who had previously taught McCullough's future artistic mentor, Edwin Forrest. McCullough eventually played second lead to Forrest, touring with him from 1861 to 1866 and then played leading roles and managed on his own in San Francisco, where a performance, which was modeled on Forrest's, received a favorable response from audiences of the West. McCullough's affiliation with Forest proved an ideal apprenticeship

Figure 5.1 "Genial John" McCullough. Image courtesy of the author.

Although framed in a similar form of portraiture to the Jacksonian images of masculinity (figures 1.1–1.4), comparatively, McCullough exudes an accessible geniality.

because the elder tragedian performed only on three or four nights a week, allowing McCullough to slowly build a repertoire and reputation as a leading actor on Forrest's off nights. Forrest viewed McCullough as his heir apparent. The younger tragedian acquired Forrest's prompt books and received blessing to perform his repertoire. In his early days as a solo star, Philadelphia's *Sunday Dispatch* (1863) saw his performance as a mere shadow of his mentor: "McCullough has now, by perfect study, made himself a Forrest in miniature. He is a picture in little—a reduced copy of a colossal figure."[2] This connection with Forrest, whether viewed positively or negatively, largely persisted even as he established himself as a viable draw in the years that followed Forrest's death in 1872, although kinder press such as the *St. Louis Republican* (1873) praised McCullough, "not as an imitator of a grand model, but as a young artist who has imbibed correct principles from a wise teacher."[3] Whether real or imagined, a stigma forever associated his performances with Forrest, regardless of how assiduously he worked to improve his craft. San Francisco's *Newsletter and California Advertiser* (1873) placed definite limitations on his appeal and potential growth: "[H]is declamation is too much of the Old Bowery stamp to allow him to rank among our best and most cultured actors."[4] Regardless, by 1880, H. P. Phelps in *Players of a Century: A History of the Albany Stage* praised McCullough as "the only fit representative of the Forrestian school of acting."[5]

An overwhelming majority of reviewers compared McCullough to Forrest, and both actors were frequently described through similar vocabulary and imagery. McCullough's performance style, according to the *New York Sun* (1877), often reflected "hints of his master, the Gothic Forrest.... As a tragedian he is vigorous and effective, but it is a muscular rather than a poetic vigor.... If he is not poetic, he is at least virile and emphatic." William Winter of the *New York Daily Tribune,* responding to the exact same performance as the *Sun,* elevated McCullough over Forrest for the former's vulnerability and tenderness: "The stately form, the massive ease of movement, the leonine repose, the rich variety of vocal treatment, the air of innate gentleness, and the winning manner—all these elements are fused, in his embodiment, by an individuality that is virtue itself." At a time when enthusiasm for the muscularity of the romantic actor waned, Winter nostalgically celebrated McCullough's performance as "a personification which, in these days, it is an astonishment to see." The *Sun* spoke kindly but more condescendingly of his efforts and the audience that appreciated him: "[H]e manages to capture the sympathies of those who like to have even their tragedies made stirring." The time for "stirring" tragedies apparently had passed for those seeking the comparatively subtle and spiritually uplifting "pathos of mind."[6]

Whereas Forrest had been described as "imposing" and "Herculean," McCullough, the last heroic tragedian, was "stately" and "leonine," suggesting a growing dignity and respectability in the masculine image. John Ranken Towse, long-time critic for the *New York Evening Post*, described McCullough as "a man of noble presence, of powerful build..., [who] could assume a lofty dignity in which Forrest was lacking, and had a notable mastery of virile pathos."[7] Most important, however, as the *Chicago Times* (1866) noted when the younger tragedian still served in his apprenticeship under Forrest, McCullough possessed an accessibility and likability described as

> [a] certain unnameable, indescribable elasticity, lightness and grace of bearing, look and utterance—always winning, and not rarely inspiring. He shows everywhere marks of general culture and of special study; but these never intrude themselves, but disappear amid the natural openness, unaffectedness and spontaneity of his nature.[8]

In his first New York appearance after Forrest's death, the *Herald* (1874) found in McCullough "a bright, genuine, winning quality which Forrest never succeeded in expressing."[9] While McCullough appeared in the same repertory and initially performed in roughly the same style as Forrest, McCullough presented a more positive, noble, and accessible image, even if he failed to thrill and inspire audiences as passionately as his mentor. Audiences worshipped Forrest; they liked McCullough.

William Winter, eventual friend and fan of McCullough, initially saw capability but no inspiration in his acting: "He worked up each scene with entirely competent mechanical skill.... He seems to have approached the part [Richelieu] through the medium of intellectual perception, and not through that of spontaneous emotional sympathy. All it means on its surface he has conveyed."[10] Whereas Winter's impressions gradually warmed and softened, he maintained reservations about the tragedian's intellectual and emotional capacity. Others articulated McCullough's limitations more bluntly. "Mr. McCullough is a good tragedian," writes Towse, "but whether he has the divine spark that lights up the soul, and is the birthright of genius, is another question."[11] As the *American and Commercial Advertiser* (1874) observed in McCullough's performance of his mentor's signature role, Spartacus, he could not match the intense fire of Forrest: "The barbarian rage and fervor which he [Forrest] cast into the part gave it a vitality which Mr. McCullough's art does not attain."[12] Even those who deplored Forrest's excesses freely acknowledged the power and passion of his performance.

McCullough maintained a loyal following, initially among Forrest's primarily working-class male audience, and eventually added middle-class families. By 1880, the *Memphis Daily Avalanche* puffed, "Mr. John McCullough has the rare faculty of pleasing every class."[13] He built his reputation in, and spent significant time touring, geographically remote outposts, performing widely throughout the entire country and in Canada, even at the height of his popularity. Even though his one- or two-night stays in small southern, western, and New England towns were financially driven, it further encouraged an image of accessibility, prompting Philadelphia's *North American* (1882) to dub him, "the people's actor."[14] However, because he catered to the less experienced and discerning, McCullough frequently played to audiences that were, in the words of the *Chicago Daily Inter-Ocean* (1875), "composed for the most part of people such as an actor of this stamp would like to play to." [15] Surrendering to baser theatrical instincts and giving the gallery gods what they wanted did little to boost his tragic stature or to enhance his legacy. He privileged applause and short-term profits over elevated reputation.

Throughout his nearly 30 years on the American stage, McCullough escaped the passionate negative responses that marred his mentor's career, in spite of multiple potentially damaging events. A 17-year-old McCullough married Letitia McClain, with whom he had two sons. His deeply religious wife strongly disapproved of his passion for the stage. Although never legally separated or divorced, from the beginning of his professional theatre career, McCullough and his wife generally lived separate lives. He eluded the public scrutiny of marital discord that plagued Forrest (and Booth, too, for that matter), which invariably influenced public perceptions of the actor and the man. In the *San Francisco Chronicle* (1885), McCullough's friend Charles Bishop framed the dissolving relationship between tragedian and wife as inevitable:

> He advanced and she did not. He acquired education, experience, polish; she remained what she was when he married her, a factory hand's companion.... He always spoke of her with utmost respect, and even, to his intimates, when speaking of her he would say, 'She deserved a better husband than I.'[16]

McCullough allowed others to assume that his commitment to self-improvement and greatness pulled him away from a limited, provincial spouse. Leaving his wife and children to pursue his passion became obligatory sacrifice rather than self-interest. In consistently articulating only a respectful and humble regret, he kept his private life private.

At variance with the controlled nobility of the roles in which he excelled, prominent California citizen and politician Samuel D. Woods revealed McCullough's unquenchable thirst for pleasure in life:

> He was genial John to everyone. He took the world at its swing, was fond of good things to eat and drink, and where good fellowship was to be found he was there also. He had the Bohemian instinct and he indulged it.... For years about town, in the robustness of his splendid figure, he lived in happy indifference to the frailty of human capacity to defy inexorable natural laws. He worked without tire in his profession, and then gave hours of needed rest to pleasures.[17]

Unlike the self-destructive heroic actors who previously emulated Forrest, and who in their offstage lives were unable to temper the excess, McCullough both withstood the self-punishment and avoided public censure. His relationship with Sacramento actress Helen Tracy remained private and discreet—made easier by the thousands of miles separating California from his Philadelphia home.[18] McCullough even avoided censure and scandal regarding the illegitimate daughter born to Tracy—named Virginia after the daughter of his greatest theatrical triumph, Virginius, the role in which Tracy made her theatrical debut under McCullough. Although some later claimed that McCullough's prodigality led to his early demise, it never impacted his popularity. Friends and audiences attributed behaviours that were derided in others merely to an excess of genial spirit.

When Forrest (sometimes called the "tyrant of the stage") agreed to do a benefit performance for the theatre manager who held McCullough's contract at the beginning of their association in 1861, America's most famous actor had not appeared in a benefit for another actor in 37 years.[19] McCullough embodied the opposite extreme—seemingly generous to, supportive of, and universally well liked by everyone in the world of the theatre. His close professional need to insert a space between "friends" and "included" John Wilkes Booth, who admired McCullough second only to his idol, Forrest: "McCullough ought to become in the future Forrest's son and heir—I mean theatrically—for he is the only one worthy of wearing the old Roman's sandals."[20] Booth's final stage appearance, in *The Apostate* at Ford's Theatre (March 18, 1865), was in a benefit for McCullough. In the days following Lincoln's assassination, authorities sought McCullough for questioning regarding a suspiciously vague telegram from Booth to McCullough. According to friend Charles Bishop, McCullough crossed into Canada to avoid arrest:

> Then McCullough telegraphed from Montreal that he would return if wanted. He did not because some friends had undertaken to quietly clear up the dispatch mystery. The fact was that the mysterious dispatch was a cipher announcement of a dinner engagement for Booth and McCullough with two women. The reason McCullough left so suddenly for Canada was that the dinner lark was with two well-known Washington ladies, and he did not want to disclose their names. So he left until the matter could be explained quietly.[21]

McCullough's telegraph, which was entered into testimony during the trial of the conspirators, established that he left Washington, DC nearly three weeks before the assassination. Even tangential connection to Booth tarnished many lives and reputations, but McCullough escaped unscathed. He even fashioned himself as a gentleman for protecting the honor of society ladies, even though these same actions shielded the dishonor of a married man who was fleeing the country to avoid responsibility. Good fortune, good manners, and good press smoothed over potentially damning personal events.

"DISPLAYING EACH YEAR A RIPER MANLINESS IN HIS ART": MCCULLOUGH'S PERPETUAL SELF-IMPROVEMENT

Far from relying on fate and geniality, however, McCullough consistently received praise for devotion to craft, continued learning, and artistic improvement. *Overland Monthly*'s 1885 obituary recalls McCullough seeking feedback from a newspaper critic after his first performance as Othello:

> When you are quite through with your work, I wish to talk with you about my performance—I saw you in the audience—and I cannot rest until I know whether I have disappointed you. Some of the blemishes that I know of I can remedy at the next performance, but I want to learn whether there are too many to justify me in keeping the character on my list.[22]

While possibly a canny attempt to cultivate critical friendship and favor, McCullough sought and heeded informed advice throughout his career. Unique for the consistency and endurance of his work ethic, McCullough eventually pursued formal training in the Delsarte system, which proffered assiduous study and complete self-control as keys to achieving "natural" performance. His commitment, if not anxiety, to better himself demonstrated dedication to craft, but also suggested dependence on validation. Willingness to transform also potentially indicated a lack of confidence in and ownership of his theatrical identity. His compulsion to improve and reinvent also could have served as a need (possibly subconscious) to separate himself from Forrest's enormous shadow.

The *Boston Globe* (1875) complimented a work ethic that was all the more extraordinary for a young man who was essentially illiterate when he arrived in the United States at the age of 15: "[T]he most conservative critics today will not hesitate to give him [McCullough] the...praise which he has earned by years of hard and conscientious study."[23] The *San Francisco Alta* (1875) praised his continued advancement in such favorite roles as Virginius, the noble Roman father who sacrifices his daughter to preserve her honor: "Not a scene but shows trace of finer elaboration and more perfect poise.... McCullough never returns to us without having learned some new lesson; he gives his every part some new finish."[24] Even late in his career, when many celebrated actors settled into expected interpretations, the *Chicago Times* (1880) lauded him for his continued improvement: "With Mr. McCullough there is neither stagnation nor retrogression. He goes on."[25] McCullough's ability to endure served him well as he weathered changing audience tastes and expectations. Addressing McCullough's continuing quest for self-mastery in the final decade of his life, William Winter initially saw the tragedian's inhibiting efforts at self-command in *Hamlet* as "too much the controller of circumstances and himself."[26] Looking back on McCullough's entire career, however, Winter described the actor's artistic journey as a methodical improvement of craft and maximization of potential:

> Animated by a distinct professional purpose and always resolute in its pursuit, he possessed in an eminent degree the calmness of a man who understands himself and the objects of his life and who means to exercise a firm and wise control over the inward resources of his nature and all outward aids to his career.[27]

Later, building on this idea of systematic self-betterment, Winter characterized McCullough as "a tragic actor of fine natural talents, thoughtfully, carefully and thoroughly cultivated."[28] McCullough attained a "cultivated" image by the end of his career, in the sense that he not only carefully and deliberately sought a level of refinement and acceptance that the brusque Forrest never achieved, but he also "cultivated" himself by developing and improving his craft through a tireless quest for self-amelioration.

McCullough joined a growing number of actors in the last quarter of the nineteenth century who sought a formal artistic education. The *New York Dramatic Mirror* (1910) later articulated this growing need for systematized instruction: "The theatre is an institution in which exact knowledge is as necessary as it is in other institutions. This profession can make no better headway without schools of instruction than can the profession of the law, or that of medicine, or that of painting."[29] Possibly motivated by a need for this "exact knowledge," McCullough took a short break from his generally lucrative and successful career to devote himself to formal training—the only prominent, mature performer of this era to make such a sacrifice and commitment. McCullough studied the Delsarte system under Steele MacKaye (1842–1894) in 1877 and credited this training with helping him achieve a higher level of dramatic discipline: "That teacher, MacKaye, has taught me more in three months than I could have learned otherwise in twenty years, and I don't care who knows it."

François Delsarte (1811–1871) created a science of the arts that was inspired by orthodox Catholic doctrine and was based on the trinitary division of man (life, mind, and soul—governed by the Father, Son, and Holy Spirit, respectively), which, in the context of performance, became vocal sound, words, and movement. Movement as expression of the soul, however, was the element of the Delsarte system that was embraced by Americans, largely because of the physical-based teachings of MacKaye, Delsarte's only American pupil, who introduced the system to America in 1871.[30] A successful actor and playwright, MacKaye simultaneously sought, through his first training program in 1872, to educate the actor and to elevate the stature of people who were drawn to the theatre: "[W]e can never be sure of fine performers until we can offer such opportunities of education for the profession as will induce people of superior moral character and natural intelligence to go upon the stage."[31] MacKaye's secular interpretation of Delsarte's system stressed physical training, and he created a system of harmonic gymnastics that were designed to give the actor complete physical and emotional control. American Delsartism sought to create a science of movement that classified consistent and predictable physical responses to emotional and sensual stimuli. MacKaye, an expert practitioner of the system, demonstrated mastery at a Boston recital in 1871, presenting what he referred to as "chromatic scales" or "gamuts" of facial expression:

> In exhibiting these gamuts, he stood perfectly motionless, except in his countenance, and, starting from the normal expression, would make his face pass very slowly through a dozen grades of emotion to some predetermined phase, and thence he would descend, reversing the previous steps, to perfect repose.... Thus, he showed a chromatic state of emotion running through satisfaction, pleasure, tenderness and love to adoration, and, having retraced his steps, descended facially through dislike, disgust, envy, and hate to fury. Again he exhibited the transitions from repose through jollity, silliness, and prostration, to utter drunkenness; and made a most astonishing but painful spectacle of his fine face, passion through all the grades of mental disturbance to insanity, and down all the stairs of mental weakness to utter idiocy.—The impression produced was at once very lively and very profound.[32]

Neither McCullough nor any other American actor or Delsarte practitioner reached MacKaye's level of technical proficiency.

Although MacKaye primarily emphasized the physical aspect of Delsarte, he couched it in terms of social and moral betterment, as well as masculine guidance:

> What we need especially in these days of indifference to nobility bearing is a Culture which will gift us with a clear insight into the degrading influence of slovenly ways and awaken the ambition to attain to more manly and womanly modes of motion. In a word the Sciences most neglected in these days of desperate devotion to money hunting is the Science of Emotion and its Expression—and yet this Science illuminates the hidden springs of Human nature—elevates our ideals of Manhood and enables us to develop its Essence by assisting us to acquire its Manners.[33]

MacKaye's justification sounds like the dictums of the conduct manuals, but he suggests that the change can, and perhaps should, begin with comportment. It is not surprising that Americans in the years following the Civil War embraced the Delsarte system as a form of model behavior and external control. The idea that "correct" external choices—"more manly...modes of motion"— could be learned and repeated with guaranteed success corresponded to the regimented behavior that was lauded in advice literature and likewise defended precepts that were based on science and nature. Implied pressure to learn what should be obvious and inherent instilled a fear of social and moral ostracism if the ignorant inadvertently violated laws of conduct. Delsarte mapped instinctive physical movements to encourage more free and natural performance, a result that was at least partially achieved by McCullough. Beginning in the 1890s, casual interpreters and poor teachers often misinterpreted and misapplied Delsarte's principles, and the system unfairly came to be associated with false, external, and mechanical acting—corresponding to the worst fears of conduct manual readers, that others would see assumed refinement as dissimulation.

While difficult to know how much of the enormously complex Delsarte system he absorbed in only three months of concentrated study, the consensus of critical response suggests that McCullough improved vocal tensions that plagued his early career but, more importantly, that he achieved more effective levels of control, moderation, and restraint. A. C. Wheeler (writing as "Nym Crinkle") commented on the complete transformation that followed McCullough's training:

> [E]veryone was amazed at the leap he made in his art. His Othello and Richelieu astonished me by being entirely unlike his former impersonations of those characters. The native vigor, resonance, and fire were there, but they were disciplined and controlled. A nicer balance of faculty was apparent. The intelligibility of the subtler emotions had been made sharper and clearer. There were noble climaxes of passion, less waste of energy in making himself felt, a cleaner adaptation of tone and gesture to the exigent thought—more repose, more dignity, more grace.[34]

Joseph Clarke of the New York *Tribune* provides a striking before-and-after comparison of McCullough's performances. Clarke found little to admire in McCullough's work shortly after his apprenticeship with Forrest: "My first impression was that his art was noisy, scorned repose, laughed at subtlety but hammered its points with a force that meant sincerity at least. It was virile without virtuosity.... It was, I take it, the 'Forrest school' going to seed." In 1878, however, Clarke proclaimed, "[T]his was a new McCullough indeed. Here was a chaste spirit, a sure, tempered emotion, utmost grace, restraint overlying power that only flashed out on the mountain tops."[35] The *Boston Globe* (1879) elevated McCullough over Forrest in his "capacity for self-control," praising him for "never overstepping the many temptations to extravagance" and comparatively exhibiting "a quiet dignified intensity."[36] William Winter identified McCullough as "a white ideal of manly purity and grace," possessing "splendid manliness of self-command."[37]

The *Boston Herald* (1883) similarly applauded his journey toward moderation and self-discipline, framed as an aesthetic compromise between the old and new:

> McCullough has cultivated that evenness of style which is the true criterion of what is best in the actor's art. There is probably no tragedian on the stage to-day more capable of bursting into moments of fury, electrifying passion if he chose; but recognizing the fact that there are other and better things to accomplish, and that "still waters run deep," McCullough has almost remodeled his older methods. Not that he has gone from one extreme to another and become a tame actor that would be impossible for him but he realizes more the possibilities of his art and uses his powers to attain those possibilities. The old moments of fire and energy are still there, but their roughness is smoothed away, and has begot a temperance which brings out more vividly the noble tenderness of the Roman father's [Virginius'] nature.

The emotional excess associated with Forrest was merely one tool in the tragedian's arsenal, and one to be used with discretion. The *Herald* went on to claim that McCullough ultimately "retains every worthy feature of what is vaguely known as the 'old school,' and at the same time embraces the better points of what is ambitiously termed 'the modern school'."[38] In his 1882 article "Success on the Stage," McCullough provided tips to young actors about finding the balance between honoring tradition and embracing innovation: "The true course for the aspirant would seem to be to learn first all that traditions enjoin, and then bend all the forces of fine intelligence and genuine feeling to the task of evolving something which, in the light of all past experience, and the scrutiny of study and reflection, shall be better than the old."[39] McCullough continued to practice and implement his Delsarte training over the following years, occasionally with MacKaye's help.

It is tempting to attribute McCullough's improvements simply to growth of experience and theatrical maturity, but no other actor of this period underwent a similar, let alone such a profound, change. Most critical responses following his training with MacKaye suggested more effective command of physical and emotional resources, but some auditors suggest a level of control and restraint that extended beyond the actor's tools to the person inside. The *Philadelphia Inquirer* (1879) praised McCullough as "a student in that school of acting in which self-repression is the very first lesson."[40] The *New York Sun* (1877), although maintaining reservations about McCullough's potential as an actor, similarly extolled this new-found mastery of self: "It may have been very far from perfection, but it had grown in the right direction. We could see that McCullough was held in check. And after that almost anything was possible to him."[41] In his self-command, McCullough had essentially saved himself from himself. The *Boston Advertiser* (1877) praised his Virginius for its "manly simplicity.... It is a worthy reproduction of that type which knew how to subdue the world because it had learned to subdue itself."[42] This self-conscious and systematic betterment, transformation, and suppression of self (personally and professionally), coupled with a willingness to abandon what he was before, suggests parallels to social chameleons of the middle classes who sought change to achieve social acceptance and success.

VALORIZING "MANLY SIMPLICITY": RISING ABOVE THE FORREST AND APPROACHING THE INAPPROACHABLE BOOTH

Although McCullough incorporated elements of contemporary refinement into his performance style, his strengths, as well as his intellectual and emotional limitations, narrowly confined his effective repertoire to the heroic characters that had been popularized by Forrest. The ennobling simplicity and sincerity of McCullough's portrayals (especially of Virginius), however, elevated perceptions of the plays and provided nostalgic comfort, if not masculine inspiration, following the Civil War. The broad appeal of McCullough's accessible simplicity provided a theatrical and manly alternative to the elegant complexity of Booth. McCullough, like Forrest, essentially played himself on stage. His charismatic geniality and sincerity influenced critical and popular perceptions, making the man indistinguishable from the roles that he assayed.

As San Francisco's *Alta* (1876) commented on his performance in Dion Boucicault's social comedy *London Assurance* (1841), "McCullough...looked strangely enough in the modern drama, and the free, swinging gestures of the classical school accord illy with broadcloth and social cigars."[43] McCullough occasionally performed in contemporary plays, and prolific fellow Irishman Boucicault specifically wrote the Civil War melodrama *Belle Lamar* for McCullough, who played it to at least moderate success. McCullough purchased new plays and even commissioned an unsuccessful adaptation of the Jack Cade story that had been popularized by Forrest, but, in comparison to the older, established vehicles, none of these contemporary works meshed as closely with

McCullough's persona. His temperament and abilities continually pushed him toward familiar tragic heroes (Virginius, Spartacus, Jack Cade, Richelieu, Damon, Brutus, Lear, Othello, Coriolanus), and he was the last significant actor to perform Forrest's repertory. The public and press, although clamoring for novelty and sensation in their theatre, showed little interest in seeing McCullough in anything other than Forrest's most popular roles. McCullough ultimately stopped fighting the reassuring masculine model of paternal nobility that audiences expected from him: "[T]he old plays are good enough for me; I like to act in them, and the public is good enough to pay liberally to see them."[44] The *Chicago Tribune* (1875) felt McCullough's success in Forrest's plays placed limitations on his growth as an artist and provided a warning judgment to an actor who wins excessive praise in such vehicles, "for it would seem to assume that his power lies principally in the representation of such parts, and that he lacks that higher spiritual insight without which no actor can gain enduring fame."[45] The fact that McCullough allowed himself primarily to revel in the adulation he received in those parts may well have influenced the fairly rapid fading of his bright particular star. McCullough embraced his association with Forrest's repertoire, yet sought to bring more nuance to the roles. As Chicago's *Daily Inter-Ocean* (1875) claimed, "Forrest did little more than picture vividly the idea of brute force." McCullough, on the other hand, "seeks to illustrate the poetic side of the character, to depict a loftier type of heroism than is to be seen in the mere exhibition of animal power."[46] Although this observation may have held some truth, like similar critical comparisons of Forrest to Booth, the *Daily Inter-Ocean* privileged the cultural superiority of the middle classes following the Civil War.

William Winter applauded both the ennobling potential of these dramas and the actor who brought them to life: "If acting ever could do good, the acting of McCullough did. If ever dramatic art concerns the public welfare, it is when such an ideal of manliness and heroism is presented in such an image of nobility."[47] Winter saw McCullough's living example on and off stage as a model and an inspiration and believed that he would be remembered "for an essential nobleness and manliness such as stimulate human hearts to a renewed devotion to duty and a fervid allegiance to high ideals of character and conduct."[48] Although Winter likely exaggerated McCullough's powers of moral suasion, as he did Edwin Booth's, the *Boston Globe* (1874) echoed these sentiments, calling McCullough's Virginius "a personation which one is better for seeing."[49] And A. C. Wheeler of the

New York World commended the healing power of McCullough's entire Forrestian repertory:

> I wonder if wholesome John McCullough knows that he is making the world better by playing *Spartacus* and *Damon* in it. It is extremely doubtful. He probably knows no more about it than the lily of the field. He seems to have been preserved in the pure California air through an era of artificiality to come and revive for us those naïve, heroic pictures of clean, vigorous work which once gladdened the dramatic gallery.[50]

Whereas many (if not most) young actors built their experience in the theatres of the West, McCullough based himself in California until after Forrest's death, making his starring New York debut in 1874 at the age of 41. Similar to the way in which English critics romanticized Forrest as a frontier backwoodsman during his London debut, eastern elites simultaneously patronized and elevated the West. Wheeler's romantic idealization of McCullough's melodramatic vehicles and the impact of his Western experiences extended to the inspiring, but uncomplicated, nature of McCullough's performance:

> There is nothing about John that your dilettante and technical scrutinizer will admire. He could have issued from no other portal than that in the Rocky Mountains with all that breezy, out-door puissance, that clear, open face, and that broad, Western romanticism. Therefore let classicality cavil. He lays hold of the multitude. He stalks robustly down from the Sierra Nevadas with the old portfolio of melodramas under his arm.... Does wholesome John clearly understand that this is all wrong? That we got past this long ago? That he has no right to move people? That we don't want to be moved? That the vigorous, manly sort of thing is exploded? That wholesomeness is as much out of place in a theatre as brimstone is in the pulpit? I think not. His ingenuousness, his innocence, and his sonority waft us back to the springtime of life. There is the freshness of youth in his aspirations, the candor and the enthusiasm of puberty are in his impersonations.[51]

Walking a fine line between adoration and paternal condescension in his praise of McCullough's unguarded geniality and the lack of sophistication in his characterizations, Wheeler suggests the promise of comfort and hope in difficult times: "Out of the stress of life, then, it is at least pleasant to turn to the freedom of illusion. It is more. It is wholesome. As we hunt romance from our thoroughfares with steam whistles and resolve passion in its organic compounds with our science, let them take refuge in the theatre."⁵² Following the horrors of the Civil War and the continued tensions associated with recovery and Reconstruction, Wheeler found that McCullough's simplicity and the calming familiarity of his characters provided a reassuring salve "to lead the imagination captive, silence all cynicism, and move us to the bottom of our hearts."⁵³ Momentarily banishing memories of the war, American audiences found escape and nostalgic comfort in McCullough's old-fashioned masculine models and the "vigorous, manly sort of thing" he represented. At the same time, the protective, parental, and sometimes demeaning attitude toward McCullough, whose healing influence Wheeler does not recognize as conscious or deliberate, limits his authority as a masculine model.

Not only were McCullough's strengths best suited to heroic tragedies like *Othello,* but, as Virginia City's *Daily Trespass* (1867) noted in his performance of Iago shortly after leaving Forrest, "[The role of] 'Othello' is better suited to his powers . . . [McCullough] can not look nor act the craft and villainy of subtle 'Honest Iago'."⁵⁴ San Francisco's *Daily Morning Call* (1868) similarly questioned his ability to play less than genial characters: "Mr. McCullough's Iago was spoiled by a certain native sincerity and simplicity which this excellent actor cannot well disguise."⁵⁵ Even in the maturity of his career, the *Chicago Tribune* (1878) confirmed his lack of harmony with such roles: "One can hardly imagine John McCullough possessed by an evil passion, by anything but what is manly and good; and it is not necessary to inquire further than his face to learn that he is incapable of doing a base or malignant act."⁵⁶ Although this incompatibility of temperament might be ascribed to his irrepressible geniality, William Winter recognized more sweeping limitations: "[H]is face can express perplexity and trouble of mind more readily than misery and conflict of the soul, and his voice is tuned to the heroic rather than the philosophic and mournful emotions."⁵⁷ The *Chicago Daily Tribune* (1877) praised him for an "impressive dignity and a noble simplicity" but questioned his ability to portray layers of subtlety and sophistication: "There was in Mr. McCullough's personation a wonderful failure to exhibit the higher and more intellectual endowments of Coriolanus. His merit lay in dealing with the ingenuous manhood and simple domestic virtue of the character."⁵⁸ These perceived limitations, whether physical, intellectual, or emotional, likely led him to pursue Delsarte training under MacKaye. But even after the improvements achieved through study, the *New York World* reaffirmed the tragedian's constraints: "He is always at his best in moments that call for an expression of the simplest and least complicated emotions. He is always at his worst when the action demands imagination or poetic feeling."[59] Following the advice of critics and the preferences of his audience, later in his career he increasingly relied on the roles most praised: Virginius and Spartacus. His most celebrated triumph as the Roman father Virginius succeeded because, as the *New York Herald* (1880) notes, he essentially played himself: "So perfectly does the part fit the man that at first the actor seems scarcely to be acting; the rendition is so natural, the dignity, force and affection so suggestive of much more in reserve, that the man seems merely to be living, not acting."[60]

Above all, audiences and critics responded to the simplicity and noble sincerity of McCullough's performances. "To be deadly in earnest is held by the populace to be better than to be exquisitely in the right," wrote a reviewer for the *New York Sun* (1877), "and Mr. McCullough is powerfully in earnest. He utterly lacks the subtle touch."[61] The *New York Times* (1880) agreed, praising McCullough for "a combination of simplicity and sturdiness guided by a broad, healthy intelligence which is but faintly tinged with either imagination or subtlety."[62] The *Boston Advertiser* (1879) elevated McCullough's uncomplicated nature: "[H]is simplicity and sweetness—'sweetness' is the only word—are beautiful, not having remotest kinship with pretense of affection."[63] A. C. Wheeler of the *New York World* found "something remarkably tender and sympathetic in the gentler moods of this actor...touching in their manly simplicity."[64] William Winter similarly praised McCullough's lack of social and theatrical sophistication as a virtue: "He was not a simpleton—he was only simple.... Such a nature offers no complexities for analysis."[65] This image could hardly have been more at odds with a competing masculine model of the stage that was fairly begging for analysis: Edwin Booth.

Critiquing McCullough's performance in Booth's favorite role, the *St. Louis Republican* (1874) praised the actor's everyman quality: "Hamlet is a flesh and blood man, and not a philosophical abstraction; his Hamlet has his five senses and his perfect mental poise, his normal affection, his sound philosophy and his vigorous manhood."[66] The *Boston Globe* (1876) agreed, calling his Dane "a much more natural being," with "nothing of the excess of refinement...a man whose warm heart feelings cannot always be kept from expression by morbid emotion or the indecision of his nature."[67] These reviews not only validate McCullough and his performance choices but also either subtly or directly condemn his lauded contemporary. Booth was irrevocably linked to the role, and his interpretation of it had become the accepted standard. But critics like the *Daily Alta California* (1874) found relief in McCullough's less complicated performance: "He makes the character that of a sensible man of the world... —not the lachrymose, driveling noodle some actors [presumably including Booth] make of him."[68] The *St. Louis Dispatch* (1874) similarly praised his less melancholy Dane for its dissimilarity to Booth as "not a lovelorn or dyspeptic twaddler who stalks lackadaisically over his kingdom, with lean cadaverous visage, and unhealthy sentimentality, a burden to himself and a perplexity to the world."[69] A. C. Wheeler felt that McCullough played Hamlet "intelligently but not intellectually," but maintained admiration for what McCullough represented in the role:

> His *Hamlet* was a gothic affair—lusty, effective, sinewy throughout. It utterly lacked the elegance of Booth.... It was devoid of the fine-spun intellectuality of the commentators. But it had a certain honest ruggedness. Without the gloss of elaboration, it wore the hue of health. Unaided by any of the spurs of the closet [i.e. theoretical ideas] it still moved with the momentum of manliness.[70]

Wheeler suggests that the solid masculine presence of McCullough should satisfy, yet the layers of complexity and emotional dissatisfaction introduced by Booth and embraced by his audience made the values and behaviors of McCullough and his followers appear insufficient. Although his portrayal may have been more accessible and reassuring than the moral ambiguity of Booth, McCullough flattened and reduced the character to a pleasant but mundane everyman—perhaps one not altogether unlike McCullough himself.

Because they shared the stage on multiple occasions, audiences and critics directly compared Booth and McCullough, who was a year older than his more celebrated theatrical counterpart. When Booth visited McCullough's California Theatre in 1876, the *San Francisco Chronicle* evaluated the passion of both actors' Othello: "[H]e [Booth] was the panther where the other type [McCullough] was the elephant—both terrible in wrath, but instinctively you feel that the first is more terrible.... The one is a club which crushes, the other is a rapier which wounds, and both have their merits and demerits."[71] McCullough is admired, but the coarse indelicacy of the elephant and club suggest a masculine image without finesse or refinement. The actors alternated as Othello and Iago, and the same critic privileged Booth in both roles:

> McCullough played 'Iago' for an admirable hypocrite and 'Othello' for a jealous fool. Booth played 'Iago' for a designing knave and 'Othello' for a man of high culture and intelligence, but blinded by passion. The latter is in both cases the pleasanter performance, as it is in both cases the more difficult.[72]

The complexity implied in Booth's pleasant difficulty directly contrasted with McCullough's simplicity, insinuating a definite ceiling on the latter's masculine potential.

When off the stage, Edwin Booth consciously cultivated an air of conscious cultivation. He deliberately elevated his intellectual and cultural status (and that of his audience), sometimes at the cost of being labeled cold, formal, and arrogant. San Francisco's *Overland Monthly* (1885) praised McCullough for complete, unaffected naturalness offstage:

> John McCullough did not pose as a student, did not wear a preoccupied air when brought in contact with people off the stage nor wrinkle his brow as if deep in thought; he laid no plans to be pointed out as 'one of the most diligent students in the profession': and thus the man who did not act out of the theatre...was rated as a 'genial gentleman and a delightful companion—he will never rank with Doleful Lugubrious [presumably Edwin Booth] as a star.'"[73]

This critic suggests that McCullough was not a star because he did not assume the elevated social expectations of a star, which meant that he was essentially being penalized for refusing to "act" offstage. The *Boston Herald* (1885) praised the unassuming nobility of McCullough in life: "In an artificial world, and a society particularly prone to all uncharitableness, McCullough managed to retain a wholesome nature and an integrity of disposition that would alone render him remarkable."[74] McCullough's persistent geniality was commendable, but its blandness hardly seems remarkable. New York's *Dramatic Mirror* (1881) found McCullough "what is popularly termed a thoroughly 'good fellow,' with a social reputation and a heart as big as his body. A princely entertainer, a genial companion, a liberal purse, these three attributes have gained John McCullough a good part of his fame, and nobody begrudges him one iota of it."[75] Shortly after his separation from Forrest, San Francisco's *Daily Evening Bulletin* (1866) found McCullough, "meritorious, without being a great actor."[76] Henry Edwards's funeral oration praised McCullough's perpetual compassion and evenness of temper: "Whether shadowed by misfortune, tortured by sickness, or hampered by the cares of a busy life...he was still the same genial friend, the same warm-hearted companion, the same kind and friendly associate as of old."[77] In an 1881 speech delivered at a banquet in his honor, McCullough communicated his love of, but not his reliance on, the theatre: "If I succeed I shall be grateful, but not unduly elated. If I fail, I shall not be soured by disappointment."[78] He exhibited (at least the appearance of) moderation on both sides of the curtain. McCullough may have too closely embodied the middle classes who longed to see the repressed spark of masculine passion (and perhaps even a hint of Forrest's danger) beneath the controlled moderation of gentility—a quality that was admired in Booth. Although rejecting overt displays (and internalizing the exuberance of their responses to theatrical stimuli), they needed to see a remarkable man behind the placid exterior.

His warm persona was so closely tied to his popularity as an actor that the *Detroit Free Press* (1879) discussed the difficulty in separating the man from the artist, as McCullough "has acted his way into the affection as well as the admiration of the people and he is now the popular idol. Possibly something of that is due to the 'Genial John' sentiment that everyone seems more or less affected with."[79] Writing after McCullough's death, Lewis Strang candidly evaluated how McCullough's personality impacted performance criticism:

> McCullough was a simple, whole-souled, lovable man, and his personal popularity was remarkable. Indeed, his friends were so numerous and so loyal that critical judgment regarding his intrinsic worth as an actor was in a measure swayed by the affection felt for the man. A fair estimate of his histrionic ability would place McCullough decidedly in the second class, but still not disgracefully so.[80]

The friendship McCullough shared with many critics likely softened their critiques, and this perceived favoritism prompted attacks, especially from hometown Philadelphia critics. The *Evening Bulletin* (1878) derided, "[I]t is Mr. McCullough's own fault if he is judged by a high standard, and it is the fault of his too fulsome friends upon the New York press if intelligent people who go to see him upon the stage suffer most grievous disappointment."[81] The *North American* (1878) echoed these sentiments: "[S]ome of the writers of the New York press have undertaken the rather ill-advised task of elevating a tolerable and conscientious actor to a pinnacle beyond the ambitious thought of artists much more than his equals in professional skill."[82] While these rebukes likely contained more than a little truth, a competitive tension between Philadelphia and New York—and the fact that the hometown boy seemed to put greater stock in the validation of the latter—may have fueled what the *Philadelphia Record* (1878) termed "the proverbial jealousy existing between Philadelphia and New York."[83]

Notwithstanding critical quibbling, the countless thousands who patronized the tragedian, and who never had an opportunity for personal contact, also felt a sense of kinship with the tragedian. Chicago's *Daily*

Tribune (1875) partially demystifies the spell McCullough cast:

> The secret lies in his own personal character, in the man's heart as well as his brain. There is in his acting a charm which is not easy to define, a spell of rich, deep earnestness, of purity, and of 'sweet good will to all mankind,' which leaves a glow of kindly warmth, and melts the mere individual into harmony with the noble thoughts and actions of the ideal he seeks to embody. His heroes are but phases of his own character,... the outward vesture of a nature singularly sweet and sunny.[84]

McCullough's ability to radiate sincere geniality was a key to his success. It may also suggest why his legacy faded so quickly. One needed to experience the man in order to fully appreciate the performance, because performance descriptions could not capture his indefinable charm. And not all were entranced. The St. Louis' *Evening Post* (1878) appeared to base a more critical opinion solely on his performance, rather than on his personality: "There are many who are unwilling to concede to him the greatness which the general run of folks consider an indisputable attribute of his, and, to be plain, Mr. McCullough does seem to be a little overrated."[85] During his 1881 appearance in London, critics such as the *Sunday Times,* who were less influenced by direct interaction with the man, typically were less impressed by the actor: "[T]hat singular gift of electricity or that combination of gifts necessary to a tragedian of intensity and electricity Mr. McCullough does not possess. He does not stir you."[86] The overall criticism of the British press, which was also not a great fan of Forrest's later performances in London, focused on the same deficiencies and faults that the American press had noted earlier in McCullough's career, which suggested that American audiences either grew accustomed to his performance or surrendered to the charm of his personality. Bringing simplicity, sincerity, nobility, and moderation to the roles so passionately portrayed by Forrest, McCullough was either praised for maintaining or resurrecting a reassuring, ennobling masculine image or criticized for failing to adjust to the complexities and sophistication of his time.

"FORLORN, FRENZIED IMAGE OF BREAKING MANHOOD": DEATH OF THE LAST TRAGIC HERO

Buoyed by critical and popular praise of his manly simplicity and geniality, McCullough survived social and professional pitfalls that destroyed most heroic actors, but he began to suffer signs of fatigue and memory loss in 1882. Newspapers throughout the country, and presumably legions of his fans, followed the rapid downward spiral of his physical and mental health over the next two years. Forced to cancel performances in March 1883, he was diagnosed with a "bilious liver," frequently associated with excessive drinking.[87] During his final year of performance, admirers such as the *Minneapolis Tribune* (1883) found greater mellowness, depth, and weight in his characterizations: "[T]hough showing visible signs of his recent illness, [McCullough] never appeared to better advantage."[88] A growing number of critics, such as the *Cincinnati Enquirer* (1883), however, lacked sympathy: "His soul did not seem to be in his work. He appeared to be acting under protest. He was in bad voice and looked and acted like a sick man."[89] Shortly after a trip to the springs of Carlsbad failed to recover his health, Kalamazoo's *Daily Gazette* (1884) reported increasingly irrational behavior as the tragedian wandered the train tracks of New York: "[A] watch was kept on him, as it was feared he would attempt suicide. After the train started, McCullough attempted to jump off, but was prevented.... [I]t seems McCullough fancies he is followed by men who want to kill him, and he keeps dodging imaginary foes constantly."[90] Days before the opening of his 1884–1885 season in Wisconsin, the *Racine Advocate* announced: "John McCullough will not appear at the Blake in *Virginius* Monday, as he is out of his mind again."[91] Response to McCullough's decline was divided sharply between sentimental support and somewhat mean-spirited attacks.

In what would prove to be the final stop of his tour, the *Chicago Daily Evening News* (1884) revealed the difficulty of focusing on the tragic character because of the obvious suffering of the man: "The lofty purpose, cruel wrongs, and terrible fate of Virginius were forgotten in absorbed interest in the actor's struggle with weakness."[92] After wandering the stage unable to remember his lines as Spartacus in *The Gladiator* (September 29, 1884), a role he had literally played thousands of times, audiences hissed and laughed at the famous tragedian, assuming him to be drunk. McCullough suffered a breakdown and had to be helped off the stage. McCullough wandered for the next several months, occasionally traveling to cities on his now canceled tour: "John McCullough came here on the Western Express from New York," related the Pittsburgh correspondent to the *New York Clipper* (1884). "He insisted he was on his way to St. Louis, Mo. to fill a date there. Several men tried to take him off the car, but he insisted on staying on the train. He will probably turn up in St. Louis."[93] Spells of delusion and incoherence were interspersed with moments of sad clarity, as he shared with playwright and producer David Belasco: "[T]he manly drama is passing."[94] His behavior became increasing erratic and sometimes violent, and he was committed to the Bloomingdale Insane Asylum in June 1885. Spending his final weeks at his wife's home in Philadelphia, McCullough passed away on November 8, 1885—less than a week before his 53rd birthday. According to the *Philadelphia Evening Bulletin* (1885), 8,000 viewed the dead actor's body and an additional 10,000 sought admittance.[95] Although one of the most popular actors in the country, earning up to $50,000 a year (equal to over $1,000,000 in today's dollars), he left an estate of only $40,000. The enormous salary indicates his great popularity, and the comparatively small amount remaining mirrors his legacy.

Close friend and fellow actor W. J. Florence blamed McCullough's early demise on the strain of the roles he portrayed:

> He was not dissipated, yet knowing his mode of life, I can but wonder that he survived so long. The parts of Lear, Othello and Virginius—impose upon the actor's vitality a severe strain and shorten his life with every appearance. So many men who have excelled in tragedy have met with similar ends that I am surprised that some people have seen fit to ransack their head to assign a cause for that which appears so natural.[96]

Despite Florence's claim, however, actors do not die from the emotional strain of acting—even in such angst-filled roles. Other friends posited that McCullough was simply too sensitive to survive the emotional strain of great acting and the financial stress of theatre management. And certainly his generous nature, as well as his desire to be liked, were often at odds with the harsh, practical necessities of managing a theatre. Although loved ones concealed the nature of his illness, McCullough suffered from general paresis, which is a result of untreated syphilis. Initially attributed to an inherent weakness, psychiatrists began to link general paresis with syphilis in the 1850s, but this connection was not definitive until the 1880s (around the time of McCullough's illness and death).[97] McCullough's onstage popularity was irrevocably linked to his reputation as an exemplary citizen. The social stigma attached to the disease, indicating madness from syphilis or inherent deficiency of character, suggested that depravity and decay laid beneath this model surface. McCullough's friends, such as fellow actor Tom Keene, actually circulated stories about his illness coming from excessive drinking, a lesser (or at least more acceptable) weakness: "It is true in one sense but not in another [McCullough drank excessively]. The man is sick and feeble. He feels that he must work, and he tries by stimulants to put himself in condition. In his enfeebled state a little of that overcomes him, and I suppose that was the trouble the other night."[98] Placing the cause of the drinking on the draining nature of his profession absolved McCullough from responsibility. Another friend, Charles B. Bishop, in addition to revealing McCullough as a high-functioning "sober drunkard," encouraged hearth and home to counter the impossible demands of the theatrical profession: "What McCullough needs is a change in his way of life. He wants domesticity, and the quiet and regularity of a well-ordered household would do much to soothe the irritation of a brain tossed hither and thither in the shifting scenes of his career."[99] Again, the world of the theatre is made culprit. The idea that McCullough must be domesticated to regain health and normalcy is intriguing. It suggests to McCullough's audience that the life they are leading is the truest path to content. It also makes McCullough something of a martyr, sacrificing himself to share the inspiration of his theatrical, idealized visions of tragic, manly nobility.

Masculinity on the nineteenth-century American stage is often reduced to an overly simplistic division: Edwin Forrest before the Civil War and Edwin Booth after it. This shift was not an abrupt revolution but rather a complex evolution in which McCullough played an integral and a unique part. While roughly the same age as Booth, McCullough achieved national prominence over a decade later, and his transformative Delsarte work occurred later still. McCullough serves as an intriguing transitional figure, artistically but not chronologically, between the unrefined muscularity of Forrest and the intellectual gentility of Booth. Whereas many young actors of the period adapted and evolved their performance skills in training or apprenticeship before they received significant critical or popular attention, McCullough appears to be the only established artist who publically and prominently refashioned himself to meet changing demands and expectations. William Winter commended the journey:

> McCullough did not try to equal the reverberant sonority…[of] Forest, and he could not have equalled it if he had tried; but he used an artistic method more conformable to Nature than that of the elder tragedian, and his action, while it had neither the ponderous precipitance of Forrest, nor the lurid, electrical, meteoric celerity that made Edwin Booth…superlatively thrilling,…was splendidly effective.[100]

Although the meager praise of "effective" may be damning, and elsewhere Winter uses the phrase "absolute adequacy" to describe the power of the tragedian's Virginius, the sincerity of McCullough's performances filled a need by presenting familiar, reassuring paternal characters.[101] His accessible geniality also provided the hope, in a competitive capitalist society, that a man could achieve success through nothing more than solidity, hard work, and good nature.

    McCullough was an emulator. He worked hard and followed directions. In his apprenticeship under Forrest, he copied the external, heightened performance of the nation's greatest passionate delineator, although he failed to capture the fiery dramatic spirit within. He was "a Moon as it were to Forrest's Sun."[102] In the Delsarte method he studied a scientific system that was largely based on the idea of recreating a perfected, idealized exterior. With the straightforward attack of a Forrest, he sought the sophistication of a Booth. The modulations in McCullough's acting style mirrored gradual elevations in American taste. He also intriguingly personified changing artistic and masculine ideals of the mid-nineteenth century. McCullough's theatrical reinvention, even if he could not completely fulfill (or perhaps even identify) the expectations of his audience, emerged from a desire to meet the needs of this rapidly changing world. McCullough's simplicity was his strength but ultimately suggests reasons for his limitations. The genial but bland nature of McCullough's real-life persona was winning but wanting in the dynamism needed to inspire emulation, providing a plausible and reassuring masculine model—one that was not exciting but got the job done. This manly ideal in many ways harkens back to the solid and admirable Manly in Royall Tyler's *The Contrast*—the ultimate anti-Chesterfield. Yet, at least in the case of McCullough, this unaffected performance was based on assiduous cultivation, which represented the ultimate invisible performance.

    McCullough's death put sudden and definitive punctuation on the end of an era. Edwin Forrest and Edwin Booth, both greater actors, faded from the spotlight as they grew old and out of fashion. McCullough died seemingly near the peak of his popularity—finally at a proper age for his greatest roles. His premature exit precluded potential years of continued artistic growth. He represented the last of his line. Forrest passed the theatrical and masculine torch to McCullough, and several actors took up the mantle of Edwin Booth. McCullough, however, was the last tragic hero. His masculine model, and the theatrical repertory associated with it, vanished from the stage with his passing.

Conclusion: Affirming White Masculinity by Deriding the Other

> *It's not the feminization [of men], just the reduction.... Our role was very simple: Find meat, bring it home. It feels... [like] what we used to do is being limited.... You get kinda backed in a corner.*[1]
>
> Tim Allen, 2011

Although my study has focused primarily on exploring attractive (and sometimes conflicting) ideals of white men, it only presents one side of the equation. Denigrating, mocking, and caricaturing nonwhite, immigrant, and lower-class models also establishes parameters of "normative" manliness by constructing nonhegemonic masculinities—essentially defining white, American manhood by negation and exclusion. Playwrights, performers, and audiences affirmed and normalized white masculinity by stigmatizing "abnormal" others, establishing and enforcing social and gender barriers of excluded men. Theatrical constructions (imagined and perceived by white American males) of Native Americans, African Americans, and immigrant Irish communicated insecurities of the dominant masculinity, both in the behaviors that were derided and in the elements that were chosen for praise. Briefly examining the framing and theatricalization of these unacceptable paradigms suggests the complexities and contradictions that are involved in gendered performance.

Changing policies toward, and national tensions involving, Native Americans began to complicate responses to *Metamora* and to Forrest's portrayal of the title character shortly after the play's premiere in 1829.[2] Andrew Jackson, an old Indian fighter who was unsympathetic to the Indian cause, enforced a strict policy of forcible removal and relocation of all tribes west of the Mississippi to the land between the Missouri River and the Rockies (thought unfit for habitation by whites)—supported by the Indian Removal Act of 1830.³ Many Native Americans lost their lives in the Black Hawk War (1832) and the Seminole War (1833). Even when the Cherokee Nation gained Supreme Court support for the right to their land (*Cherokee Nation v. Georgia*—1831; *Worcester v. Georgia*—1832), Jackson refused to enforce the rulings. In the winter of 1838, thousands of Native Americans died on their enforced trek from Georgia to Oklahoma— known as the "Trail of Tears." George Caitlin, who was sympathetic to Native Americans, detailed the discursive changes that were associated with white perceptions of Indians by the mid-nineteenth century. For example, Indians were once described as "Temperate," but by 1857 they are "Dissipated." "Independent" changes to "Dependent," "Proud" becomes "Humble," and "Stout-hearted" shifts to "Broken-hearted."⁴

As America's Indian problems escalated and sympathy toward their plight decreased, less noble images of Native Americans emerged on

Figure 6.1 John Vanderlyn, *The Death of Jane McCrea*, 1804. Image courtesy of the author.

The fierce, sensual muscularity of Vanderlyn's Indian warriors resembled Edwin Forrest's portrayal of Metamora, although Forrest's character acted as a defender of white women, saving his attacks primarily for evil British aristocrats. This troubling image of Native American men fetishized their power, while simultaneously denigrating them as "savage barbarians."

theatrical stages. An advertisement for The Grand Saloon of the Arcade on Chestnut Street in Philadelphia announced the following entertainment for February 7, 1842:

> A Company of Real Indian Warriors and their Squaws; Exhibiting the various Modes and Ceremonies of Savage Life.... On the rise of the Curtain, will be presented the Scenic Scene of the Murder of Miss M'Crea. In this Scene a beautiful young Lady will represent Miss M'Crea, who fell prey to the Savages during the dark days of the American Revolution...Act Fifth. THE WHITE TRADER—In this Scene a white man will appear on the Stage, and show the manner in which the white people trade with the Indians, giving them mere trifles for large quantities of Furs, after getting them drunk, and show the manner of torturing and killing him.... The whole to conclude with the thrilling scene of the Chace [sic], Capture, MASSACRE and SCALPING of the Mail Rider and his Wife...fully represented by the Indians on the Stage.[5]

A short 12 years after the acclaim of Forest's noble warrior, the Indian had been reduced to a pathetic display of savages in a saloon. Under the guise of displaying real history, this presentation underscored the clever deception of whites and the brutal violence of Indians against pure, defenseless foes. This equivocal narrative contained no identifiable hero and neither side of the conflict acted with honor. The performance description most tellingly demonstrated the nation's ambivalence about the role of native people in its history—ambivalence unsuited either to Forrest's talents or to the form of melodrama. John Brougham's burlesque, *Metamora; or, The Last of the Pollywogs* (1847), followed roughly the same plot as Stone's play, but Brougham's hero ("a favorite child of the Forrest") was reduced to a ridiculous, grunting savage gleefully dreaming of carnage:

> Methought the pale-faces were gathered all,
> Unarmed, defenceless; on them I did fall.
> Pile after pile of dead I sent to sleep,
> Their red scalps streaming in a gory heap.
> From the gray morning to the set of sun,
> I killed and killed.[6]

By the time of Brougham's burlesque, nearly 20 years after the original, Stone's *Metamora* no longer presented an acceptable picture of the Native American Indian. Brougham replaced the ideal of Forrest's noble American savage with an object of loathing that was stigmatized as a brutal, gullible, and wholly unpalatable "other."

While Forrest continued to perform the role throughout his career, by the time of the Civil War, Washington's *Daily National Intelligencer* (1864) viewed *Metamora,* and the Native American male, with distaste:

> Well, the 'poor Indian' is fast losing his romance. He is ceasing to be an 'institution.' Doomed by the cruelly kind policy of our government to revel in the isolated pomp, arrogance, and indolence of the wilds, which are fast receding from him; too vain and too lazy to work; the victim of bad whiskey and the smallpox; the buffalo, his last resource, failing him;... what is left of him appears to be reserved to feed on occasional excitement in Washington.... We wish that our eminent tragedian would drop him from his *repertoire*.... [T]he Indian is getting to be understood as very little more than an inveterate nuisance.[7]

The sympathetic disdain for the Indian, summed up by their "cruelly kind" treatment, demonstrates the impossibility of finding a proper emotional response to Stone's play, as audiences were simultaneously drawn and repulsed by the hero. Forrest's biographer Alger identified double vision in white perceptions of the Indian:

> The North American Indian seen from afar is a picturesque object. When we contemplate him in the vista of history, retreating, dwindling, soon to vanish before the encroachments of our stronger race, he is not without mystery and pathos. But studied more nearly, inspected critically in the detail of his character and habits, the charm for the most part disappears and is replaced with repulsion.[8]

Forrest's appeal as a masculine model, which was becoming increasingly limited by the class division of his audience, faded along with this "more nearly inspected" vision of the Native American. Both Forrest and the noble Indian chief he embodied remained on stage, but they did so largely through the power of theatrical reputation, as something of a museum piece, drawing an audience that remembered with nostalgic relish the simplicity of an earlier generation. Whereas Forrest's protégé "Genial John" McCullough respectfully maintained his mentor's other dramatic triumphs, he quickly abandoned *Metamora*.[9] By 1876, San Francisco's *Alta* lamented, "the glamour of romance has so faded from Lo! the poor Indian, that it has become a difficult task to make him even interesting."[10]

Roughly contemporaneous with Forrest's creation of his noble Indian warrior, Thomas D. Rice (1808–1860) originated the Jim Crow character, inspiring the minstrel show, which evolved into one of the most popular forms of variety entertainment through the end of the century and into the the first distinctly American form of theatrical entertainment.[11] In *Records of the New York Stage*, Joseph Ireland claimed, "His [Rice's] popularity was unbounded, and he probably drew more money to the Bowery treasury than any other American performer in the same period of time."[12] In the 1840s and 50s, the Virginia and Christy Minstrels built upon Rice's success, formalizing a three-act structure of music and humor, variety entertainment, and scenes from plantation life (or burlesques of popular plays). Appealing across class lines, the minstrel show employed archetypal characters, created derogatory and fictitious pictures of African American males, and provided a lens through which whites viewed blacks. W. T. Lhamon Jr. argues that minstrelsy presented images of "complex blackness" that represented an ultimately liberating cultural ritual, which revealed blacks' ability to endure, and even sometimes outwit, unjust treatment.[13] Within the time period, however, Frederick Douglass described the purveyors of minstrel entertainment as "the filthy scum of white society, who have stolen from us a complexion denied to them by nature, in which to make money, and pander to the corrupt taste of their white fellow citizens."[14]

Minstrelsy relied on the promise of presenting "real" Southern life. An advertisement for "Sanford's Great Philadelphia Nigger Opera Troupe" recounted a minstrel performance in Richmond, at which a respected citizen insisted that the black-faced Sanford was his "lost darkie,... recently absconded to parts unknown," and had him arrested. Sanford replied, "Massa...please let me wash de dust out of my eyes, and take off dese good close.... Sanford was metamorphosed in an instant. His color, voice, gait and demeanor were all changed in a twinkle, and from an old greasy Negro, he came out a finished gentleman, as everybody knows him to be."[15] The stark masculine contrast between "old greasy negro" and "finished gentleman" reassured reader and audience of the multifarious differences between white gentility and the one-way impersonation of shuffling slavery. According to Eric Lott, the minstrel show placed the African American male in a manageable context, defining the supremacy and power of the white masculine image:

> [Minstrelsy] was cross-racial desire that coupled a nearly insupportable fascination and a self-protective derision with respect to black people and their cultural practices, and that made blackface minstrelsy less a sign of absolute white power and control than of panic, anxiety, terror, and pleasure.... Underwritten by envy as well as repulsion, sympathetic identification as well as fear, the minstrel show continually transgressed the color line even as it made possible the formation of a self-consciously white working class.[16]

This complex relationship between white audiences and their colored creations revealed simultaneous obsession with and stigmatization of a passive and inherently inferior "other," which strengthened and defined parameters of white manhood. Perpetuating the "authenticity" of minstrel stereotypes proved vital to Sanford's success, "thus defending their [the South's] institutions and showing the slaves in their proper light, and not the abuse as written by Mrs. Beecher Stowe."[17]

Giving a human face to the inhuman system for which the Fugitive Slave Act (1850) now required the conflicted North to take active responsibility, Stowe's *Uncle Tom's Cabin* (1852) proved an effective tool of abolitionist propaganda, although Lincoln's famous (and possibly apocryphal) quote exaggerated her practical impact: "So this is the little lady who made this big war!"[18] The novel sold over 1 million copies by 1860, but dramatizations of *Uncle Tom's Cabin* likely reached 50 people for every person who read Stowe's book.[19] The most popular sensation in American theatre history, with some conservatively estimating 300,000 performances, dramatic incarnations called "Tom Shows," which were written by a variety of playwrights, subsequently influenced Northern white perceptions of black masculinity.[20] The *New York Herald* (1852), writing shortly after the Compromise of 1850, spoke for Northern conservatives and Unionists who condemned the play as "a more extended agitation of the slavery question—than any that has heretofore imperiled the peace and safety of the Union,...[calculated] to poison the minds of our youth with the pestilent principles of abolitionism." The *Herald* also found little comfort in the initial audience response: "True, the audience appears to be pleased with the novelty, without being troubled about the moral of the story, which is mischievous in the extreme."[21] The potential moral suasion of the drama, here pleasantly masked in sentiment and novelty, presented real political danger.

George L. Aiken's adaptation, which was the most popular stage version, emphasized comedy, and its subsequent "happy ending" (reuniting Uncle Tom with little Eva in angelic tableau) weakened its attack on slavery.[22] The villain Legree murders St. Clare and is shot while resisting arrest, providing poetic justice and effectively destroying the evil of slavery, while simultaneously maintaining the "peculiar institution" and absolving viewers of responsibility. This choice affirmed the moral rightness of black subjugation and the stability and dominance of white men. Both Stowe and Aiken, however, created sympathetic black characters, in some small way providing a comparatively viable alternative to firmly entrenched minstrel stereotypes. The play's two principal male slaves, George Harris and Uncle Tom, represented sharply contrasting views of black masculinity.

George, an articulate light-skinned mulatto, behaved like a typically assertive melodramatic hero: "[I]f any man tries to stop me, let him take care, for I am desperate. I'll fight for my liberty, to the last breath I breathe! You say your fathers did it; if it was right for them, it is right for me!"[23] His sentiments could easily have sprung from any of Forrest's republican heroes, and his slavery was framed as a melodramatic contrivance to part two lovers, implying that he might offer a tentative blueprint for manly black behavior—although the fact that George had to flee to Canada to find freedom and happiness suggests that such positive models were barred from participating in America's masculine culture. Elizabeth Ammons suggests that Uncle Tom, in his emotional self-sacrifice, essentially fulfilled the role of sentimental, melodramatic heroine.[24] Tom also acted as a martyred Christ figure (complete with ascension), even in the face of torture by the evil personified in Legree: "Mas'r, if you was sick, or in trouble, or dying, and I could save [you], I'd *give* you my heart's blood; and, if taking every drop of blood in this poor old body would save your precious soul, I'd give 'em freely."[25] Although it represented a feminized and spiritualized ideal, the extreme nature of Uncle Tom's suffering and forbearance disconnected him from the men in Aiken's audience.

Business-minded theatre managers refused to promote a controversial political agenda or encourage perceptions of slave masculinity outside the bourgeois comfort zone. *The Octoroon* (1859), Dion Boucicault's melodramatic treatment of slavery, played successfully both in the North and in the South. Producing the play during the Civil War, Philadelphia's Chestnut Street Theatre privileged authenticity in portraying slave life over any comment on slavery as an institution:

> [T]he manager begs to say that he disclaims all intention of making CAPITAL OUT OF POLITICAL SENTIMENT. He is actuated solely by the very great popularity of the Play.... *The Octoroon* presents a faithful picture of Slavery in Louisiana in its least objectionable form, and has never been equaled for its truthful portraiture of Life in the Far South-West![26]

The principal male slave characters in Boucicault's drama, a mischievous young boy (similar to Stowe's Topsy) and a shuffling, comic old man, proved more lively than Aiken's and Stowe's slaves (although dramatically less active) but differed little from minstrel models, reasserting the "least objectionable," and least threatening, masculine paradigms.

The theatrical prevalence of the Irish immigrant vied with the minstrel character for popularity on the antebellum stage. Mr. and Mrs. Barney

Williams, "the Legitimate Exponents of Irish Drama," exhibited "Artistic Excellence and Identification in the Peculiarities of Irish and Yankee Life!"[27] This zoo-like display of immigrant "peculiarities" resembles the exhibition of multiple types of excluded "others," including the theatricalizations of "genuine" Indian and slave life. Irish immigration in the 1840s flooded densely populated urban centers, competing for jobs with the native-born working classes and sparking violent ethnic conflict. The stigma placed on the "Irish savage," reflected in the stage portrayal of Irish characters as lazy, intemperate thieves, created a separation within *white* masculinity.[28] By the 1850s, however, immigrants composed a sizable portion of working-class audiences, so stage characterizations gradually became more favorable. Brougham's *The Irish Emigrant; or, Temptation* (1856) and Boucicault's *The Colleen Bawn* (1860)—both works of Irish dramatists and actors—created comparatively sympathetic, multi-dimensional Irish characters. As William Winter argues, Brougham consciously addressed social issues in his work yet kept the tone of his dramas and his performances light:

> His thoughts, and often his talk, dwelt upon the great disparity of conditions in society, the struggles and sufferings of the poor, and the relation of evil to the infirmities of human nature.... In his writing as in his acting the characteristic quality was a sort of off-hand dash and glittering merriment, a commingling bluff, breezy humor with winning manliness. The atmosphere of his works was always that of sincerity, but it never had the insipidity of strenuous goodness.[29]

Hiding his agenda behind entertainment and good humor, Brougham slowly nudged perceptions of the Irishman toward "winning manliness." Boucicault's dramas, on the other hand, pointedly ignored social conflicts in New York's working-class culture, working *within* the Irish stereotype to create appealing, lovable rogues. Boucicault and Brougham created more nuanced and sympathetic Irish characters, allowing immigrant audiences to see positive masculine images onstage, but their theatricalizations never rose above a certain class—primarily garnering laughs rather than admiration.

America's comic actors not only presented and defined masculine ideals but also ridiculed other conceptions of manhood, stigmatizing men because of race, class, social standing, or political affiliation. James Henry Hackett and William Evans Burton were men of elevated social standing, famous for portraying immigrant and lower-class roles, primarily for middle-class and elite audiences.[30] Whether their comedy was broad or subtle, raucous or reserved, they maintained an emotional, intellectual, and aesthetic separation between themselves and the "inferior" characters they portrayed. Because they made clear distinctions between themselves and their profession, as well as their objects of satire, these comic actors often successfully entered respected society. They placed excluded men on display for ridicule, mutually negotiating with their audiences visions of laughable masculinity to further define and separate their own mannerly manhood.

James H. Hackett (1800–1871) was primarily known for the development of the stage Yankee and for his didactic portrayal of Falstaff as a moral lesson against vice.[31] Praised as scholar and intellectual, Hackett published his *Notes, Criticisms, and Correspondence Upon Shakespeare's Plays and Actors* (1863) and frequently rebutted critical comments in newspaper reviews. He even corresponded with John Quincy Adams on *Hamlet*. The first important American actor to perform on the English stage (1827), Hackett enjoyed at least moderate success but was considered a bit gloomy as Falstaff.[32] Joseph Ireland placed him in the highest social pantheon: "[H]is cultivated mind and refined manners brought him into close intercourse with the most accomplished critics and highest social circles both in England and America."[33] Hackett, a staunch nationalist champion, albeit with aristocratic sympathies, actively encouraged the American drama. He managed the Astor Place Opera House at the time of the riot and championed Macready as "the most intellectual and generally effective actor of the time."[34] Performing at the aristocratic Park Theatre when in New York, Hackett also specialized in dialect characters (Yankee, "Kentuckian," English, German, Dutch, Scotch, French), which the *New York Mirror* (1832) claimed, "always fills the house, and elicits hearty plaudits.... It [Hackett's performance of the Yankee] is new, fresh from life, full of humor.... We have seen nothing for many a day more ludicrous and yet more correct."[35] Hackett presented the Yankee Jonathan Swap as an object of amusement, and an elite crowd joined in the laughter at the "ludicrous" and "correct" masculine image. Hackett crafted a successful and dignified career out of comedy, because he fully separated himself from the buffoons he portrayed, making him the first successful intellectual American actor to look at lower-class models from the outside.

English-born William E. Burton (1804–1860) arrived in Philadelphia in 1834 and became one of America's most popular comedians. Francis Wemyss describes the power that Burton held over his viewers: "We have seen him keep an audience in roars of inextinguishable laughter, for minutes in succession, while an expression of ludicrous bewilderment, of blank confusion, or pompous inflation, settled upon his countenance." Wemyss also suggests that Burton's mocking presentation of characters from the lower order elicited a divided response: "[W]hilst thus ever fortunate in winning golden opinions from the masses [of respectable audiences], his ceaseless enterprise has made him enemies among portions of the less fortunate of mankind."[36] The objects of Burton's mockery understood his derision, suggesting a working-class audience that was fully capable of reading performers' motivations and sympathies. Burton founded and published the *Gentleman's Magazine* (later to become *Graham's Magazine*) in 1836 and edited the *Literary Souvenir* and the *Cambridge Quarterly Review*. The initial president of the prestigious Shakespeare Club, he also possessed one of the country's largest private libraries, including a collection of dramatic and theatrical literature. Burton was the first manager in America to emulate the full, lavish, "historically authentic" Shakespearean productions of Charles Kean that primarily appealed to genteel audiences.[37] Burton presented an oddly conflicting masculine image—a man of high ideals, who specialized in coarse comedy. Naked emotions and ribald humor earned hearty laughs from a "respectable" crowd, painting a nonthreatening picture of the base nature of immigrant and working-class masculinity.

Audiences, actors, dramatists, and theatre managers mutually constructed a range of positive and negative masculine models, validating the superiority of their respective ideals. Theatrical treatments of Native Americans and African Americans marked and mocked men who visibly differed from the white masculine norm. Comic visions of undesirable foreigners, rural rustics, and the undeserving poor exiled and made fools of "inferior" white manhood. Effective constructions and performances of elevated white masculinities relied on "othering" to establish definite, unassailable barriers of gendered identity. Dominant forms of "normal," white masculinity could not, in fact, exist without constructing the "problem" and differences of nonhegemonic manhoods. However, increasing class separation, a proliferation of immigrants (including Chinese, German, Jewish, Italian, and Irish), and growing African American populations, filled theatres with a range of audiences. Each theatrical constituency demanded to see their own values and models of behavior portrayed on stage, while simultaneously searching for a sense of masculine, communal belonging. As these individual groups became more influential in and out of the theatre auditorium, performances of manhood shifted to address their diversity. Yet, ultimately, by the end of the Civil War, not only had the nation's masculine identity fragmented, but the individual's *own* identity fragmented as well. He could not be entirely a man of action nor a man of feeling, yet he was pushed to make a choice—with the inevitable result that something would be lost in the process. That something, I suggest, was any hope of creating either a unified political body or a unified culture.

AN ENDURING SPECTER OF MASCULINITY: A CODA TO THE LIFE OF MCCULLOUGH

To varying degrees, memories of great individuals live on past death. Three years after the passing of Genial John McCullough, a number of theatrical luminaries dedicated a 36-foot granite monument to the tragedian at Philadelphia's Mt. Moriah Cemetery—the first and still the largest monument to an actor in the country, "such a monument as might perpetuate his honored name, transmitting it to future times and indicating to future generations the esteem in which he was held by his contemporaries."[38] The monument featured a bronze bust "of colossal size," which depicted the actor as Virginius, and two engraved quotes that specifically referenced the complexity of his masculine image—the first from *Julius Caesar*:

> His life was gentle, and the elements
> So mixed in him that Nature might stand up
> And say to all the world, "This was a man."

The second quote, taken from a poem by American Quaker abolitionist and activist John G. Whittier in tribute to British Quaker abolitionist and activist Joseph Sturge, emphasizes a similarly soft and subdued manhood:

> Tender as woman; manliness and meekness
> In him were so allied
> That they who judged him by his strength or weakness
> Saw but a single side.[39]

Exemplifying the difficulty in evaluating manliness in general, this quote also frames McCullough in the feminized mold of Edwin Booth, although this delicate quality was not frequently emphasized during his life.

The introductory address delivered at the dedication of McCullough's monument by friend William F. Johnson sought to justify the immortalizing of this particular actor, "the last and not the least of a long line of delineators of the romantic and heroic characters of poetry."[40] McCullough represented the end of a theatrical era. No actor waited in the wings to portray Spartacus, nor to embody the masculine model that was originated by Forrest and muted by McCullough. Johnson lists the types of men who were typically memorialized (heroes, poets, rulers), noting that "few are honored, as our dead friend is to-day, for personal worth, unostentatious charities, and a beneficent life."[41] Johnson does not suggest that McCullough be remembered as a great actor, but as a kind man; however, kindness, especially that of an unostentatious variety, rarely warrants monuments.

Steele MacKaye, in his oration, similarly explores the reasons for honoring McCullough: "Was it because he was greater or more skillful in his art that those who passed before him to the tomb? No! Few would care to press such a claim." Instead of memorializing a noted actor, this monument "demonstrates the lasting hold that true manhood can obtain, through loyal service on the stage, upon the affectionate remembrance of our race." The rare union of earnest actor and simple man, MacKaye argues, deserves commemoration: "[T]he stainless integrity and sensitive tenderness of an unaffected man was blended with the undying devotion of an unpretentious artist in the noble personality of John McCullough."[42] Rather than solely celebrating the tragedian, this monument, then, served as a beacon of hope and potential reward to all the gentle, tender, beneficent, true, loyal, and worthy. McCullough stands in for all potentially forgotten men, but the benefactors, who expected his masculine image to live in perpetuity, could have no idea how future generations would frame their champion. Although his monument still stands, the bronze bust of the actor no longer inhabits it. His faded name lingers, but his image is lost.

As interest shifted to Edison's phonograph in the 1890s, a recording entitled "The Ravings of John McCullough" enjoyed marked popularity. Ostensibly a re-creation of McCullough's actual delirium in the insane asylum, the text includes a great deal of self-referential madness ("Oh, I am mad!") interspersed with maniacal laughter and pitiful moans. It also contextualizes and quotes from McCullough's three greatest roles: *Othello*, *The Gladiator*, and *Virginius*. His performances of Lear and his signature role of Virginius almost certainly inspire the recording. McCullough's performance of Lear's mad scene, which is described by critic John Ranken Towse after the actor's death and is potentially clouded by memory of the actor's mental deterioration, presented "pictures of utter wreck and desolation. The vacant eye, the foolish, smiling face, the restless hand aimlessly grasping at the air for naught, all spoke of intellect dethroned and prostrate. Now and again there was a flash of the royal spirit... but these glimmerings of light were few and only served to intensify the prevailing darkness."[43] Critics praised McCullough for revealing different colors of madness in

Lear (simple and childlike), Hamlet (clearly feigned), and his masterpiece, Virginius. In the final act of *Virginius*, written by Sheridan Knowles in 1820 for William Charles Macready, a grief-stricken father descends into madness after killing his daughter so as to preserve her honor. In outlining McCullough's performance, the *Baltimore American and Commercial Advertiser* (1877) could just as easily be describing the recording: "[L]ucid intervals are followed by incoherent ravings and meaningless laughter."[44] The more detailed portrait of the *Nashville Daily American* (1877) foreshadowed McCullough's real-life descent and provided direction to performers of his ravings:

> It was finely portrayed by the symptoms of intense nervous disorder—nervous clutching, the rolling eye and wandering vision—the far look, the painful effort to recall and concentrate the faculties whose use is not forgotten—the sudden recall, the struggling to gather up the lost threads, and the terrible cachinnation of a demented man were rendered with remarkable fidelity and naturalness.[45]

The recording crudely dramatized the striking similarity between *Virginius's* final act and the final chapter of the actor's life, letting audiences in on the cosmic joke. As late as 1914, nearly 30 years after the tragedian's death, vaudevillian Eddie Foy used "The Ravings of John McCullough" as a punch line, suggesting a continued familiarity with the figure of mockery.[46] McCullough's rapid descent from tragic heroism to real-life tragedy trumped his theatre contemporaries' struggles to justify dedicating a monument to honor a man who was primarily noted for geniality. His fall from fame and fortune to penury and ridicule obscured the memorialized picture of perfection. His madness provided the more lasting legacy.

Although major critics of the day, including Towse and Winter, included chapters on McCullough in books that explored the theatre of their time, 20 years would pass before a biography was published. A woman who never met him, nor likely ever viewed him on stage, took on the task. This worshipful life history does more than simply chronicle the tragedian's life and career. The final third of the book focuses on McCullough after death. Spiritualist Susie Champney Clark interviewed McCullough through mediums and even allowed his spirit to select the title for his biography: *John McCullough as Man, Actor and Spirit* (1905).

Jon Butler, author of *Awash in a Sea of Faith: Christianizing the American People,* argues that a religious eclecticism (defined as a "belief in and resort to superhuman powers, sometimes beings, that determine the course of natural and human events") marked nineteenth-century religion in the United States as "a widening range of spiritual alternatives... turned antebellum America into a unique spiritual hothouse."[47] The popularity of American Spiritualism emerged with the publication of *The Principles of Nature, Her Divine Revelation, and a Voice to Mankind* (1847) by seer, clairvoyant, and healer Andrew Jackson Davis.[48] In 1848, the Fox Sisters of New York began communicating with the dead through rapping noises, which (although later admitted as a hoax) further popularized a spiritualist craze, often taking on a political bent and advocating the abolition of slavery and women's suffrage. The movement enjoyed enormous popularity, especially with middle- and upper-class women, and provided comfort to mourning families during the Civil War. Grieving over the death of their son, President Lincoln attended séances organized by his wife. Increased publicity of fraud, most famously by magician Harry Houdini, dampened spiritualism's popularity in the 1920s. Part of the New Thought movement, which flourished in the 1890s and into the first decades of the twentieth century, Clark was a mental healer and an author in topics ranging from biography to travel, although she was most prolific in spiritualism and mental healing. New Thought, inspired by Ralph Waldo Emerson's Transcendentalism, championed the divinity of true selfhood and the spiritual and practical power of "right" or positive thinking. Through mediums, McCullough apparently spoke to Clark of his life and art but also expounded on spiritual messages that were in line with Clark's beliefs, although the tragedian had not been a terribly religious man while alive. In writing his biography, his spirit urged her to "make the story simple, rugged, sweet," which certainly reflected the life he lived.[49]

Clark and McCullough might initially seem an unlikely match. McCullough's somewhat profligate lifestyle and the stigma attached to his insanity, however, are given short shrift (when not expunged completely) in Clark's account. She fleetingly references and discounts the "fraudulent phonograph" and shares McCullough's beyond-the-grave explanation for his mental instability and demise: a blow to the head when exiting a Philadelphia stage in 1877. Her uncritical exploration of his life and career idealizes the tragedian and provides no separation between the man and the heroic characters he portrayed. The man's extraordinary qualities, featuring "great force of character," "deeply passionate nature," "stanchest [sic] honor," "great moral emotions, an intense love of nature, in short, every quality which endowed him with the possibilities of a great actor," all were present in the roles he portrayed: "Thus he could give the finest renditions of genius because it existed within him, and found its fitting outlet of expression."[50] Whereas Clark details the astrological contributions and significance of McCullough's life, she concludes by championing the power of hard work and free will to achieve masculine potential: "Man, as a spirit, transcends the ruling of the stars..., and thus is he free, the sovereign occupant of the throne of his own enfranchised manhood."[51] Simply by ignoring anything objectionable or inconsistent in his character, Clark constructs a model of the perfect man at the dawn of the twentieth century.

Clark likely first encountered McCullough through the medium Reverend Frederick A. Wiggin, D. D., later, "pastor of the Unity Church [Boston] and a spiritualist well known throughout the country," who first channeled John McCullough's spirit a year after the tragedian's death in the autumn of 1886.[52] The spiritual link between Reverend Wiggin and McCullough, whose identity was confirmed definitively by two well-known actor friends (Walter Hubbell and Thomas W. Keene), continued for decades. In 1921, through the organism of Wiggin, McCullough acted as a conduit for the spirit of the Great Teacher, who was later revealed to be Jesus Christ. Providing comfort and reassurance in the years following the devastation of World War I, these messages were published under the title, *The Living Jesus: The Words of Jesus of Nazareth Uttered through the Medium Frederick A. Wiggin from February 11 to June 1, 1921*.[53] Acting as a twentieth-century John the Baptist, McCullough foretold the arrival of Christ's spirit and always appeared immediately before and after the Great Teacher's preachings. As McCullough communicated through Wiggin, "The object of mediumship is to further the need of a spiritualized manhood."[54] Regardless of whether Wiggin selected McCullough or vice versa, the simplicity and purity of McCullough continued to fill a need. His spirit, apparently both literally and figuratively, outlasted memories of his madness and disgrace, providing solace and guidance even at the start of the Jazz Age.

A strangely persistent rumor of McCullough's death actually continues into the twenty-first century. The National Theatre in Washington, DC still tells an apocryphal story of the tragedian, who was allegedly shot by a rival actor and buried beneath the stage, whose friendly ghost continues to watch paternally and genially over performances. His spirit lives on.

A MASCULINE EPILOGUE

From the nation's beginnings, American men struggled with the paradox of fraternal sameness versus competitive individualism. What is the frontiersman (or Spartacus or Metamora) but the quintessential individual? How then can that self-determined and self-sufficient character learn to cooperate in civilized society? Forrest's dramas precariously straddled this fence of sameness and individuality, presenting a world in which all men could potentially be individuals together (at least until the Astor Place Riot), but Booth's Hamlet was a solo artist who could not collaborate and could *not* fit into society. Edwin Forrest, like Jack Cade, fought for a personal and communal cause—independence and respect in the face of oppression and elitism—just as the nation sought a unique identity and the men who lived in it craved a new vision of American manhood. Yet his masculine image could not keep pace with the changing nation. Following the death of McCullough, Forrest's brand of masculinity, which was no longer desirable in the playhouse, went to the sporting arena to seek new audiences and free avenues of expression. Edwin Booth emblemized the struggle facing Lincoln and the nation, gaining masculine respect and status from his ability to bear sorrows in silence. The feminized gentility of Booth's Hamlet held up a mirror to the emerging middle-class man. Booth internalized his masculine performance, changing and diffusing the obvious signs and signifiers of ideal manhood that were so easily read in Forrest.

Forrest, Booth, and McCullough each modeled masculine ideals that were based on personal strengths and limitations that felicitously corresponded with the crises of his time. What exactly did audiences get from each of these masculine models? In Forrest, audiences vicariously reveled in the thrill of his unwavering strength, leadership, and power. Booth provided the tantalizing promise that each individual possessed great spiritual depth and the ability to endure hardship and tragedy. The accessible and reassuring McCullough gave hope that nice guys can triumph through hard work and goodwill. In the wake of the Civil War, the impeachment of Johnson, a succession of fairly lackluster presidencies, and the failure of Reconstruction contributed to a period of profound national disillusionment.. The collapse of Reconstruction suggests that the nation, once divided, cannot be reconciled successfully. It can be pieced together, but the cracks still show. The struggle to define and establish masculine identity in antebellum America informs an understanding of the problems of the late-nineteenth century.

Michael Kimmel, in *Manhood in America,* suggests that the journey of American men, throughout the country's history, reflects an almost perpetual crisis of masculinity: "It is a story of a chronically anxious, temperamentally restless manhood—a manhood that carries with it the constant burdens of proof." Kimmel observes a consistency in the struggle to provide this proof: "[T]he current malaise among men has a long history, and... the way men are responding these days bears a startling resemblance to men's responses over the course of American history."[55] Men seek the refuge and validation of an ideal, but they are pulled between at least two conflicting, incompatible visions. The bifurcation of masculinity, which is reflected in the disparity between Forrest and Booth on the antebellum stage, represents two dominant acts of manhood.

The reciprocal relationship of entertainment and masculine identity continued through the twentieth century and endures to the present day, although theatre has had a decreasing impact on the course of manly identity. Although theatre may still reflect a range of masculine identities and struggles, its influence on them is marginal. Marlon Brando's electric performance in Tennessee Williams's *Streetcar Named Desire* (1947) not only popularized a revolutionary acting style but also reawakened a raw, animal masculinity that was somewhat reminiscent of Forrest, while incorporating elements of vulnerability. Brando's performance in the film version in 1951, and his abandonment of the live stage, completed the shift to film and television as the most dominant and influential media for gender models. Contrasting visions of ideal manhood have vied for approval, dominance, and box office ever since.

A familiar polarity of competing masculine images—established by the brawny passion of Forrest and the spiritual refinement of Booth—filled screens, big and small, of the twentieth century. Following World War II, the stoic strength of John Wayne and Gary Cooper (later joined by the disaffected rebellion of Brando and James Dean) vied with the vulnerable warmth of Jimmy Stewart and Henry Fonda and the debonair elegance of Cary Grant and Fred Astaire. The muscular anti-intellectualism of Sylvester Stallone and Arnold Schwarzenegger and the tortured explosiveness of Al Pacino and Robert De Niro contrasted with the New-Age sensitivity of Dustin Hoffman and Alan Alda in the post-Vietnam era. The arrogant entitlement of Tom Cruise and Bruce Willis jockeyed with the quirky, feminized vulnerability of Tom Hanks, Johnny Depp, and Leonardo DiCaprio from the 1980s into the 1990s. Competing aspirants for the twentieth-century White House revealed similar masculine tensions—from the big stick of Teddy Roosevelt vs. Judge Alton B. Parker to the midcentury election of war hero Eisenhower vs. the erudite Adlai Stevenson to the charismatic folksiness of Reagan vs. intellectual peacemaker Carter to the dawn of the twenty-first century when the good-old-boy image of George W. Bush rivaled the comparatively subdued intellectualism of Al

Gore. Although these familiar contrasts continue, they remain only part of the complex web of masculinity, as the strands and complexities of viable manly models continue to multiply.

As I write this conclusion, the 2011 fall television season features no less than three shows (*Last Man Standing, Man Up!,* and *How to Be a Gentleman*) that reveal and capitalize on the latest crisis of masculinity—the struggle between the metrosexual and the retrosexual. *Last Man Standing* follows a traditional, "manly" father in a house and world that is dominated by women. Star Tim Allen, when asked about the multiple shows featuring "the feminization of men," opined, "It's not the feminization, just the reduction.... Our role was very simple: Find meat, bring it home. It feels... [like] what we used to do is being limited.... You get kinda backed in a corner."[56] *How to Be a Gentleman,* which is based on the 1998 male etiquette bestseller, similarly struggles with conflicting visions of manhood as a genteel intellectual seeks help from a macho Neanderthal: "The notion of the series is Bert helping me [series creator and star David Hornsby] take the *gentle* out of the *gentleman* a little bit and me adding a little *gentle* to his *man.*"[57] *Man Up!,* as framed by *Entertainment Weekly,* takes for granted the alienation of the contemporary male: "[A] generation of demasculinized men...search[es] for a balance between old and new male ideals."[58] The series' actors suggest that these characters "live in a world where 'they just don't know how to be men anymore.'.... 'Your grandfather fought in World War II, your father fought in Vietnam, but you play video games and use pomegranate body wash.'"[59] The irreconcilable dichotomy of mythical masculine ideals and the complex negotiations of actual manly existence still challenges and frustrates attempts to act like a man.

Notes

INTRODUCTION: A NEW RACE OF MEN

1. J. Hector St. John de Crevecoeur, *Letters from an American Farmer,* ed. Albert Stone (New York: Penguin, 1981), 69–70.
2. Jonathan Oldstyle, "Letter IV—Audiences," *Morning Chronicle,* December 4, 1802.
3. Royall Tyler, *The Contrast,* in *Early American Drama,* ed. Jeffrey H. Richards (New York: Penguin Books, 1997), 25, 26.
4. Ibid., 17.
5. Ibid., 57.
6. *Jacobellis v. Ohio,* 378 U.S. 184 (1964).
7. For Judith Butler's discussion of this idea, see *Bodies that Matter* (New York: Routledge, 1993), 1–5, 27–31.
8. Michael S. Kimmel, *Manhood in America: A Cultural History,* 2nd ed. (New York: Oxford University Press, 2006), 4.
9. Amy S. Greenberg, *Manifest Manhood and the Antebellum American Empire* (New York: Cambridge University Press, 2005), 11–14.
10. Beginning with Robert Staples's foundational study, the last 30 years have seen enormous growth in works directly and indirectly addressing the African-American masculine experience: Monica L. Miller, *Slaves to Fashion: Black Dandyism and the Styling of Black Diasporic Identity* (Durham, NC: Duke University Press, 2009); David R. Roediger, *The Wages of Whiteness: Race and the Making of the American Working Class* (Brooklyn, NY: Verso, 2007); E. Patrick Johnson, *Appropriating Blackness: Performance and the Politics of Authenticity* (Durham, NC: Duke University Press, 2003); Devon Carbado, *Black Men on Race, Gender, and Sexuality: A Critical Reader* (New York: New York University Press, 1999); Don Belton, *Speak My Name: Black Men on Masculinity and the American Dream* (Boston, MA: Beacon Press, 1997); Robert Staples, *Black Masculinity: The Black Man's Role in American Society* (San Francisco: Black Scholar Press, 1982). Specific to the world of the theatre, see the following works that directly and indirectly address issues of black masculinity: Heather S. Nathans, *Slavery and Sentiment on the American Stage, 1787–1861: Lifting*

the *Veil of Black* (New York: Cambridge University Press, 2009); Daphne A. Brooks, *Bodies in Dissent: Spectacular Performances of Race and Freedom, 1850–1910* (Durham, NC: Duke University Press, 2006); and Marvin McAllister, *White People Do Not Know How to Behave at Entertainments Designed for Ladies and Gentlemen of Colour: William Brown's African and American Theater* (Chapel Hill: University of North Carolina Press, 2002. For the treatment, portrayal, and performance of Native-American identities, see Philip J. Deloria, *Indians in Unexpected Places* (Lawrence: University of Kansas Press, 2006); and Philip J. Deloria, *Playing Indian* (New Haven, CT: Yale University Press, 1999).

11. Bruce McConachie and Lawrence Levine both indirectly make links between changing visions of national masculinity and transformations in theatrical preferences and practices: Bruce A. McConachie, *Melodramatic Formations: American Theatre and Society, 1820–1870* (Iowa City: University of Iowa Press, 1992); Lawrence W. Levine, *Highbrow/Lowbrow: The Emergence of Cultural Hierarchy in America* (Cambridge: Harvard University Press, 1988).

12. For recent works that have explored the construction of American masculine identity, see the following: Kimmel, *Manhood in America;* Greenberg, *Manifest Manhood* ; David Greven, *Manhood, Sex, and Violation in American Literature* (New York: Palgrave Macmillan, 2005); Dana D. Nelson, *National Manhood: Capitalist Citizenship and the Imagined Fraternity of White Men* (Durham, NC: Duke University Press, 1998); E. Anthony Rotundo, *American Manhood: Transformations in Masculinity from the Revolution to the Modern Era* (New York: Basic Books, 1993); David G. Pugh, *Sons of Liberty: The Masculine Mind in Nineteenth-Century America* (Wesport, CT: Greenwood Press, 1983).

13. For examinations of masculinity in the context of post–World War II American drama, see Carla J. McDonough, *Staging Masculinity: Male Identity in Contemporary American Drama* (Jefferson, NC: McFarland, 1997); Robert Vorlicky, *Act Like a Man: Challenging Masculinities in America* (Ann Arbor: University of Michigan Press, 1995). For issues of gender, men (including Edwin Forrest) and women, up to 1969, see Robert A. Schanke and Kim Marra, eds.,in *Passing Performance: Queer Readings of Leading Players in American Theater History* (Ann Arbor: University of Michigan Press, 1998). For an examination of women assuming the roles of men on the nineteenth-century American stage, see Elizabeth Reitz Mullenix, *Wearing the Breeches: Gender on the Antebellum Stage* (New York: Palgrave Macmillan, 2000). The following monographs and anthologies explore American manhood in film, television, and occasionally, theatre: Hamilton Carroll and Donald E. Pease, eds., *Affirmative Reaction: New Formations of White Masculinity* (Durham, NC: Duke University Press, 2011); Elwood Watson and Marc E. Shaw, eds., *Performing American Masculinities: The 21st-Century Man in Popular*

Culture (Bloomington: Indiana University Press, 2011); Rebecca Feasey, *Masculinity and Popular Television* (Edinburgh: Edinburgh University Press, 2009); Kenneth MacKinnon, *Representing Men: Maleness and Masculinity in the Media* (London: Bloomsburg, 2003); and David Savran, *Take It Like a Man: White Masculinity, Masochism, and Contemporary American Culture* (Princeton, NJ: Princeton University Press, 1998).

14. Paul Connerton, *How Societies Remember* (Cambridge: Cambridge University Press, 1989), 72–75.
15. Nelson, *National Manhood*, x. Nelson connects evolving attitudes of nation, race, and gender to the ideological formation of manliness and identifies an anxiety and alienation that are inherent in the simultaneously democratic and antidemocratic nature of white masculinity.
16. McConachie, *Melodrama Unveiled*, 75.
17. Alexis de Tocqueville, *Democracy in America*, vol. 2, trans. Henry Reeve (1850, reprint New York: A. S. Barnes, 1858), 145.
18. Edmund Kean, quoted in *Actors on Acting*, ed. Toby Cole and Helen Krich Chinoy (New York: Crown, 1970), 327–28. Joseph R. Roach, who places the historical study of acting within evolving understandings of physiology and psychology from the seventeenth to the twentieth centuries, describes the difference between perceptions of spontaneity—"coming freely without premeditation or effort, growing naturally without cultivation or labor"—and the ways in which artists consciously employed technique—"a coincidence of meaning that evokes not the free overflow of emotions but their progressive canalization into habit...Reflection shapes memory into an expressive illusion—an illusion of feelings spontaneously overflowing as if for the first time. This is not Nature, then; it is second nature" (*The Player's Passion: Studies in the Science of Acting* [Ann Arbor: University of Michigan Press, 1993], 162–63).
19. Richard Butsch provides tables that trace changes in Admission Prices for Stage Entertainments and Population and Income. "During the colonial period...the cheapest seats in the gallery cost a half-day's wages for an artisan and more than a full day's for a laborer. During the early republic, admission became more affordable, the gallery being about a third of a laborer's daily wage. The pit where an artisan might be expected to sit cost about a third of his daily wage" (*The Making of American Audiences From Stage to Television, 1750–1990* [Cambridge: Cambridge University Press, 2000], 298–99, 301, 296).
20. Prior to Cooper, actors such as Lewis Hallam, Jr., John Hodgkinson, and James Fennel transitioned from British to American stages. Each had performance strengths and raised the artistic credibility of American stages, but all presented problematic manly models. Hallam, whose family formed the first major professional theatre company in the New World, developed a reputation for jealousy and dishonesty. Hodgkinson presented a fine model onstage

but a suspicious figure offstage. Fennell had the potential for greatness but spent time in jail because of financial misdealings.
21. James E. Murdoch, *The Stage or, Recollections of Actors and Acting From an Experience of Fifty Years; A Series of Dramatic Sketches* (Philadelphia PA: J.M. Stoddart, 1880), 87. For a thorough examination of Cooper's life and career, see F. Arant Maginnes, *Thomas Abthorpe Cooper: Father of the American Stage, 1775–1849* (Jefferson, NC: McFarland, 2004).
22. *New York Commercial Advertiser,* March 2, 1798.
23. Henry Dickinson Stone, *Personal Recollections of the Drama; or, Theatrical Reminiscences* (Albany, NY: C. Van Bentuysen, 1873), 207.
24. Francis Courtney Wemyss, *Twenty-Six Years in the Life of an Actor and Manager* (New York: Burgess, Stringer, and Company, 1847), 75.
25. Murdoch, *The Stage,* 79, 82. For the most detailed biography of Cooke, see Don B. Wilmeth, *George Frederick Cooke: Machiavel of the Stage* (Westport, CT: Greenwood Press, 1980).
26. William Dunlap, *Memoirs of George Frederick Cooke* (New York: D. Longworth, 1813), 2: 157.
27. William Hazlitt, *Hazlitt on Theatre,* ed. William Archer and Robert W. Lowe (New York: Hill and Wang, 1957), 8.
28. *New York Evening Post,* November 30, 1820.
29. *Boston Galaxy,* May 26, 1821.
30. Following inflammatory newspaper reports that Kean had insulted the country, a reported 5000 Bostonians attacked the theatre in which Kean performed, forcing him off the stage. They attempted to hunt him down and threatened to kill him, but he escaped the city in disguise. No fatalities or serious injuries were reported, although the theatre was significantly damaged.
31. John W. Francis, *Old New York, or, Reminiscences of the Past Sixty Years* (New York: Charles Roe, 1858), 218.
32. *Spirit of the Times,* March 11, 1848.
33. *National Advocate,* October 8, 1821.
34. Francis, *Old New York,* 245.
35. William Charles Macready, *Macready's Reminiscences and Selections from His Diaries and Letters,* ed. Frederick Pollock (New York: Harper, 1875), 527.
36. James Sheridan Knowles, *Lectures on Oratory, Gesture and Poetry* (London, n.p., 1873), 134.
37. Macready, *Reminiscences,* 301.
38. William Charles Macready, *The Diaries of William Charles Macready, 1831–1851,* ed. W. Thompson, (New York: Putnam's, 1912), 1: 282.
39. George Henry Lewes, *On Actors and the Art of Acting* (New York: Holt, 1878), 3.
40. For theatrical performance in Colonial America, see Jason Shaffer, *Performing Patriotism: National Identity in the Colonial and Revolutionary American Theater* (Philadelphia: University of Pennsylvania Press, 2007); Jared Brown,

The Theatre in America During the Revolution (Cambridge: Cambridge University Press, 1995); and Hugh F. Rankin, *The Theater in Colonial America* (Chapel Hill: University of North Carolina Press, 1960).
41. Tyler, *The Contrast*, 15.
42. Kimmel, *Manhood in America*, 13.
43. *Pennsylvania Journal*, quoted in Richard Moody, *Dramas From the American Theatre, 1762–1909* (Cleveland, OH: World Publishing, 1966), 31.
44. Philip Dormer Stanhope, *Letters to his Son by the Earl of Chesterfield on the Fine Art of Becoming a Man of the World and a Gentleman*, ed. Joseph R. Seabury (New York: Silver, Burdett and Company, 1902).
45. Quoted in James Boswell, *The Life of Samuel Johnson* (1791), ed. William Wallace (Edinburgh: William P. Nimmo, 1873), 73.
46. James Dana, *A Sermon, Preached before the General Assembly* (Hartford: n.p., 1779), 27.
47. *Charleston National Gazette*, March 6, 1793. Also see Heather Shawn Nathans, "'All of the Federalist School?': Choosing Sides and Creating Identities in the Boston Theatre Wars," *New England Theatre Journal* 11 (2000): 1–18.
48. William Dunlap, *Andre*, in *Early American Drama*, ed. Jeffrey H. Richards (New York: Penguin Books, 1997), 90.
49. *Darby's Return*, quoted in Arthur Hobson Quinn, *A History of the American Drama From the Beginning to the Civil War* (New York: Harper and Brothers, 1923), 77.
50. Tyler, *Contrast*, 21–22, 24.
51. Henry Brooke, *Gustavus Vasa, The Deliverer of his Country* (London: R. Dodsley, 1739), 81.
52. Quoted in Richard Moody, *Edwin Forrest: First Star of the American Stage* (New York: Alfred A. Knopf, 1960), 16. *Douglas* was based on the Scotch ballad *Gil Morrice*.

1 ACT LIKE A MAN: IMAGES AND RHETORIC OF RECONSTRUCTED MANHOOD

1. Hezekiah Niles, *Principles and Acts of the Revolution in America* (Baltimore: William Ogden Niles, 1822), ii. The phrase "reconstructed manhood" comes from Henry Ward Beecher (*Yale Lectures on Preaching* [New York: J.B. Ford, 1872–1874], 6).
2. Niles, *Principles and Acts*, iv.
3. *The Complete Works of Ralph Waldo Emerson*, vol. 7 (Boston, MA: Houghton Mifflin, 1903–04), 115, 126.
4. Jay Fliegelman, *Declaring Independence: Jefferson, Natural Language, and the Culture of Performance* (Stanford, CA: Stanford University Press, 1993), 2, 89, 94.

5. Thomas Paine, "Common Sense," in *The Writings of Thomas Paine*, vol. 1, ed. Moncure Daniel Conway (New York: Putnam's, 1894), 71.
6. *Massachusetts Spy*, quoted in *The History of Printing in America*, vol. 2, 2nd ed., ed. Isaiah Thomas (Albany, NY: n.p., 1874), 63.
7. Kenneth Cmiel, *Democratic Eloquence: The Fight Over Popular Speech in Nineteenth-Century America* (New York: William Morrow, 1990), 14.
8. Paine, "Common Sense," 91.
9. J. Hector St. John de Crèvecoeur, *Letters from an American Farmer*, ed. Albert Stone (New York: Penguin, 1981), 69.
10. After the debacle of the 1800 election in which Federalist John Adams was defeated but Democratic-Republicans Thomas Jefferson and Aaron Burr received the same number of electoral votes (and the House of Representatives went through 36 ballots before electing Jefferson), the 12th Amendment supposedly eliminated future election problems and controversies.
11. By the 1824 election, John Quincy Adams's party, which was composed of anti-Jacksonians and many old Federalists, was called the National Republicans (by the early 1830s it would come to be known as the Whig Party). Suspicion of New England elite dated back to the Federalist Party and the War of 1812. Much of New England opposed the war and yet profited significantly by it. Rumors of secession and treason surrounded the "secret" Hartford Convention in 1814 and hurt the Federalist Party (of which Adams and his father were members), which disbanded soon after.
12. Lynn Hudson Parsons explores the innovations introduced in the 1828 election: *The Birth of Modern Politics: Andrew Jackson, John Quincy Adams, and the Election of 1828* (New York: Oxford University Press, 2009).
13. The published lectures of Adams, Harvard's first Boylston Chair of Rhetoric and Oratory, represented the country's first significant writings on the subject. John Quincy Adams, *Lectures on Rhetoric and Oratory*, 2 vols. (Cambridge, MA: Hilliard and Metcalf, 1810).
14. Cmiel, *Democratic Eloquence*, 15. For further discussion on the impact of elevated oratory, see Alexander Saxton, *The Rise and Fall of the White Republic: Class Politics and Mass Culture in Nineteenth-Century America* (London: Verso, 1990), 46. Paul C. Nagel explores Adams's personal side and the ways it influenced his political actions in *John Quincy Adams: A Public Life, A Private Life* (New York: Knopf, 1997).
15. John Quincy Adams, quoted in *Great Debates in American History*, vol. 4, ed. Marion M. Miller (New York: Current Literature, 1913), 123.
16. Thurlow Weed, *The Life of Thurlow Weed*, vol. 1, ed. H. A. Weed (Boston, MA: Houghton Mifflin, 1883), 178. Joseph Wheelan examines Adams's political life after presidency in *Mr. Adams's Last Crusade: John Quincy Adams's Extraordinary Post-Presidential Life in Congress* (New York: Public Affairs, 2008).
17. *Address of the Republican General Committee of Young Men of the City and County of New York* (New York: A. Ming, Jr., 1828), 41.

18. *New York Times,* October 8, 1834. The scholarship on Jackson is vast. Robert V. Remini's three-volume *Andrew Jackson* (Baltimore: Johns Hopkins University Press, 1998) most thoroughly details Jackson's political and personal journey. H. W. Brands effectively examines the controversial aspects of Jackson's life and politics in *Andrew Jackson: His Life and Times* (New York: Anchor, 2006). Sean Wilenz's biography provides perhaps the most balanced view of Jackson: *Andrew Jackson* (New York: Times, 2005).
19. Willis Hall, *An Address Delivered August 14, 1844, Before the Society of Phi Beta Kappa in Yale College* (New Haven, CT: Hamlen, 1844), 30.
20. Quoted in Richard Hofstadter, *Anti-intellectualism in American Life* (New York: Alfred A. Knopf, 1963), 162. Hofstadter convincingly demonstrates a mistrust of abstract, theoretical intellectualism, seen as an unfair advantage of power and privilege, in preference of common sense, functional thought, and pragmatic action through the country's history.
21. "Antinullification proclamation, Washington, D.C., December 10, 1832," in *The Statesmanship of Andrew Jackson as Told in his Writings and Speeches,* ed. Francis Newton Thorpe (New York: Tandy-Thomas, 1909), 232–36.
22. Nowhere did Jackson more obviously fashion himself as the nation's patriarch than in his dealings with the American Indians, claiming their actions, "compelled your Father the President to send his white children to chastise and subdue you, and thereby give peace to his children both red and white" (Andrew Jackson, quoted in Paul Michael Rogin, *Fathers and Children: Andrew Jackson and the Subjugation of the American Indian* [New York: Knopf, 1975], 199). In his troubling relationship with Native Americans, Jackson limits the father role to harsh punishment (Indian removal, ethnic cleansing, and enforced treaties) in preference of his favored children, the whites.
23. James Fennimore Cooper (1789–1851) implemented a similar mixture of high and low in his *Leatherstocking Tales* (*The Pioneers* [1823], *The Last of the Mohicans* [1826], *The Prairie* [1827], *The Pathfinder* [1840], and *The Deerslayer* [1841]). Natty Bumppo's speech combines high and low language, yet every chapter begins with a quotation from an "elevated" source (Shakespeare, the Bible, Sir Walter Scott, as well as comparatively obscure poets like William Somerville), suggesting a simultaneous accessibility to multiple audiences.
24. *Memoirs of John Quincy Adams, Comprising Portions of his Diary from 1795 to 1848,* vol. 8 ed. Charles Francis Adams (Philadelphia, PA: 1876), 547.
25. Andrew Jackson, quoted in Amos Kendall, *Autobiography,* ed. William Stickney (Boston, MA: Lee and Shepard, 1872), 631.
26. Andrew Jackson, quoted in Richard Hofstadter, *The American Political Tradition and the Men Who Made It* (New York: Alfred A. Knopf, 1948), 57.
27. *Ralph Waldo Emerson,* 8: 124; 7: 65. In his study of nineteenth-century speech, Cmiel suggests widespread implementation and success of the high and the low: "Everywhere you looked—the popular press, political oratory,

courtroom forensics, and religious homiletics—the story was the same: All combined the refined and crude" (*Democratic Eloquence*, 15).

28. Cmiel, *Democratic Eloquence*, 14.
29. For a comparative examination of these three figures, see Merrill D. Peterson, *The Great Triumvirate: Webster, Clay and Calhoun* (New York: Oxford University Press, 1988). Calhoun was the second man to serve as vice president under two presidents. George Clinton served under both Jefferson and Madison. Calhoun was the first vice president to resign (1832), leaving office toward the end of Jackson's first term to return to the Senate.
30. John C. Calhoun, quoted in John S. Jenkins, *The Life of John Caldwell Calhoun* (Auburn, AL: James Alden, 1858), 277.
31. John C. Calhoun, quoted in Arthur Styron, *The Cast Iron Man: John C. Calhoun and American Democracy* (New York: Longmans, Green, 1935), 199–200. James H. Read examines the complexity of Calhoun's political contributions in *Majority Rule Versus Consensus: The Political Thought of John C. Calhoun* (University Press of Kansas, 2009). For exploration of Calhoun as man and politician, see Irving H. Bartlett, *John C. Calhoun: A Biography* (New York: W. W. Norton, 1994); John Niven, *John C. Calhoun and the Price of Union: A Biography* (Baton Rouge: Louisiana State University Press, 1993).
32. Andrew Jackson and John C. Calhoun (1830), quoted in Warren Choate Shaw, *History of American Oratory* (Indianapolis, IN: Bobbs-Merrill Company, 1979), 179.
33. John C. Calhoun, "Speech on Slavery," U.S. Senate, *Congressional Globe*, 24th Congress, 2nd Sess (Feb. 6, 1837), 158.
34. Calhoun quoted in Styron, *Cast Iron Man*, 120.
35. John Wentworth, *Congressional Reminiscences: Adams, Benton, Calhoun, Clay, and Webster* (Chicago, IL: Fergus Printing, 1882), 35.
36. Quoted in Joseph M. Rogers, *The True Henry Clay* (Philadelphia, PA: Lippincott, 1905), 286.
37. Henry Clay, *The Works of Henry Clay*, vol. 6, ed. Calvin Colton (New York: Putnam, 1904), 412.
38. Ernest J. Wrage, "Henry Clay," in *History and Criticism of American Public Address*, vol. 2, ed. Marie Kathryn Hochmuth (New York: Russell and Russell, 1955), 612. Two recent works explore Clay's complex politics and image: David S. Heidler and Jeannie T. Heidler, *Henry Clay: The Essential American* (New York: Random House, 2010); Robert V. Remini, *At the Edge of the Precipice: Henry Clay and the Compromise That Saved the Union* (New York: Basic, 2010).
39. *Works of Henry Clay*, 566–67.
40. Lincoln on Clay, quoted in Shearer Davis Bowman, "Comparing Henry Clay and Abraham Lincoln," *Register of the Kentucky Historical Society* 106 (2008): 496.
41. Henry Clay, quoted in Irvin G. Wyllie, *The Self-Made Man in America: The Myth of Rags to Riches* (New Brunswick, NJ: Rutgers University Press,

1954), 10. Clay defined self-made manhood primarily in terms of the right to hold property, rather than social mobility.
42. Henry Clay, quoted in *Modern Eloquence,* ed. Thomas B. Reed (Philadelphia, PA: John D. Morris, 1903), 15: vi.
43. Robert V. Remini explores the contradictions in Webster's life and career, specifically addressing Webster's elitism in *Daniel Webster: The Man and His Time* (New York: W. W. Norton, 2009), 352. As a practical model of masculine performance, the imposing physical and vocal presence of Forrest more closely resembled Webster than Jackson.
44. Nathaniel Parker Willis, *Hurry-graphs: or, Sketches of Scenery, Celebrities and Society, Taken from Life* (Auburn, AL: Alden, Beardsley, 1853), 191.
45. Daniel Webster, quoted in *Great Debates in American History,* 4, 219.
46. Daniel Webster, "Description of the Eloquence of John Adams from his Eulogy of Adams and Jefferson, August 2, 1826," quoted in Shaw, *History of American Oratory,* 134–35. Webster's oratory could disappoint when the occasion failed to arouse his interest and passion, which was similar to romantic actors "playing points" and only giving their whole passion to a play's most heightened moments.
47. Halford Ryan, ed., *U.S. Presidents as Orators: A Bio-Critical Sourcebook* (Westport, CT: Greenwood Press, 1995), xiv. Of the twenty-one speakers featured, only five (Jefferson, Madison, Adams, Jackson, and Lincoln) served during the nineteenth century. Space does not allow an exploration into the masculine and rhetorical impact of such potent political speakers as Thomas Hart Benton, Stephen Douglas, Jefferson Davis, Wendell Phillips, Frederick Douglass, William Lloyd Garrison, Martin Delany, and Charles Sumner, among others.
48. William Henry Harrison died 32 days after assuming the presidency. Zachary Taylor died about 16 months into his presidency. It is possible that either or both of these war heroes could have established a stronger political personality if they had served a full term.
49. *Boston Daily Journal,* February 29, 1860. Ronald C. White, Jr. examines Lincoln's personal, political, and moral evolution: *A. Lincoln: A Biography* (New York: Random House, 2009).
50. Carl Schurz, *Reminiscences of Carl Shurz,* vol.2 (New York: McClure, 1909), 90. Schurz based his description on recollections of Lincoln during the Douglas debates in 1858.
51. *Illinois State Register,* November 23, 1839.
52. Edward H. Rollins, quoted in Elwin L. Page, *Abraham Lincoln in New Hampshire* (Boston, MA: Houghton Mifflin, 1929), 39.
53. *Comic Monthly,* reprinted in Mildred Freburg Berry "Abraham Lincoln: His Development in the Skills of the Platform," in *A History and Criticism of American Public Address,* vol. 2, ed. W. Norwood Brigance (New York: McGraw-Hill, 1943), 829.

54. Abraham Lincoln, quoted in Shaw, *History of American Oratory*, 383. Eric Foner explores Lincoln's complex view toward slavery in *The Fiery Trial: Abraham Lincoln and American Slavery* (New York: W. W. Norton, 2010).

55. Abraham Lincoln, quoted in John G. Nicolay and John Hay, *Abraham Lincoln: A History*, vol. 3 (New York: Century Company, 1890), 343. These authors present an earlier draft of this conclusion that was written by William H. Seward, which illustrates Lincoln's efforts to simplify language while retaining poetic elements (327–44).

56. The worshipful, posthumous praise of Lincoln is illustrated by Warren Choate Shaw, who described an oratorical magnetism "that led captive rich and poor, learned and unlearned, in a way that challenges comparison with the preaching of Christ in the parables or in the *Sermon on the Mount*" (Shaw, *History of American Oratory*, 2: 376). Although lauded by foreign presses, America's rhetoricians, newsmen, and general populace ignored many of the speeches that are now most admired. Neither Lincoln's Gettysburg Address nor the Second Inaugural Address received much attention. British critics lavishly praised both speeches, and the *Edinburgh Review* called the Gettysburg Address "an address without a parallel since the eulogy by Pericles on the heroic dead of the Peloponnesian War" (quoted in Shaw, *History of American Oratory*, 2: 398). While generally opposing slavery, England relied on the cotton produced by the South, complicating their response to Lincoln and the war. Amanda Foreman explores the complex relationship between American and England in *A World on Fire: Britain's Crucial Role in the American Civil War* (New York: Random House, 2011).

57. *New York Herald*, September 17, 1865. "Taking him for all in all" is borrowed from Hamlet's reminiscences on his late father: "He was a man, take him for all in all, / I shall not look upon his like again." I will further explore Lincoln's connection to Hamlet in my discussion of the era's greatest portrayer of the role, Edwin Booth.

58. Alexander Hamilton Stephens, *A Constitutional View of the Late War Between the States; its Causes, Character, Conduct and Results. Presented in a Series of Colloquies at Liberty Hall*, vol. 2 (Philadelphia, PA: National Publishing, 1868–70), 447.

59. Beecher, *Yale Lectures on Preaching*, 6.

60. Henry Ward Beecher, quoted in Harry Emerson Fosdick, *The Power to See It Through* (New York: Harper, 1935), 64.

61. Jon Butler, *Awash in a Sea of Faith: Christianizing the American People* (Cambridge, MA: Harvard University Press, 1990), 238.

62. Henry Ward Beecher, quoted in Harriet Beecher Stowe, *The Lives and Deeds of our Self-Made Men* (Hartford, CT: Worthington, Dustin, 1872), 568; Altina L. Waller, *Reverend Beecher and Mrs. Tilton: Sex and Class in Victorian America* (Amherst: University of Massachusetts Press, 1982), 148.

63. Henry Ward Beecher, quoted in Constance Mayfield Rourke, *Trumpets of Jubilee* (New York: Harcourt and Brace, 1927), 177.

64. Henry Ward Beecher, quoted in N. A. Shenstone, *Anecdotes of Henry Ward Beecher* (Chicago, IL: R. R. Donnelley, 1887), 434.
65. Lionel Crocker, "Henry Ward Beecher," in *History and Criticism of American Public Address*, 1: 280.
66. Henry Fowler, *The American Pulpit* (New York: J. M. Fairchild, 1856), 141.
67. Henry Ward Beecher, quoted in Crocker, "Henry Ward Beecher," in *A History and Criticism of American Public Address*, 274.
68. Paxton Hibben, *Henry Ward Beecher: An American Portrait*, with a foreword by Sinclair Lewis, vol. vii (New York: George H. Doran, 1927; reprint, New York: Readers Club, 1942), 19. Lewis was born two years before Beecher died, so his observation was not a first-hand account.
69. William H. Smith, *The Drunkard; or, The Fallen Saved*, in *Early American Drama*, ed. Jeffrey H. Richards (New York: Penguin, 1997), 295–96.
70. Jeffrey D. Mason, *Melodrama and the Myth of America* (Bloomington: Indiana University Press, 1993), 73. Mason's chapter on the temperance melodrama (60–87) provides an overview of drinking in America, the temperance movement, and the effectiveness of moral reform drama. For the most thorough treatment of theatre and the temperance movement, see John W. Frick, *Theatre, Culture, and Temperance Reform in Nineteenth-Century America* (Cambridge: Cambridge University Press, 2003). See also Michael R. Booth, "The Drunkard's Progress: Nineteenth-Century Temperance Drama," *Dalhousie Review* 44 (1964): 205–12; Jill Siegel Dodd, "The Working Classes and the Temperance Movement in Ante-Bellum Boston," *Labor History* 19 (1978): 510–31.
71. Maud Skinner and Otis Skinner, *One Man in His Time: The Adventures of H. Watkins, Strolling Player, 1845–1863, from His Journal* (Philadelphia: University of Pennsylvania Press, 1938), 70. For more on John Bartholomew Gough, see John Marsh, *Temperance Recollections* (New York: Charles Scribner, 1866), 127–28. For more on Barnum's production of *The Drunkard*, see P. T. Barnum, *Struggles and Triumphs: Or, Forty Years' Recollections* (Hartford, CT: J. B. Burr, 1869; reprint, New York: Arno, 1970), 264–65.
72. For more on the Beecher-Tilton Affair, see Altina L. Waller, *Reverend Beecher and Mrs. Tilton: Sex and Class in Victorian America* (Amherst: University of Massachusetts Press, 1982).
73. Bruce A. McConachie, *Melodramatic Formations: American Theatre and Society, 1820–1870* (Iowa City: University of Iowa Press, 1992), 32. For discussion of the evolving role of the young man in the nineteenth-century urban environment see Richard Stott, *Workers in the Metropolis: Class, Ethnicity and Youth in Antebellum New York City* (Ithaca, NY: Cornell University Press, 1990); Sean Wilentz, *Chants Democratic: New York City and the Rise of the American Working Class, 1788–1850* (New York: Oxford University Press, 1984).
74. As described by the *Analectic Magazine*, "only when it [history] deviates into biography, in portraying the actions of some extraordinary man, does it afford

those practical models of conduct, or exhibit the consequences of ill regulated ambition, the consideration of which teaches philosophy by examples, and is truly the 'school of life'" (*Analectic Magazine* 1 [January 1820]: 462). According to the *Connecticut Courant* (1849), Kellogg Company presses "run off daily from 3000 to 4000 copies of various popular prints...More than 100,000 copies have been sold from a single design. The portrait of Washington takes the lead and next to him stands Old Rough and Ready" (Quoted in Wendy Wick Reaves, "Portraits for Every Parlor: Albert Newsam and American Portrait Lithography," in *American Portrait Prints: Proceedings of the Tenth Annual American Print Conference* [Charlottesville: University Press of Virginia, 1984], 85.

75. Arthur M. Schlesinger provides statistics on the publication of advice manuals in *Learning How to Behave: A Historical Study of American Etiquette Books* (New York: Macmillan, 1947), 18. Additional studies that specifically address etiquette manuals, conduct books, and advice literature include: Sarah E. Newton, *Learning to Behave: A Guide to American Conduct Books Before 1900* (Westport, CT: Greenwood Press, 1994); Andrew St. George, *The Descent of Manners: Etiquette, Rules and The Victorians* (London: Chatto and Windus, 1993). The study of the transformations in social practices, niceties, and identities—the historical importance of which was largely unrealized until recently—have been undertaken in the following: C. Dallett Hemphill, *Bowing to Necessities: A History of Manners in America* (Oxford: Oxford University Press, 1999); John F. Kasson, *Rudeness and Civility: Manners in Nineteenth-Century Urban America* (New York: Hill and Wang, 1990); Lawrence W. Levine, *Highbrow/Lowbrow: The Emergence of Cultural Hierarchy in America* (Cambridge, MA: Harvard University Press, 1988); Karen Halttunen, *Confidence Men and Painted Women: A Study of Middle-Class Culture in America, 1830–1870* (New Haven, CT: Yale University Press, 1982).

76. Newton, in *Learning to Behave*, 10, claims that 90 percent of the texts she surveyed sought to provide gender role instruction.

77. Henry Lunettes [Margaret C. Conkling], *The American Gentleman's Guide to Politeness and Fashion* (New York: Derby and Jackson, 1857), 330.

78. Frances Trollope, *Domestic Manners of the Americans*, ed. Donald Smalley (1832; New York: Knopf, 1949), 263–64. Frances Anne Kemble, *The American Journals*, ed. Elizabeth Mavor (London: Weidenfeld and Nicolson, 1990).

79. See Michael Denning, *Mechanic Accents: Dime Novels and Working Class Culture in America* (New York: Verso, 1987).

80. Review of *Bazar Book of Decorum,* by Robert Tomes, reprinted in *Atlantic Monthly* 26 (July 1870): 122.

81. *The Art of Good Behavior; and Letter Writer on Love, Courtship, and Marriage: A Complete Guide for Ladies and Gentlemen, particularly Those Who Have Not Enjoyed the Advantages of Fashionable Life* (New York: C.P. Huestis, 1846), viii-ix.

82. Anna Cora Mowatt, *Fashion; or, Life in New York*, in *Early American Drama*, ed. Jeffrey H. Richards (New York: Penguin, 1997), 366, 311. The play provides two models of ideal American manhood in the aptly named Trueman and the young Colonel Howard.
83. Henry Ward Beecher, *Twelve Lectures to Young Men on Various Important Subjects* (New York: George H. Doran, 1879), 196; Maurice Francis Egan, *A Gentleman*, 2nd ed. (New York: Benziger Brothers, 1893), 15.
84. Rev. J. W. Kasey, *The Young Man's Guide to True Greatness* (Big Springs, KY: J.W. Kasey, 1858), 224.
85. John Todd, *The Young Man: Hints Addressed to the Young Men of the United States* (Northampton, UK: J.H. Butler, 1845), 22, 33.
86. Robert de Valcourt, *The Illustrated Manners Book and Manual of Good Behavior and Polite Accomplishments* (New York: Leland, Clay, 1855), 205.
87. Harvey Newcomb, *How to Be a Man* (Boston, MA: Gould, Kendall, and Lincoln, 1847), 101.
88. Beecher, *Twelve Lectures*, 123.
89. Smith, *The Drunkard*, 275, 289.
90. Samuel Robert Wells, *How to Behave: A Pocket Manual of Republican Etiquette* (New York: Fowler and Wells, 1856), 124.
91. Karen Halttunen, *Confidence Men and Painted Women*, 192.
92. Tocqueville, *Democracy in America*, 1: 3, 2: 146–47.
93. Charles William Day, *Hints on Etiquette and the Usages of Society* (Boston, MA: Otis Broaders, 1844), 3.
94. Abby Buchanan Longstreet, *Social Etiquette of New York* (New York: D. Appleton, 1887), 9.
95. Mowatt, *Fashion*, 333.
96. de Valcourt, *Illustrated Manners Book*, 14.
97. Lunettes, *American Gentleman's Guide*, 145.

2 "A GLORIOUS IMAGE OF UNPERVERTED MANHOOD": EDWIN FORREST AS MASCULINE IDEAL

1. *Edinburgh Review, Or Critical Journal* 23 (January 1820), 79.
2. *New England Galaxy*, February 16, 1827.
3. *Boston Daily Bee*, November 10, 1856.
4. *Dayton Journal*, September 30, 1865.
5. William Rounseville Alger, *Life of Edwin Forrest, The American Tragedian* (Philadelphia, PA: J. B. Lippincott), 259.
6. In 1947, the bibliophile Grolier Club credited Alger's novel as one of the most influential 100 American novels written before 1900 (Gary Scharnhorst and Gary Bales, *The Lost Life of Horatio Alger, Jr.* [Bloomington: Indiana University Press, 1985], 86–87).

7. *The History of Edwin Forrest, the Celebrated American Tragedian. Written by an Individual Who Has Known Him from His Boyhood* (New York: n.p., 1837), 19.
8. Quoted in Richard Moody, *Edwin Forrest: First Star of the American Stage* (New York: Alfred A. Knopf, 1960), 250.
9. John Carboy, "Theatrical Reminiscences: Edwin Forrest," Harvard Theatre Collection, n.d.
10. Moody, *Edwin Forrest*, 346–47.
11. Kerry Dean Carso discusses the theatrical architecture and nationalist implications of Forrest's Fonthill in "The Theatrical Spectacle of Medieval Revival: Edwin Forrest's Fonthill Castle," *Winterthur Portfolio* 39 (Spring 2004): 21–42.
12. Moody, *Edwin Forrest*, 249.
13. For records of the court trial and some contemporary commentary, see *The Forrest Divorce Case: Catherine Norton Forrest vs. Edwin Forrest Before the Superior Court of New York, Chief Justice Oakley Presiding. Case Tried in December, 1851, and January, 1852* (Boston, MA: n.p, 1852); *Report of the Forrest Divorce Case, Containing the Full and Unabridged Testimony of All the Witnesses, the Affidavits and Depositions, Together with the Consuelo and Forney Letters* (New York: n.p., 1852).
14. *Forney's Weekly Press* (Philadelphia), December 21, 1872.
15. "American Actors in England," *The United States Magazine and Democratic Review* 19 (September 1846): 187.
16. Montrose J. Moses, *The Fabulous Forrest: The Record of an American Actor* (Boston, MA: Little, Brown, and Co., 1929), 134.
17. John Foster Kirk, "Shakespeare's Tragedies upon the Stage: Remarks and Reminiscences of a Sexagenarian," *Lippincott's Magazine* (June 1884), 604.
18. Fanny Elssler, quoted in Moses, *Fabulous Forrest*, 195.
19. Charles T. Congdon, *Reminiscences of a Journalist* (Boston, MA: James R. Osgood, 1880), 190; *The Age* (Philadelphia), October 11, 1872.
20. Mark Twain, "Lisle Lester on Her Travels," *The Daily Dramatic Chronicle* (San Francisco), October 30, 1865; Lisle Lester, "Edwin Forrest. His Art and Manhood," *Leslie's Popular Monthly* (December 1887), 686.
21. *New York Sunday Times*, September 22, 1860.
22. Alger, *Life of Edwin Forrest*, 251–52. It is tempting to read a homoerotic tone into this passage. Ginger Strand's "'My Noble Spartacus:' Edwin Forrest and Masculinity on the Nineteenth-Century Stage" (in *Passing Performances: Queer Readings of Leading Players in American Theater History*, ed. Robert A Schanke and Kim Marra [Ann Arbor: University of Michigan Press, 1998], 19–40) suggests a "queer" reading of portions of Forrest's career and specifically his longtime friendship with James Oaks. Although this interpretation may read too literally into Forrest's masculine imagery, it highlights the unabashed sensuality of the sexually charged celebration of his manhood.

23. *New York World,* September 29, 1862.
24. Moody, *Edwin Forrest,* 44. For a discussion of prize fighting and its relation to nineteenth-century masculine identity, see Elliot J. Gorn, *The Manly Art: Bare-Knuckle Prize Fighting in America* (Ithaca, NY: Cornell University Press, 1986).
25. Quoted in Moody, *Edwin Forrest,* 15–16. Colonel John Swift (1790–1873), a leader of the Philadelphia Whig party, served as mayor on three separate occasions (1832–1838, 1839–1841, and 1845–1849) and in 1840 became the first popularly elected Philadelphia mayor.
26. *New York Mirror,* July 1, 1826.
27. Charles Durang, "Life of Edwin Forrest," Harvard Theatre Collection, 11.
28. *History of Edwin Forrest,* 18.
29. Multiple biographers claim that Forrest studied elocution with "the father of American ornithology," Alexander Wilson. A largely unsuccessful poet, Wilson had no training or experience relating to elocution and worked tirelessly during Forrest's life on his multivolume *American Ornithology.* Wilson died when Forrest was seven, so any interaction or instruction must have been limited.
30. Moody, *Edwin Forrest,* 16.
31. Moody, *Edwin Forrest,* 40, 47–48.
32. James Murdoch, *The Stage, or, Recollections of Actors and Acting From an Experience of Fifty Years; a Series of Dramatic Sketches* (Philadelphia, PA: J. M. Stoddart, 1880), 294–95.
33. Joe Cowell, *Thirty Years Passed among the Players in England and America,* vol. 2 (New York: Harper and Brothers, 1844), 74.
34. Gabriel Harrison, quoted in Alger, *Life of Edwin Forrest,* 543.
35. *Albion* (New York), September 2, 1848.
36. Lisle Lester, *Leslie's Popular Monthly,* December 1887, 686.
37. "Editor's Easy Chair," *Harper's Magazine,* December 1863.
38. *Courier and Enquirer,* March 30, 1847.
39. *Knickerbocker Magazine,* December 1837. Romantic poet and critic Samuel Taylor Coleridge famously said of Edmund Kean: "Seeing him act was like reading Shakespeare by flashes of lightning" (*Table Talk,* April 27, 1823).
40. Alger, *Life of Edwin Forrest,* 260–61.
41. *The Age* (Philadelphia), December 13, 1872.
42. Lawrence Barrett, "Edwin Forrest," in *Actors and Actresses of Great Britain and the United States,* ed. Brander Matthews and Laurence Hutton, vol. 4 (New York: O. M. Dunham, 1886), 45.
43. Kirk, "Shakespeare's Tragedies," 615.
44. *New York Herald,* September 11, 1860. Forrest's connection to Jacksonian Democracy and its influence on his stage work is most effectively discussed in Bruce A. McConachie's "The Theatre of Edwin Forrest and Jacksonian Hero Worship" in *When They Weren't Doing Shakespeare: Essays*

on *Nineteenth-Century British and American Theatre,* ed. Judith L. Fisher and Stephen Watt (Athens: University of Georgia Press, 1989), 3–18.
45. Edwin Forrest, "Oration Delivered at the Democratic Republican Celebration, Fourth of July, 1838" (New York: Jared W. Bell, 1838), 23, 8.
46. Alger, *Life of Edwin Forrest,* 159.
47. Eliza Ware Farrar, *The Young Lady's Friend* (Boston, MA: American Stationers' Company, 1837), 102.
48. *Albion* (New York), September 2, 1848.
49. *Boston Daily Bee,* November 10, 1856.
50. "Mr. Forrest's Second Reception in England," *United States Magazine and Democratic Review* 16 (April 1845), 386.
51. *Philadelphia Press,* December 27, 1861.
52. *The Critic* (New York), November 22, 1828.
53. *New York Mirror,* March 8, 1828.
54. The twenty-two-year spread from start to finish of the nine playwriting contests is somewhat misleading. The first seven contests took place in a span of less than five years.
55. *The Critic* (New York), November 22, 1828. Leggett edited this weekly review. David Grimsted provides charts of the "Popularity of Particular Plays" and "Percentages of Types of Plays Given" (for Charleston, Philadelphia, New Orleans, and St. Louis). American drama never totaled more than 16 percent of the total dramas performed (*Melodrama Unveiled,* 249–61).
56. *New York Mirror,* March 8, 1834.
57. Cornelius Matthews, *The Sun* (New York), July 5, 1881.
58. McConachie, "Theatre of Edwin Forrest," 3.
59. The overtly political *Caius Marius* lacked dramatic action. *Pelopidas,* which Forrest never performed, failed to provide a substantive enough title role. The overly moralistic *Oralloossa, Son of the Incas* suffered from structural problems. Written by the same author as *Metamora, The Ancient Briton* may have had greater literary merit, but it never enjoyed its popular success. Forrest sporadically performed *The Broker of Bogota,* frequently considered Bird's finest play, but its popular appeal was limited. Although he acknowledged it as well written, Forrest never performed *Mohammed,* which was awarded the prize for the final competition, and felt it unsuitable for the stage.
60. *Brooklyn Daily Eagle,* December 26, 1846.
61. Jeffrey Mason suggests that, as theatricalized history, "Stone's white audience could admire Metamora and sympathize with him, but as audience, they were not required to act on his behalf" ("*Metamora* and the Indian Question," in *Melodrama and the Myth of America* [Bloomington: Indiana University Press, 1993], 46). Also see Scott C. Martin, "Interpreting *Metamora*: Nationalism, Theater, and Jacksonian Indian Policy," in *Journal of the Early Republic* 19 (Spring 1999): 73–101.

62. John Augustus Stone, *Metamora; or, The Last of the Wampanoags*, in *Dramas From the American Theatre, 1762–1909*, ed. Richard Moody (Cleveland, OH: World Publishing, 1966), 207, 224.
63. Robert Montgomery Bird, *The Gladiator*, in *Early American Drama*, ed. Jeffrey H. Richards (New York: Penguin, 1997), 240.
64. Robert T. Conrad, *Aylmere, or the Bondman of Kent; and Other Poems* (Philadelphia, PA: E. H. Butler, 1852), 132.
65. *Aylmere*, 165. Forrest, at the urging of manager Frances Wemyss, changed the title to *Jack Cade*.
66. *Metamora*, 207.
67. *Metamora*, 224–25.
68. *Gladiator*, 224.
69. *Aylmere*, 148.
70. Bruce McConachie points out some of the parallels to Christ in these works. He also suggests a contrast in the English romantic tragedies of this era, all of which lack the providential hand that require the martyrdom of their hero (*Melodramatic Formations: American Theatre and Society, 1820–1870* [Iowa City: University of Iowa Press, 1992], 103–04). McConachie and Richard Fletcher both suggest that the memory and fear of Napoleonic ambition and tyranny inspire and demand the endings of these romantic tragedies (McConachie, "The Theatre of Edwin Forrest," 11; Richard M. Fletcher, *English Romantic Drama, 1795–1843: A Critical History* [Hicksville, NY: Exposition Press, 1966] 106, 152).
71. *Boston Daily Atlas*, November 7, 1833.
72. *New England Galaxy* (Boston), November 9, 1833.
73. From a letter to a literary society in Albany, January 8, 1834, quoted in Alger, *Life of Edwin Forrest*, 179.
74. *New England Galaxy*, November 19, 1831.
75. Robert Montgomery Bird, quoted in Richard Harris, "A Young Dramatist's Diary: The Secret Records of Robert Montgomery Bird" in Library Chronicle of the Friends of the University of Pennsylvania Library (vol. 25, 1959), 16. Bird wrote this diary entry on August 27, 1831, just one month before the opening of *The Gladiator*.
76. William Winter, quoted in Clement E. Foust, *The Life and Dramatic Works of Robert Montgomery Bird* (New York: Knickerbocker, 1919), 67.
77. Edgar Allan Poe, "A Chapter on Autobiography [part II]," in *Graham's Magazine* 19 (December 1841), 281.
78. Alger, *Life of Edwin Forrest*, 361.
79. Arthur Herman Wilson, *A History of the Philadelphia Theatre, 1835–1855* (New York: Greenwood Press, 1968). *Jack Cade* has understandably been linked to *Metamora* and *The Gladiator*, and the three plays have been explored as a group in the following: Gary A. Richardson, "Plays and Playwrights: 1800–1865," in *The Cambridge History of American Theatre*, ed. Don

B. Wilmeth and Christopher Bigsby (Cambridge: Cambridge University Press, 1998), 1: 267–70; McConachie, *Melodramatic Formations*, 97–110; Moody, *Edwin Forrest*, 90–91; Montrose J. Moses, ed., *Representative Plays by American Dramatists From 1765 to the Present Day* (New York: Benjamin Blom, 1925), 2: 427–30.

80. T. Allston Brown, *A History of the New York Stage From the First Performance in 1732 to 1901*, vol. 1 (New York: Benjamin Blom, 1903), 105–06. *Jack Cade* opened on December 9, 1835 for a three-show run, averaging a respectable $290 per night, and was revived the following year for another three consecutive performances (Francis Courtnay Wemyss, *Twenty-Six Years of the Life of an Actor and Manager* [New York: Burgess, Stringer, and Co., 1847], 244–50). Augustus A. Addams (?-1851) openly but artfully imitated Forrest, and actor Walter Leman ranked his potential higher: "In stature he excelled Forrest, and was not unlike him in manner and method. He died young, otherwise I think Mr. Forrest would have found in him a dangerous rival" (Walter M. Leman, *Memories of an Old Actor* [San Francisco, CA: A. Roman, 1886], 37).
81. Richard Hofstadter, *Anti-intellectualism in American Life* (New York: Alfred A. Knopf, 1963), 400.
82. *New York Evening Post*, December 18, 1834, reprinted in *A Collection of the Political Writings of William Leggett*, vol. 1, ed. Theodore Sedgwick, Jr. (New York: Taylor and Dodd, 1840), 132–33, 126.
83. Conrad, *Aylmere*, 282.
84. Edgar Allan Poe, *Graham's Magazine*, December 1841; Ellis Paxson Oberholtzer, *The Literary History of Philadelphia* (Philadelphia, PA: George W. Jacobs, 1906), 264.
85. Poe, "Chapter on Autobiography," 281.
86. Poe, "Our Contributors—Number 12. Robert T. Conrad," *Graham's Magazine* 25 (June 1844), 242.
87. Wemyss, *Twenty-Six Years*, 245–50.
88. Robert T. Conrad, *Aylmere; or, The Kentish Rebellion*, "Property of Edwin Forrest," Marked for Mr. Forrest by D. A. Sarzedas, Prompter, Park Theatre May 24th 1841 New York (University of Pennsylvania, Forrest Collection). For ease of reference, I will refer to this version of Conrad's script as *Jack Cade*. This script, in which Forrest marked cuts, requested changes, and included a few brief notes to Conrad, resides in the Forrest Collection at the University of Pennsylvania Library. *Jack Cade* moderates *Aylmere*'s most gruesome descriptions of famine, whipping, immolation, death, and spearing babies—most likely out of sensitivity to the few women in the audience. Some changes lack any apparent artistic justification. For example, as Aylmere rhapsodizes on the beauty of Italy in his exile, he brief exults on the four seasons. *Jack Cade* cuts off the speech in the middle of Summer, completely eliminating Autumn and Winter (*Jack Cade*, 25).

89. *Jack Cade*, 25.
90. Poe, "Robert T. Conrad," 242.
91. Ibid.
92. *Aylmere*, vii-viii.
93. Ibid., 22.
94. Ibid., 44.
95. Ibid., 62.
96. Ibid., 104.
97. Ibid., 106–07.
98. Ibid., 83.
99. Ibid., 149.
100. Ibid., 80.
101. Ibid., 20.
102. Ibid., 72.
103. Ibid., 36.
104. Ibid., 55–58.
105. *Jack Cade*, 31.
106. For the history of women's struggles for recognition and equality through the nineteenth century, see the following: Jean V. Matthew, *The Rise of the New Woman: The Women's Movement in American, 1875–1930* (Chicago, IL: Ivan R. Dee, 2004); Jean V. Matthew, *Women's Struggle for Equality* (Chicago, IL: Ivan R. Dee, 1998). For Ibsen's role in evolving notions of womanhood, see Joan Templeton, *Ibsen's Women* (New York: Cambridge University Press, 1997).
107. Mary Wollstonecraft, *A Vindication on the Rights of Woman: With Strictures on Political and Moral Subjects* (Cambridge: Cambridge University Press, 2010).
108. Marion Reid, *A Plea for Woman* (Chester Springs, PA: Dufour Editions, 1989).
109. Quoted in Moses, *Fabulous Forrest*, 287. Bruce McConachie similarly argues that Forrest saw women as "inferior…and hence dependent upon men," while his upper-class wife felt that "men and women were natural equals and should work together for moral progress" (McConachie, *Melodramatic Formations*, 71–72).
110. *Aylmere*, 66.
111. *Jack Cade*, 36.
112. *Aylmere*, 67, 120.
113. Patricia Cline Cohen, *The Murder of Helen Jewett: The Life and Death of a Prostitute in Nineteenth-Century New York* (New York: Vintage Books, 1998), 210. In the early part of the century, Patricia Cline Cohen argues, "Women were now construed to be the victims of seduction, not complicit participants." Cohen goes on to discuss the increase in court actions in defense of "jilted brides and desolate or pregnant lovers," from 1815 to 1830 (210). In

addition to Cohen's discussion of class-based seduction, see the following for evolving societal and legal attitudes toward seduction and fallen women: Jane H. Pease and William H. Pease, *Ladies, Women, and Wenches: Choices and Constraint in Antebellum Charleston and Boston* (Chapel Hill: University of North Carolina Press, 1990); Christine Stansell, *City of Women: Sex and Class in New York, 1789–1860* (Chicago: University of Illinois Press, 1982).

114. Nancy Cott discusses the personal impact of seduction on women: "Passionlessness: An Interpretation of Victorian Sexual Ideology, 1790–1850," *Signs: Journal of Women in Culture and Society* 4 (1978): 219–36.

115. William Hill Brown, *The Power of Sympathy*, ed. William S. Kable (Columbus: Ohio State Univeristy Press, 1969). In her analysis of *The Power of Sympathy*, Cathy N. Davidson argues "that seduction... is a metaphor not just of women's status in the Republic but of... a range of problems that arise when moral value and social responsibility are outweighed by the particular desires, no matter how basely self-serving, of privileged individuals or classes" (*Revolution and the Word: The Rise of the Novel in America* [Oxford: Oxford University Press, 1986], 108).

116. *Aylmere*, 119.
117. *Jack Cade*, 61.
118. *Aylmere*, 125.
119. *Jack Cade*, 66.
120. Alexis de Tocqueville, *Democracy in America*, vol. 1 (New York: Barnes, 1858), 248.
121. E. Anthony Rotundo identifies communal and self-made manhoods as historical phases of masculine development, along with passionate manhood (*American Manhood: Transformations in Masculinity from the Revolution to the Modern Era* [New York: Basic Books, 1993], 2–7).
122. Roland Barthes discusses the deceptive power of myth consumption: "We reach here the very principle of myth: it transforms history into Nature. We now understand why, *in the eyes of the myth consumer,* the intention, the abhomination [sic] of the concept can remain manifest without however appearing to have an interest in the manner: what causes mythical speech to be uttered is perfectly explicit, but it is immediately frozen into something natural; it is not read as a motive, but as a reason" ("Myth Today," in *A Barthes Reader*, ed. Susan Sontag [New York: Hill and Wang, 1996], 116).

3 A MASCULINE IDENTITY WORTH DYING FOR: THE ASTOR PLACE RIOT

1. Francis Courtney Wemyss, *Twenty-six Years in the Life of an Actor and Manager* (New York: Burgess, Stringer and Company, 1847), 117. For the evolving relationship between the United States and England, see *Britain*

and the Americas: Culture, Politics, and History, ed. Will Kaufman and Heidi Slettedahl Macpherson (Santa Barbara, CA: ABC-CLIO, 2005).
2. *Spirit of the Times,* April 7, 1860. In the bare-knuckle prizefighting of the day, a round lasted until one of the opponents was knocked down. A round rarely lasted more than a minute.
3. Beecher, *Yale Lectures on Preaching* (New York: J. B. Ford, 1872–1874), 6.
4. David Humphreys, quoted in Francis Hodge, *Yankee Theatre: The Image of America on the Stage, 1825–1850* (Austin: University of Texas Press, 1964), 54. As David Grimsted suggests, "This Jonathan was largely an Americanization of the Irishmen and Yorkshireman of the English stage, and clearly...a descendant of the Jonathan in *The Contrast*" (*Melodrama Unveiled: American Theater and Culture, 1800–1850* [Berkeley: University of California Press, 1987], 186).
5. Benjamin A. Baker, *A Glance at New York: A Local Drama in Two Acts* (New York: Samuel French, 1857). Pierce Egan, *Life in London, or, the Day and Night Scenes of Jerry Hawthorn, Esq.: And His Elegant Friend Corinthian Tom: Accompanied by Bob Logic, the Oxonian, in Their Rambles and Sprees through the Metropolis* (London: Printed for Sherwood, Nealy, and Jones, 1821).
6. Francis Courtney Wemyss, *Theatrical Biography of Eminent Actors and Authors* (New York: William and Taylor, n.d.), 57.
7. Charles Gayler, "Early Struggles of Prominent Actors," reprinted in *Famous Actors and Actresses on the American Stage: Documents of American Theatre History,* vol. 1, ed. William C. Young (New York: R. R. Bowker Company, 1975), 174–75. Gayler (1820–1892) also composed a series of articles on actors for the *New York Dramatic Mirror* in the 1870s.
8. The most thorough treatment of America's mob behavior during this period is David Grimsted's *American Mobbing, 1828–1861: Toward Civil War* (New York: Oxford University Press, 1998). For an exploration of the differing modes of communication at work in the events leading up to the Astor Place Riot, see Gretchen Sween, "Rituals, Riots, Rules, and Rights: The Astor Place Theater Riot of 1849 and the Evolving Limits of Free Speech," in *Texas Law Review* 81 (2002), 679–713.
9. Sometimes conflicting accounts of the riot are presented in the following: Nigel Cliff, *The Shakespeare Riots: Revenge, Drama, and Death in Nineteenth-Century America* (New York: Random House, 2007); Richard Moody, *The Astor Place Riot* (Bloomington: Indiana University Press, 1958); *Account of the Terrific and Fatal Riot at the New York Astor Place Opera House, on the Night of May 10th, 1849* (New York: H. M. Ranney, 1849); *A Rejoinder to "The Replies From England, etc. to Certain Statements Circulated in this Country Respecting Mr. Macready." Together with an Impartial History and Review of the Lamentable Occurrences at the Astor Place Opera House, on the 10th of May, 1849. By an American Citizen* (New York: Stringer and Townsend, 1849).

10. *Account of the Terrific and Fatal Riot,* 19.
11. Unidentified newsclip, 1825, quoted in Alan S. Downer, *The Eminent Tragedian: William Charles Macready* (Cambridge: Harvard University Press, 1966), 72.
12. Walt Whitman, "The Gladiator—Mr. Forrest—Acting," *Brooklyn Eagle,* December 26, 1846.
13. Henry James, quoted in Montrose J. Moses, *Fabulous Forrest: The Record of an American Actor* (Boston, MA: Little, Brown, and Company, 1929), 245–46.
14. *New York Herald,* April 28, 1849.
15. It should be noted that Washington was sometimes shown in a toga in portraits, and Forrest also appeared in a toga in roles such as Virginius, Brutus, and Coriolanus.
16. Richard Butsch provides tables that trace changes in Admission Prices for Stage Entertainments and Population and Income. "During the colonial period... the cheapest seats in the gallery cost a half-day's wages for an artisan and more than a full day's for a laborer. During the early republic, admission became more affordable, the gallery being about a third of a laborer's daily wage. The pit where an artisan might be expected to sit cost about a third of his daily wage" (*The Making of American Audiences: From Stage to Television, 1750–1990* [Cambridge: Cambridge University Press, 2000], 298–99, 301, 296).
17. George C. Odell's 15-volume *Annals of the New York Stage* (New York: Columbia University Press, 1927) details all major New York productions of the period. David Grimsted also has compiled appendices and tables that categorize the most performed plays (*Melodrama Unveiled,* 249–61).
18. Quoted in Butsch, *Making of American Audiences,* 46. David Grimsted discusses the 1820's origins of the soon-to-be common practices of demanding favorite songs, curtain calls, and encores (*Melodrama Unveiled,* 64).
19. *Spirit of the Times,* October 24, 1846.
20. For the growing class separation of opera audiences, see the following: Lawrence Levine, *Highbrow/Lowbrow: The Emergence of Cultural Hierarchy in America* (Cambridge: Harvard University Press, 1988), 101; Bruce McConachie, "New York Opera-going, 1825–1850," in *American Music* 6 (Summer 1988), 184.
21. "The Italian Opera House and the Bowery, New York," *Spirit of the Times,* February 6, 1847.
22. George Foster, *New York by Gaslight* (New York: Dewitt and Davenport, 1850), 90–91.
23. *New York Herald,* May 3, 1848.
24. *A Rejoinder to "The Replies From England,"* 68.
25. *New York Times,* October 3, 1826.
26. *New York Mirror,* October 3, 1826.

27. Wemyss, *Twenty-six Years,* 118.
28. William Charles Macready, *Macready's Reminiscences and Selections from His Diaries and Letters,* ed. Frederick Pollock (New York: Harper, 1875), 230–231.
29. Quoted in Joseph Norton Ireland, *Record of the New York Stage, From 1780 to 1860,* vol 1. (New York: T. H. Morrell, 1867), 479.
30. William Charles Macready, *The Diaries of William Charles Macready,* vol. 2, ed. William Thompson (New York: Putnam's, 1912), 230, 405.
31. *London Morning Advertiser,* October 18, 1836; *London Atlas,* October 18, 1836.
32. *London Sun,* October 18, 1836.
33. William Bayle Bernard, *The Kentuckian, or, a Trip to New York* (London, 1833). Hackett previously performed the Nimrod Wildfire character in his playwriting competition winner *The Lion of the West; or, A Trip to Washington* (1831) by James Kirke Paulding (later revised by John Augustus Stone).
34. *London Sun,* October 18, 1836.
35. *London Examiner,* February 12, 1837; March 5, 1837.
36. Edwin Forrest, quoted in William Rounseville Alger, *Life of Edwin Forrest: The American Tragedian,* (Philadelphia: J. B. Lippincott, 1877), 317.
37. Ibid.
38. William Charles Macready, quoted in Downer, *Eminent Tragedian,* 254.
39. *St. Louis Republican,* June 13, 1844.
40. *American Advocate* (Philadelphia), September 10, 1844.
41. Letter to Mrs. Letitia Puckle, October 27, 1843, quoted in Downer, *Eminent Tragedian,* 258.
42. Moody, *Astor Place Riot,* 45.
43. Macready, *Diaries,* 230–31.
44. Macready, *Reminiscences,* 512; Macready, *Diaries,* 229–30.
45. Macready, *Reminiscences,* 512.
46. Ibid., 533.
47. Macready, *Diaries,* 274.
48. *London Spectator,* February 22, 1845; March 29, 1845.
49. *London Examiner,* March 1, 1845.
50. Charlotte Cushman, quoted in Joseph Leach, *Bright Particular Star: The Life and Times of Charlotte Cushman* (New Haven, CT: Yale University Press, 1970), 150.
51. Alger, *Life of Edwin Forrest,* 391–92.
52. *A Rejoinder to "The Replies From England,"* 37.
53. Alger, *Life of Edwin Forrest,* 392–93; Downer, *Eminent Tragedian,* 276.
54. "Behavior, in a word, is an ultimately democratic criterion for gentility that had aristocratic origins…, the essence of the definition is contained in the reference cited from *The Tatler:* 'The Appellation of Gentleman is never to be affixed to a Man's Circumstances but to his behaviour in them'" (David

Castronovo, *The English Gentleman: Images and Ideals in Literature and Society* [New York: Ungar, 1987], 31).
55. Macready, *Reminiscences,* 553.
56. Sheriff Gordon, quoted in *Replies from England,* 31.
57. Letter printed in *London Times,* March 21, 1846.
58. Letter printed in *London Times,* April 4, 1846.
59. *American Magazine and Critical Review* 2 (November 1817): 63.
60. Macready, *Diaries,* 327.
61. Ibid., 334.
62. *Boston Mail,* November 22, 1848.
63. Curtain speech and Bryant's toast quoted in Moody, *Edwin Forrest,* 236, 237.
64. Edwin Forrest to Catherine Forrest, November 25, 1848, quoted in *Report of the Forrest Divorce Case, Containing the Full and Unabridged Testimony of All the Witnesses, the Affidavits and Depositions, Together with the Consuelo and Forney Letters* (New York: n.p., 1852), 121.
65. Macready, *Reminiscences,* 529.
66. *New York Herald,* May 9, 1849. For the nationalistic tensions surrounding Charles Dickens, see Sidney P. Moss, *Charles Dickens' Quarrel with America* (New York: Whitstone, 1984).
67. *Boston Mail,* November 22, 1848.
68. Moody, *Astor Place Riot,* 72.
69. *Public Ledger* (Philadelphia), November 22, 1848.
70. Reprinted in *Replies From England,* 9–10.
71. Quoted in *Rejoinder to 'The Replies',* 37. The *Herald* traditionally supported Forrest.
72. *Rejoinder to 'The Replies,'* 42.
73. Philip Hone, *The Diary of Philip Hone,* ed. Allan Nevins (New York: Dodd, Mead, 1927), 876. Phillip Hone (1780–1852) was mayor of New York 1826–1827.
74. *Morning Express,* May 9, 1849.
75. Henry James, quoted in Moses, *Fabulous Forrest,* 246.
76. Handbill, reprinted in Moody, *Astor Place Riot,* 130.
77. See Jay Monaghan, *The Great Rascal: The Life and Adventures of Ned Buntline* (Boston, MA: Little, Brown and Company, 1952).
78. Robert Montgomery Bird, *The Gladiator,* in *Early American Drama,* ed. Jeffrey H. Richards (New York: Penguin, 1997), 198.
79. Letter to James Oaks, May 11, 1849, quoted in Moody, *Edwin Forrest,* 281.
80. *Boston Daily Evening Traveller,* November 21, 1856.
81. *Rejoinder to 'The* Replies', 3.
82. Mayor's proclamation, May 11, 1849, reprinted in Moody, *Astor Place Riot,* 185.
83. *Philadelphia Public Ledger,* May 14, 1849.

84. *Home Journal,* May 12, 1849.
85. For an exploration of the Draft Riots and their impact on society, see Barnet Schecter, *The Devil's Own Work: The Civil War Draft Riots and the Fight to Reconstruct America* (New York: Walker, 2003).
86. "Mr. Forrest's Second Reception in England," *United States Magazine and Democratic Review* 16 (April 1845): 385. For more on the development of urban police, see James Richardson, *The New York Police: Colonial Times to 1901* (New York: Oxford University Press, 1970); Roger Lane, *Policing the City: Boston, 1822–1885* (Cambridge: Harvard University Press, 1967). David Grimsted argues that the actions of the elite represented "the first precedent to set bounds to the sovereignty of the theatrical audience" (Grimsted, *Melodrama Unveiled,* 68).
87. *New York Tribune,* May 9, 1849.

4 DECORUM AND DELICACY: THE FEMINIZED MANLINESS OF EDWIN BOOTH

1. William Winter, *The Life and Art of Edwin Booth* (New York: Macmillan, 1893), 1–2.
2. George William Curtis, "Editor's Easy Chair," *Harper's New Monthly Magazine* 28 (December 1863): 132–33.
3. Ibid., 133.
4. Ibid.
5. *New York Tribune,* March 30, 1855.
6. Ann Douglas, *The Feminization of American Culture* (New York: Alfred A. Knopf, 1977), 10.
7. Lawrence W. Levine, *Highbrow/Lowbrow: The Emergence of Cultural Hierarchy in America* (Cambridge: Harvard University Press, 1988), 146.
8. "Philadelphia Area Theatre Playbills," in Library Company of Philadelphia, 12: 80. This announcement appeared for the Chestnut Street Theatre on February 20, 1864. Boston audiences represented the epitome of taste and refinement.
9. Reprinted in Arthur Herman Wilson, *A History of the Philadelphia Theatre, 1835 to 1855* (Philadelphia: University of Pennsylvania Press, 1935), 26. Actor-manager W. E. Burton announced the opening of the Arch Street Theatre in Philadelphia in June 1844. Richard Butsch argues that American melodrama began to change gender roles radically: "In striking contrast to the virile male heroes favored in the 1830s, sensation melodrama often featured vigorous heroines opposite passive and conflicted male leads" (*The Making of American Audiences: From Stage to Television, 1750–1990* [Cambridge: Cambridge University Press, 2000], 77). Augustine Daly's *Under the Gaslight* (1867) provides the quintessential example of tables turning as the brave heroine rescues a helpless man tied to the railroad tracks.

10. "Theater and Things Theatrical," *Spirit of the Times*, October 26, 1861.
11. "Editor's Easy Chair," *Harper's Monthly*, March 1870, 605.
12. *Sanford's Serenader*, November 1856, in "Philadelphia Area Theatre Playbills," 24: 128. The *Serenader* was an advertisement flyer for Sanford's Opera House, which specialized in family minstrel entertainment.
13. Chestnut Street Theatre, March 24, 1864, in "Philadelphia Area Theatre Playbills," 12: 124; Chestnut Street Theatre, March 7, 1864, in "Philadelphia Area Theatre Playbills," 12: 88. The misprinted word almost certainly is *toilette*.
14. *Sanford's Serenader*, 24: 128.
15. Walnut Street Theatre, February 4, 1864, in "Philadelphia Area Theatre Playbills," 22: 6.
16. "Americans at the Theater," *Every Saturday*, May 18, 1871.
17. "Theaters and Things Theatrical," *Spirit of the Times*, October 27, 1866. For the shifting patronage of masculine entertainments, see Richard Stott, *Workers in the Metropolis: Class, Ethnicity and Youth in Ante-bellum New York City* (Ithaca, NY: Cornell University Press, 1990), 272–75; Elliot Gorn, *The Manly Art: Bare-Knuckle Prize Fighting in America* (Ithaca: Cornell University Press, 1986).
18. James E. Murdoch, *The Stage, or, Recollections of Actors and Acting From an Experience of Fifty Years; A Series of Dramatic Sketches* (Philadelphia, PA: J. M. Stoddart, 1880).
19. *Spirit of the Times*, October 25, 1845.
20. Joseph Jefferson, *The Autobiography of Joseph Jefferson* (New York: Century, 1889), 153.
21. Ibid., 152.
22. Anna Cora Mowatt, quoted in Edwin Francis Edgett, *Edward Loomis Davenport* (New York: Dunlap Society Publications, 1902), 23.
23. Henry Dickinson Stone, *Personal Recollections of the Drama, or, Theatrical Reminiscences, Embracing Sketches of Prominent Actors and Actresses, Their Chief Characteristics, Original Anecdotes of Them, and Incidents Connected Therewith*. (Albany, NY: Charles Van Benthuysen, 1873); 121.
24. O. A. Roorbach, Jr., *Actors As They Are; a Series of Sketches of the Most Eminent Performers Now on the Stage* (New York: O. A. Roorbach, Jr., 1856), 47.
25. Adam Badeau, *The Vagabond* (New York: Rudd and Carleton, 1859), 74. Badeau is most famous now for his three-volume *Military History of Ulysses S. Grant*.
26. Henry P. Goddard, "Recollections of Edward L. Davenport," in *Lippincott's Magazine* (April 1878): 466. Goddard is now known for his Civil War experiences, which are published in *The Good Fight That Didn't End*.
27. Austin Brereton, *Dramatic Notes, 1883–1886* (London: Longman, 1886), 26.
28. Henry P. Phelps, *Players of a Century* (Albany, NY: Joseph McDonough,1880), 338; Alfred Ayres, *Acting and Actors* (New York: D. Appleton, 1894), 87.

29. *New York Tribune,* August 3, 1886.
30. Sometimes identified as Edwin Forrest Booth, his actual middle name was Thomas. For additional information on Booth's early life and career, see the following: L. Terry Oggel, *Edwin Booth: A Bio-Bibliography* (Westport, CT: Greenwood Press, 1992); Eleanor Ruggles, *Prince of Players: Edwin Booth* (New York: W. W. Norton, 1953); Richard Lockridge, *Darling of Misfortune: Edwin Booth, 1833–1893* (New York: Century, 1932); Katherine Goodale[Kitty Molony], *Behind the Scenes with Edwin Booth* (Boston, MA: Houghton Mifflin, 1931); Winter, *Life and Art of Edwin Booth.*
31. Letter to friend, quoted in Oggel, *Edwin Booth,* 16.
32. *New York Tribune,* May 15, 1857.
33. The technical innovations of Booth's theatre are described in O. B. Bunce, "Behind, Below, and Above the Scenes," in *Appleton's Journal* 3 (May 28, 1870): 589–94.
34. Charles Shattuck discusses the popularity and influence of the Booth-Barrett tours (*Shakespeare on the American Stage,* vol. 2 [Washington, D.C: Folger Books, 1987], 31–53). Booth's detailed correspondence with Winter about the promptbooks is reprinted in *Between Actor and Critic: Selected Letters of Edwin Booth and William Winter,* ed. Daniel J. Watermeier (Princeton, NJ: Princeton University Press, 1971), 84–131.
35. Nat Goodwin, quoted in Goodale, *Behind the Scenes,* 75. For a thorough examination of Fox's career, see Laurence Senelick, *The Age and Stage of George L. Fox, 1825–1877* (Hanover, NH: Tufts University by University Press of New England, 1988).
36. *New York Daily Tribune,* November 21, 1876.
37. Karen Halttunen, *Confidence Men and Painted Women: A Study of Middle-Class Culture in America, 1830–1870* (New Haven, CT: Yale University Press, 1982), 93.
38. William Winter, *Edwin Booth in Twelve Dramatic Characters* (Boston, MA: James R. Osgood, 1872), 48.
39. E. C. Stedman, "Edwin Booth," *Atlantic Monthly* 17 (May 1866): 593, 587.
40. *Boston Traveller,* May 2, 1857.
41. Adam Badeau, *New York Sunday Times,* June 14, 1858. Badeau's prescient essay suggested that Booth would single-handedly elevate the serious drama to a higher plane.
42. Winter, *Life and Art of Edwin Booth,* 2.
43. See Watermeier, *Between Actor and Critic.*
44. Winter, *Life and Art of Edwin Booth,* 129. For more on the social impact of bereavement see Mary Louise Kete, *Sentimental Collaborations: Mourning and Middle-Class Identity in Nineteenth-Century America* (Durham, NC: Duke University Press, 1999).
45. *New York Herald,* January 6, 1870.

46. Ferdinand C. Ewer, *San Francisco Daily Placer Times and Transcript,* April 29, 1853.
47. *Boston Transcript,* April 28, 1857.
48. Stedman, "Edwin Booth," 588.
49. Nym Crinkle, *New York World,* June 9, 1893.
50. Nym Crinkle, *New York World,* January 9, 1870; *New York World,* January 16, 1870.
51. Arthur Matthison, *Booth's Theatre: Hamlet,* quoted in Charles H. Shattuck, *The Hamlet of Edwin Booth* (Urbana: University of Illinois Press, 1969), 72.
52. Edwin Booth, quoted in Laurence Hutton, "A Century of Hamlet," in *Harper's New Monthly Magazine* (November 1889), 870.
53. Edwin Booth, quoted in Goodale, *Behind the Scenes,* 59–60.
54. William Winter, quoted in Tice Miller, *Bohemians and Critics: American Theatre Criticism in the Nineteenth Century* (Metuchen, NJ: Scarecrow Press, 1981), 85.
55. "Editor's Easy Chair," *Harper's New Monthly Magazine,* April 1865.
56. Chestnut St. Theatre, August 31, 1863, in "Philadelphia Area Theatre Playbills," 5: 54.
57. *New York World,* January 9, 1870.
58. *New York Times,* January 7, 1870. See Halttunen's discussion of "genteel performance" in the social sphere in *Confidence Men and Painted Women.* Erving Goffman addresses similar issues in *The Presentation of Self in Everyday Life* (Garden City, NY: Doubleday Anchor Books, 1959).
59. Stedman, "Edwin Booth," 593, 589.
60. Charles Clarke, quoted in Shattuck, *Shakespeare on the American Stage,* 145. Albert Furtwangler demonstrates that Clarke was not alone in his close study of Booth: "[S]ome individuals also responded deeply and long afterward. Some returned again and again until they knew Booth so well that they could repeat his words and gestures" (*Assassin on Stage: Brutus, Hamlet, and the Death of Lincoln* [Urbana: University of Illinois Press, 1991], 134).
61. Goodale, *Behind the Scenes,* 60.
62. Ibid., 61. Goodale was recalling a backstage conversation with Booth.
63. "Edwin Booth as Hamlet," *New York Daily Tribune,* November 21, 1876.
64. Halttunen, *Confidence Men and Painted Women,* 124.
65. Harriet Beecher Stowe, *Uncle Tom's Cabin* (1852), ed. Elizabeth Ammons (New York: W. W. Norton, 1994), 72–73.
66. *New York Evening Post,* March 16, 1870.
67. *New York Times,* January 7, 1870.
68. John Rankin Towse, *Sixty Years of the Theatre* (New York: Funk and Wagnall, 1916), 182.
69. *New York Daily Tribune,* November 21, 1876.
70. *Hamlet,* Act I, scene v.
71. Stedman, "Edwin Booth," 589.

72. *Harper's Weekly,* January 13, 1866.
73. Biographer Richard Lockridge even suggested that Booth augmented the appearance of his suffering to encourage his identification with the character: "When he [Booth] found out fully what the audience expected, he was showman enough to supply by art such slight cementing as nature required to make its façade perfect" (*Darling of Misfortune,* 7). Lockridge suggests that audiences were drawn to Booth more because of his high-profile misfortunes than his prodigious talents.
74. Winter, *Twelve Dramatic Characters,* 51.
75. Towse, *Sixty Years,* 190. Towse references the Brutus in Payne's tragedy, rather than in Shakespeare's *Julius Caesar.*
76. Edwin Booth, quoted in Otis Skinner, *Footlights and Spotlights: Recollections of My Life on the Stage* (Indianapolis, IN: Bobbs, 1924), 172.
77. Personal letter, quoted in Eleanor Ruggles, *Prince of Players,* 144.
78. Towse, *Sixty Years,* 184.
79. Winter, *Life and Art of Edwin Booth,* 198, 200.
80. *New York Daily Tribune,* April 9, 1880. Karen Halttunen details the nation's enthrallment with the villain in the middle of the nineteenth century: "In the emerging social system, authority could be seized by any charismatic figure who emerged from the masses as a man of magnetic personal power.... [T]hese men held the fascinated attention of the American people because, in the absence of a clearly defined, hierarchical authority structure, they used the power of charisma to bend others to their will" (*Confidence Men,* 24).
81. Towse, *Sixty Years of the Theatre,* 190–91.
82. Skinner, *Footlights and Spotlights,* 171. Skinner acted with Booth in 1880.
83. *New York Tribune,* March 20, 1855. "Two stars keep not their motion in one sphere" is from Shakespeare's *Henry IV,* Part 1, Act V, scene iv.
84. Lawrence Levine discusses the bifurcation of Shakespeare—indicating the growing separation between "'serious' and 'popular' culture," and the two contrasting visions of Shakespeare, "the humble, everyday poet who sprang from the people...[versus] the towering genius" (*Highbrow/Lowbrow,* 68–69). See also Furtwangler, *Assassin on Stage,* 51.
85. Towse, *Sixty Years,* 180.
86. Stedman, "Edwin Booth," 592. Although not directly naming Forrest, the description certainly points to him.
87. Edwin Booth, quoted in Oggle, *Edwin Booth,* 17.
88. Edwin Booth to William Winter, printed in Watermeier, *Between Actor and Critic,* 203–04.
89. Edwin Booth, quoted in Oggel, *Edwin Booth,* 7.
90. John William Ward, *Andrew Jackson: Symbol for an Age* (New York: Oxford University Press, 1955), 193.
91. Daniel Kilham Dodge, "Lincoln and Hamlet," *The Mid-West Quarterly* 1 (April 1914): 221.

92. Edwin Forrest, quoted in Montrose J. Moses, *The Fabulous Forrest: The Record of an American Actor* (Boston, MA: Little, Brown, and Co., 1929), 327.
93. Laurence Hutton, "A Century of Hamlet," 873.
94. *Daily Missouri Democrat,* February 13, 1866.
95. Curtis, "Editor's Easy Chair," 132.
96. *New York Daily Tribune,* April 9, 1880.
97. Laura Keene, quoted in John Creahan, *The Life of Laura Keene* (Philadelphia, PA: Rodgers, 1897), 90.
98. John F. Kasson, *Rudeness and Civility: Manners in Nineteenth-Century Urban America* (New York: Hill and Wang, 1990), 7.
99. "Mr. Forrest in Charleston," *Spirit of the Times,* January 23, 1841.

5 IMPOSSIBLY GENIAL: THE MASCULINE TRANSFORMATIONS OF JOHN MCCULLOUGH

1. William Winter, *In Memory of John McCullough* (New York: De Vinne, 1889), 30.
2. *Philadelphia Sunday Dispatch,* November 29, 1863.
3. *St. Louis Republican,* October 2, 1873.
4. *Newsletter and California Advertiser* (San Francisco), April 5, 1873.
5. Henry P. Phelps, *Players of a Century: A History of the Albany Stage* (Albany, NY: Joseph McDonough, 1880), 343.
6. *New York Sun,* April 3, 1877; *New York Daily Tribune,* April 3, 1877.
7. John Towse, *Sixty Years of the Theatre* (New York: Funk and Wagnall, 1916), 222.
8. *Chicago Times,* January 17, 1866.
9. *New York Herald,* May 5, 1874.
10. *New York Tribune,* May 19, 1874.
11. *New York Evening Post,* May 16, 1874.
12. *American and Commercial Advertiser* (Baltimore), October 27, 1874.
13. *Memphis Daily Avalanche,* March 5, 1880.
14. *North American* (Philadelphia), December 26, 1882.
15. *Chicago Daily Inter-Ocean,* January 19, 1875.
16. *San Francisco Chronicle,* November 9, 1885.
17. S. D. Woods, *Lights and Shadows of Life on the Pacific Coast* (New York: Funk and Wagnalls, 1910), 199.
18. Bruce E. Woodruff discusses McCullough's relationship with Helen Tracy in his dissertation "'Genial' John McCullough: Actor and Manager" (Ph.D. diss., University of Nebraska, 1984), 228–31, 283–85.
19. *San Francisco Bulletin,* July 27, 1895.
20. John Wilkes Booth, quoted in Asia Booth Clarke, *John Wilkes Booth: A Sister's Memoir,* ed. by Terry Alford (Jackson: University Press of Mississippi,

1999), 79. Booth's sister, Asia Booth Clarke, wrote her memoir in 1874, but it was not published until 1938.
21. *San Francisco Chronicle,* November 9, 1885.
22. Susie C. Clark, *John McCullough as Man, Actor and Spirit* (Boston, MA: Murray and Emery, 1905), 65; *Overland Monthly* (San Francisco), December 1885.
23. *Boston Globe,* December 2, 1875.
24. *San Francisco Alta,* March 28, 1876.
25. *Chicago Times,* October 10, 1880.
26. *New York Tribune,* May 19, 1874.
27. Winter, *In Memory of John McCullough,* 29.
28. William Winter, *Other Days* (New York: Moffat and Yard, 1908), 204.
29. *New York Dramatic Mirror,* October 26, 1910. Benjamin McArthur suggests that this trend toward professionalism indicated both a desire for artistic advancement and a social legitimization of the theatrical career: *Actors and American Culture, 1880–1920* (Iowa City: University of Iowa Press, 2000), 86.
30. McCullough quoted in Percy MacKaye, *Epoch: The Life of Steel MacKaye,* vol. 1 (New York: Boni and Liveright, 1927), 270. For more on the Delsarte system and MacKaye's American permutation, see Nancy Lee Chalfa Ruyter, *The Cultivation of Body and Mind in Nineteenth-Century American Delsartism* (Westport, CT: Greenwood Press, 1999); Claude L. Shaver, "Steel MacKaye and the Delsartian Tradition," in *History of Speech Education in America,* ed. Karl R. Wallace (New York: Appleton-Century-Crofts, 1954), 202–18. Forrest's biographer, William Rounseville Alger, most ardently championed the spiritual component of Delsartism in America.
31. Steele MacKaye, "A Plea for a Free School of Dramatic Art" (1871), quoted in Ruyter, *Cultivation of Body and Mind,* 21.
32. *Boston Advertiser,* March 22, 1871.
33. Steele MacKaye, "Gesture as a Language," quoted in Ruyter, *Cultivation of Body and Mind,* 82.
34. Wheeler, quoted in MacKaye, *Epoch,* 270–71.
35. Joseph I. C. Clarke, *My Life and Memories* (New York: Dodd and Mead, 1925), 266, 267.
36. *Boston Globe,* January 24, 1879.
37. William Winter, *The Wallet of Time* (New York: Benjamin Blom, 1913), 266, 267.
38. *Boston Herald,* January 16, 1883.
39. John McCullough, "Success on Stage," in *North American Review* (December 1882), 582.
40. *Philadelphia Inquirer,* December 30, 1879.
41. *New York Sun,* April 17, 1877.
42. *Boston Advertiser,* February 6, 1877.

43. *San Francisco Alta,* May 28, 1876.
44. McCullough, quoted in *Boston Herald,* January 15, 1882.
45. *Chicago Tribune,* October 17, 1875.
46. *Chicago Daily Inter-Ocean,* October 16, 1875.
47. Winter, *Wallet of Time,* 266–67, 268.
48. William Winter, "John McCullough," in *Actors and Actresses of Great Britain and the United States From the Days of David Garrick to the Present Time,* vol. 3, ed. Brander Matthews and Laurence Hutton (New York: Cassell and Company, 1886), 282.
49. *Boston Globe,* quoted in Clark, *John McCullough,* 123.
50. *New York World,* May 31, 1874.
51. *Ibid.* Wheeler further accentuates the inspiring impact of McCullough's youth: "It is the privilege of youth not only to climb but to disregard all who have gone before. If there is anything that distinguishes the spring time of life from all the other seasons it is the noble consciousness that the world is very bright and hopeful and revolves about one individual. Something of this early impulse, this fledgling fervor, shines in John's acting." As McCullough established a national reputation following the death of Forrest, many reviewers emphasized his youthful potential. At the time of his New York debut in 1874, McCullough was 41. While not old, McCullough, who entered the profession later than most, had still been acting professionally for 17 years and had been managing the most prominent theatre on the West Coast for the past 8 years. Because his performance style and repertory resembled that of Forrest, he may have appeared younger by comparison.
52. *Ibid.*
53. *New York Sun,* November 17, 1880.
54. *Virginia City Daily Trespass* [NV], June 4, 1867.
55. *Daily Morning Call,* March 25, 1868.
56. *Chicago Tribune,* September 11, 1878.
57. *New York Tribune,* May 19, 1874.
58. *Chicago Daily Tribune,* January 9, 1877.
59. *New York World,* April 15, 1877.
60. *New York Herald,* November 17, 1880.
61. *New York Sun,* April 3, 1877.
62. *New York Times,* December 4, 1880.
63. *Boston Advertiser,* January 14, 1879.
64. *New York World,* May 21, 1874.
65. Winter, "John McCullough," 281.
66. *St. Louis Republican,* March 19, 1874.
67. *Boston Globe,* February 14, 1876.
68. *Daily Alta California* (San Francisco), December 29, 1874.
69. *St. Louis Dispatch,* March 18, 1874.
70. *New York World,* May 19, 1874; *New York World,* May 31, 1874.

71. *San Francisco Chronicle,* September 15, 1876.
72. *San Francisco Chronicle,* September 17, 1876.
73. *Overland Monthly* (San Francisco), December 1885.
74. *Boston Herald,* November 25, 1885.
75. *New York Dramatic Mirror,* November 20, 1881.
76. *Daily Evening Bulletin,* August 2, 1866.
77. Henry Edwards, quoted in *In Memory of John McCullough,* 41, 42.
78. John McCullough, quoted in *In Memory of John McCullough,* 25.
79. *Detroit Free Press,* September 21, 1879.
80. Lewis C. Strang, *Players and Plays of the Last Quarter Century,* vol. 1 (Boston, MA: L. C. Page, 1903), 125. Lewis Clinton Strang (1869–1935) was from New England and wrote for the Boston *Journal* and later for the Washington *Times.* If ever he saw McCullough on stage, it would have been as a youth.
81. *Philadelphia Evening Bulletin,* December 31, 1878.
82. *North American,* December 31, 1878.
83. *Philadelphia Record,* December 31, 1878.
84. *Chicago Daily Tribune,* January 24, 1875.
85. *St. Louis Evening Post,* November 2, 1878.
86. *London Sunday Times,* May 1, 1881.
87. *New York Clipper,* March 24, 1883.
88. *Minneapolis Tribune,* September 15, 1883.
89. *Cincinnati Enquirer,* May 1, 1883.
90. *Kalamazoo Daily Gazette,* September 12, 1884.
91. *Racine Advocate,* September 11, 1884.
92. *Chicago Daily Evening News,* September 20, 1884.
93. *New York Clipper,* November 15, 1884.
94. David Belasco, "My Life's Story," in *Hearst's Magazine* (June 1914), 769.
95. *Philadelphia Evening Bulletin,* November 13, 1885.
96. W. J. Florence, quoted in Clark, *John McCullough,* 193.
97. Doctors first recognized general paresis as a distinct disease (with consistent physical and mental symptoms) in the 1820s. Syphilographer Alfred Fournier definitely established general paresis as a result of syphilis. This degenerative and ultimately fatal disease impacts memory, mood, personality, judgment, mental function, muscle strength, and speech. Typically beginning 15 to 20 years after syphilis infection, general paresis eventually leads to complete incapacitation, with death resulting 3 to 5 years after the onset of symptoms. Nineteenth-century victims of the disease, almost exclusively male, typically died in lunatic asylums. Julius Wagner-Jauregg discovered the malarial cure for general paresis in 1921, for which he received the Nobel Prize in 1927. See Edward M. Brown, "Why Wagner-Jauregg Won the Nobel Prize for Discovering Malaria Therapy for General Paresis of the Insane," in *History of Psychiatry* 11 (December 2000): 371–82.

224   Notes

98. *San Francisco Examiner,* October 2, 1884.
99. *San Francisco Morning Call,* May 3, 1885.
100. William Winter, *Shakespeare on the Stage,* series 2 (New York: Moffat, Yard, 1915), 458–59.
101. *New York Tribune,* April 3, 1877.
102. *San Francisco News Letter and California Advertiser,* April 18, 1868.

6   CONCLUSION: AFFIRMING WHITE MASCULINITY BY DERIDING THE OTHER

1. Tim Allen, quoted in *TV Guide,* September 12–18, 2011, 29.
2. Matthew Rebhorn explores the complexity of Forrest's performance in "Edwin Forrest's Redding Up: Elocution, Theater, and the Performance of Frontier," *Comparative Drama* 40 (Winter 2007): 455–81.
3. B. Donald Grose discusses the complex relationship between *Metamora* and the American viewpoint toward Native Americans in "Edwin Forrest, *Metamora,* and the Indian Removal Act of 1830," *Theatre Journal* 37 (May 1985): 181–91. Jackson's treatment of the Indians is analyzed in the following: Anthony F. C. Wallace, *The Long, Bitter Trail: Andrew Jackson and the Indians* (New York: Hill and Wang, 1993); and Michael Paul Rogin, *Fathers and Children: Andrew Jackson and the Subjugation of the American Indian* (New York: Knopf, 1975).
4. George Caitlin, *Letters and Notes on the Manners, Customs, and Condition of the North American Indians,* vol. 2 (Philadelphia, PA: Willis P. Hazard, 1857), 792.
5. Chestnut St. Theatre, February 7, 1842, in "Philadelphia Area Theatre Playbills," Library Company of Philadelphia, 29: 38.
6. John Brougham, *Metamora; or, The Last of the Pollywogs,* in *Staging the Nation: Plays from the American Theater, 1787–1909,* ed. Don B. Wilmeth (Boston, MA: Bedford Books, 1998), 107. The Irish-born Brougham came to America in 1842. He is now known principally for his comic burlesques, for which Laurence Hutton dubbed him the American Aristophanes (Hutton, *Curiosities of the American Stage* [New York: Harper and Row, 1891], 164).
7. *Daily National Intelligencer,* April 30, 1864.
8. William Rounseville Alger, *Life of Edwin Forrest, The American Tragedian* (Philadelphia: J. B. Lippincott, 1877), 127.
9. The *New York Clipper* (June 2, 1877) reports that McCullough sold the rights to *Metamora* shortly after his only New York performance of the play.
10. *Daily Alta California* (San Francisco), April 9, 1876.
11. American blackface performance and the minstrel show have received a great deal of scholarly attention over the last 20 years. Key works include the following: W. T. Lhamon, Jr., *Raising Cain: Blackface Performance from*

Jim Crow to Hip Hop (Cambridge, MA: Harvard University Press, 2000); William J. Mahar, *Behind the Burnt Cork Mask: Early Blackface Minstrelsy and Antebellum American Popular Culture* (Champaign: University of Illinois Press, 1998); Dale Cockrell, *Demons of Disorder: Early Blackface Minstrels and Their World* (New York: Cambridge University Press, 1997); Eric Lott, *Love and Theft: Blackface Minstrelsy and the American Working Class* (New York: Oxford University Press, 1995). Marvin McAllister explores African Americans who turn the tables and perform white identities: *Whiting Up: Whiteface Minstrels and Stage Europeans in African American Performance* (Chapel Hill: University of North Carolina Press, 2011).

12. Joseph Norton Ireland, *Records of the New York Stage*, vol. 2 (New York: T. H. Morrell, 1867), 56.
13. Lhamon, *Raising Cain*, 258.
14. Frederick Douglass, *North Star,* October 27, 1848. Frederick Douglass (1818–1895), the most visible and eloquent African American in the antebellum, effectively employed oratory as a persuasive abolitionist weapon. However, the American stage had no room for positive masculine images of free blacks. Ira Aldridge (1807–1867) made his theatrical debut a few years before Forrest but left America forever at the age of 17, which makes his impact difficult to gauge. The combination of prejudice and blackface performance made Aldridge an impossible masculine model on the American stage, although he received an enthusiastic reception in Europe. For more on Aldridge, see Bernth Lindfor's two books, *Ira Aldridge: The Early Years, 1807 to 1833* (Rochester, NY: University of Rochester Press, 2011) and *Ira Aldridge: The African Roscius* (Rochester, NY: University of Rochester Press, 2007) as well as Herbert Marshall and Mildred Stock, *Ira Aldridge: The Negro Tragedian* (Carbondale: Southern Illinois University Press, 1968).
15. S. S. Sanford, "Our Day: Devoted to Choice Literature, Business, The News and Commerce," October 22, 1860, in "Philadelphia Area Theatre Playbills," 14: 3.
16. Lott, *Love and Theft,* 6, 8.
17. Sanford, "Our Day," in "Philadelphia Area Theatre Playbills," 14: 4.
18. For the cultural and political impact of Stowe's novel, see Barbara Hochman, *Uncle Tom's Cabin and the Reading Revolution: Race, Literacy, Childhood, and Fiction, 1851–1911* (Amherst: University of Massachusetts Press, 2011); David S. Reynolds, *Mightier Than the Sword: Uncle Tom's Cabin and the Battle for America* (New York: W. W. Norton, 2011); and Thomas F. Gossett, *Uncle Tom's Cabin and American Culture* (Dallas, TX: Southern Methodist University Press, 1985).
19. Gossett, *Uncle Tom's Cabin,* 260. For further examination of the theatricalization of Stowe's novel, see John Frick's forthcoming book from Palgrave Macmillan, *Staging Tom: Uncle Tom's Cabin on the American Stage and Screen.*

20. Monroe Lippman, "Uncle Tom and His Poor Relations: American Slavery Plays," in *Southern Speech Journal* 28 (1963): 194. Stowe's own dramatic adaptation, *The Christian Slave* (1855), omitted the more unseemly aspects of slavery, which included the slave auction, and completely eliminated the runaway slave, George Harris.
21. *New York Herald,* September 3, 1852.
22. Several characters (Ophelia, Topsy, Phineas Fletcher) possess less emotional depth and become overtly comic, and Aiken creates other characters (Gumption Cute, Deacon Perry) and scenes solely to spark laughter. As the stage production became an attraction that was separate from the novel, spectacle increased. Bloodhounds chasing Eliza across the ice became obligatory, although no dogs appear in Aiken's script. Acting in *Uncle Tom's Cabin* became something of a theatrical necessity in the latter half of the nineteenth century due to the sheer volume of productions; however, once actors became successful, they refused to act in the show, which suggested a marginalization of black characters on the stage as much as in life.
23. George L. Aiken, *Uncle Tom's Cabin; or, Life Among the Lowly,* in *Early American Drama,* ed. Jeffrey H. Richards (New York: Penguin Books, 1997), 396.
24. Elizabeth Ammons makes a strong case for the feminization of Uncle Tom as "pious, domestic, self-sacrificing, emotionally uninhibited in response to people and ethical questions,... [insinuating] Tom into the nineteenth-century idolatry of feminine virtue" ("Heroines in *Uncle Tom's Cabin,*" in *Critical Essay on Harriet Beecher Stowe,* ed. Elizabeth Ammons [Boston, MA: G. K. Hall, 1980], 172).
25. Aiken, *Uncle Tom's Cabin,* 442.
26. Chestnut St. Theatre, March 28, 1864, in "Philadelphia Area Theatre Playbills," 12: 98.
27. Arch Street Theatre, March 14, 1864, in "Philadelphia Area Theatre Playbills," 3: 71. Dale T. Knobel examines the evolving Irish stereotype in *Paddy and the Republic: Ethnicity and Nationality in Antebellum American* (Middletown, CT: Wesleyan University Press, 1986).
28. The pejorative "Irish savage" is used in John Brougham, *The Irish Emigrant; or, Temptation* (Brooklin, ME: Feedback Theatrebooks and Prospero Press, 2001), 22.
29. William Winter, *Brief Chronicles* (New York: Dunlap Society, 1889), 29–30.
30. Additional comic actors who are famous for a range of similar roles include Henry Placide, John Gilbert, George Handel "Yankee" Hill, William Warren, and John Brougham.
31. Hackett intellectually justified his moralistic portrayal of Falstaff: "Shakespeare has invested that philosophic compound of vice and sensuality, with no amiable or tolerable quality to gloss or cover his moral deformity" ("Mr. Hackett's Analysis of Falstaff," *Spirit of the Times,* April 4, 1840).

32. For Hackett's reception in England, see Brander Matthews, *Scribner's Magazine* (July 1879), reprintted in *Actors and Actresses of Great Britain and the United States,* vol. 3, ed. Brander Matthews and Laurence Hutton (New York: Cassell and Company, 1886), 165–66.
33. Ireland, "James H. Hackett," in *Actors and Actresses of Great Britain,* 164.
34. James Henry Hackett, *Notes, Criticisms, and Correspondence Upon Shakespeare's Plays and Actors* (New York: Carleton, 1863; reprint New York: Benjamin Blom, 1968), 139.
35. *New York Mirror,* October 13, 1832. The review refers to Hackett's adaptation of George Colman's *Solomon Gundy,* entitled *Jonathan in England*—first performed in 1828. Some reviews refer to the leading character as Solomon (instead of Jonathan) Swap.
36. Francis Courtney Wemyss, *Theatrical Biography of Eminent Actors and Authors* (New York: William Taylor, n.d.), 40, 38. Wemyss' comments on Burton were written in the 1840s.
37. William L. Keese, *William E. Burton: A Sketch of His Career Other Than That of Actor* (New York: Dunlap Society, 1891), 28–36. Keese also wrote a biography that focused on Burton's artistic accomplishments: *William E. Burton, Actor, Author, and Manager: A Sketch of His Career* (New York: G. P. Putnam's Sons, 1881). For a more contemporary treatment of Burton, see David L. Rinear, *Stage, Page, Scandals, and Vandals: William E. Burton and Nineteenth-Century American Theatre* (Carbondale: Southern Illinois University Press, 2004).
38. Winter, *In Memory of John McCullough,* 48.
39. Ibid.
40. Ibid., 54.
41. Ibid., 53.
42. Ibid., 56, 55, 58.
43. *New York Evening Post,* April 24, 1887.
44. *Baltimore American and Commercial Advertiser,* November 13, 1877.
45. *Nashville Daily American,* November 2, 1877.
46. *New York Dramatic Mirror,* July 22, 1914.
47. Jon Butler, *Awash in a Sea of Faith: Christianizing the American People* (Cambridge, MA: Harvard University Press, 1990), 2–3.
48. Andrew Jackson Davis, *The Principles of Nature, Her Divine Revelation, and a Voice to Mankind* (Boston, MA: Colby and Rich, 1847).
49. Susie C. Clark, *John McCullough as Man, Actor and Spirit* (Boston, MA: Murray and Emery, 1905), 355.
50. Ibid., 180, 178–79, 66–68.
51. Ibid., 367.
52. *New York Sun,* June 24, 1912.
53. Frederick A. Wiggin, *The Living Jesus: The Words of Jesus of Nazareth Uttered through the Medium Frederick A. Wiggin From February 11 to June 1, 1921* (New York: George Sully and Company, 1921). Wiggin discusses his

association with McCullough and the testimony of the tragedian's actor friends in the book's foreword (xiv-xviii). The method of communication between Wiggin, McCullough, and the Great Teacher is discussed in the introduction that is composed by the two women who transcribed the messages (xxii-xl).

54. Clark, *John McCullough*, 288.
55. Michael Kimmel, *Manhood in America: A Cultural History*, 2nd ed. (New York: Oxford University Press, 2006), x, viii.
56. Allen, quoted in *TV Guide*, September 12–18, 2011, 29.
57. Hornsby, quoted in *Entertainment Weekly*, September 9, 2011, 94.
58. *Entertainment Weekly*, September 9, 2011, 75–76.
59. *TV Guide*, September 12–18, 2011, 30.

Works Cited

Account of the Terrific and Fatal Riot at the New-York Astor Place Opera House, on the Night of May 10th, 1849. New York: H. M. Ranney, 1849.
Adams, John Quincy. *Lectures on Rhetoric and Oratory.* 2 vols. Cambridge, MA: Hilliard and Metcalf, 1810; Reprint, New York: Russell and Russell, 1962.
———. *Memoirs of John Quincy Adams, Comprising Portions of his Diary from 1795 to 1848.* Edited by Charles Francis Adams. 12 vols. Philadelphia: 1876.
Address of the Republican General Committee of Young Men of the City and County of New York. New York: A. Ming, Jr., 1828.
Aiken, George L. *Uncle Tom's Cabin; or, Life Among the Lowly.* In *Early American Drama,* ed. Jeffrey H. Richards, 305–67. New York: Penguin Books, 1993.
Alger, William Rounseville. *Life of Edwin Forrest: The American Tragedian.* Philadelphia, PA: J. B. Lippincott, 1877.
"American Actors in England." In *The United States Magazine and Democratic Review* 19 (September 1846): 186–192.
Ammons, Elizabeth. "Heroines in *Uncle Tom's Cabin.*" In *Critical Essays on Harriet Beecher Stowe,* ed. Elizabeth Ammons, 152–65. Boston, MA: G. K. Hall, 1980.
Anderson, Benedict. *Imagined Communities: Reflections on the Origins and Spread of Nationalism.* London: Verso, 1983.
The Art of Good Behavior; and Letter Writer on Love, Courtship, and Marriage: A Complete Guide for Ladies and Gentlemen, Particularly Those Who Have Not Enjoyed the Advantages of Fashionable Life. New York: C. P. Huestis, 1846.
Ayres, Alfred. *Acting and Actors.* New York: D. Appleton, 1894.
Badeau, Adam. *The Vagabond.* New York: Rudd and Carleton, 1859.
Baker, Benjamin A. *A Glance at New York: A Local Drama in Two Acts.* New York: Samuel French, 1857.
Barnum, P. T. *Struggles and Triumphs: Or, Forty Years' Recollections.* Hartford: J. B. Burr, 1869. Reprint, New York: Arno, 1970.
Barrett, Lawrence. "Edwin Forrest." In *Actors and Actresses of Great Britain and the United States,* vol. 4, edited by Brander Matthews and Laurence Hutton, 33–68. New York: O. M. Dunham, 1886.
Barthes, Roland. *A Barthes Reader.* Edited by Susan Sontag. New York: Hill and Wang, 1996.

Works Cited

Bartlett, Irving H. *John C. Calhoun: A Biography*. New York: W. W. Norton, 1994.
Beecher, Henry Ward. *Twelve Lectures to Young Men on Various Important Subjects*. New York: George H. Doran, 1879.
———. *Yale Lectures on Preaching*. New York: J. B. Ford, 1872–1874.
Belasco, David. "My Life's Story." In *Hearst's Magazine* (June 1914): 767–79.
Belton, Don. *Speak My Name: Black Men on Masculinity and the American Dream*. Boston, MA: Beacon Press, 1997.
Bernard, William Bayle. *The Kentuckian, or, a Trip to New York*. London, 1833.
Bird, Robert Montgomery. *The Gladiator*. In *Early American Drama*, edited by Jeffrey H. Richards, 166–242. New York: Penguin, 1997.
Booth, Michael R. "The Drunkard's Progress: Nineteenth-Century Temperance Drama." In *Dalhousie Review* 44 (1964): 205–12.
Boswell, James. *The Life of Samuel Johnson*. Edited by William Wallace. Edinburgh: William P. Nimmo, 1873.
Bowman, Shearer Davis. "Comparing Henry Clay and Abraham Lincoln." In *Register of the Kentucky Historical Society* 106 (2008): 495–512.
Brands, H. W. *Andrew Jackson: His Life and Times*. New York: Anchor, 2006.
Brereton, Austin. *Dramatic Notes, 1883–1886*. London: Longman, 1886.
Brigance, William Norwood, ed. *A History and Criticism of American Public Address*, 2 vols. New York: McGraw-Hill, 1943.
Brooke, Henry. *Gustavus Vasa, the Deliverer of His Country*. London: R. Dodsley, 1739.
Brooks, Daphne A. *Bodies in Dissent: Spectacular Performances of Race and Freedom, 1850–1910*. Durham, NC: Duke University Press, 2006.
Brougham, John. *The Irish Emigrant; or, Temptation*. Brooklin, ME: Feedback Theatrebooks and Prospero Press, 2001.
———. *Metamora; or, the Last of the Pollywogs*. In *Staging the Nation: Plays from the American Theater, 1787–1909,* ed. Don B. Wilmeth, 101–23. Boston, MA: Bedford Books, 1998.
Brown, Edward M. "Why Wagner-Jauregg Won the Nobel Prize for Discovering Malaria Therapy for General Paresis of the Insane." In *History of Psychiatry* 11 (December 2000): 371–82.
Brown, Jared. *The Theatre in America during the Revolution*. Cambridge: Cambridge University Press, 1995.
Brown, T. Allston. *A History of the New York Stage: From the First Performance in 1732 to 1901*. 3 vols. New York: Benjamin Blom, 1903.
Brown, William Hill. *The Power of Sympathy*. Edited by William S. Kable. Columbus: Ohio State Univeristy Press, 1969.
Bunce, O. B. "Behind, Below, and Above the Scenes." In *Appleton's Journal* 3 (May 28, 1870): 589–94.
Butler, Jon. *Awash in a Sea of Faith: Christianizing the American People*. Cambridge, MA: Harvard University Press, 1990.

Butler, Judith. *Bodies that Matter*. New York: Routledge, 1993.
Butsch, Richard. *The Making of American Audiences: From Stage to Television, 1750–1990*. Cambridge: Cambridge University Press, 2000.
Caitlin, George. *Letters and Notes on the Manners, Customs, and Condition of the North American Indians*. 2 vols. Philadelphia, PA: Willis P. Hazard, 1857.
Carbado, Devon. *Black Men on Race, Gender, and Sexuality: A Critical Reader*. New York: New York University Press, 1999.
Carboy, John. "Theatrical Reminiscences: Edwin Forrest." In *Harvard Theatre Collection*, n.d.
Carroll, Hamilton and Donald E. Pease, eds. *Affirmative Reaction: New Formations of White Masculinity*. Durham, NC: Duke University Press, 2011.
Carso, Kerry Dean. "The Theatrical Spectacle of Medieval Revival: Edwin Forrest's Fonthill Castle." In *Winterthur Portfolio* 39 (Spring 2004): 21–42.
Castronovo, David. *The English Gentleman: Images and Ideals in Literature and Society*. New York: Ungar, 1987.
Clark, Susie C. *John McCullough as Man, Actor and Spirit*. Boston, MA: Murray and Emery, 1905.
Clarke, Asia Booth. *John Wilkes Booth: A Sister's Memoir*. Edited by Terry Alford. Jackson: University Press of Mississippi, 1999.
Clarke, Joseph I. C. *My Life and Memories*. New York: Dodd and Mead, 1925.
Clay, Henry. *Works of Henry Clay*. Edited by Calvin Colton. 10 vols. New York: Putnam, 1904.
Cliff, Nigel. *The Shakespeare Riots: Revenge, Drama, and Death in Nineteenth-Century America*. New York: Random House, 2007.
Cmiel, Kenneth. *Democratic Eloquence: The Fight Over Popular Speech in Nineteenth-Century America*. New York: William Morrow and Company, 1990.
Cockrell, Dale. *Demons of Disorder: Early Blackface Minstrels and Their World*. New York: Cambridge University Press, 1997.
Cohen, Patricia Cline. *The Murder of Helen Jewett: The Life and Death of a Prostitute in Nineteenth-Century New York*. New York: Vintage Books, 1998.
Cole, Toby and Helen Krich Chinoy. *Actors on Acting*. New York: Crown, 1970.
Congdon, Charles T. *Reminiscences of a Journalist*. Boston, MA: James R. Osgood, 1880.
Connerton, Paul. *How Societies Remember*. Cambridge: Cambridge University Press, 1989.
Conrad, Robert T. *Aylmere, or The Bondman of Kent; and Other Poems*. Philadelphia, PA: E. H. Butler, 1852.
Conrad, Robert T. *Aylmere; or, The Kentish Rebellion*, "Property of Edwin Forrest," Marked for Mr. Forrest by D. A. Sarzedas, Prompter, Park Theatre May 24th 1841 New York. University of Pennsylvania. Forrest Collection.
Cooper, James Fennimore. *The Leatherstocking Tales*. Edited by Blake Nevius. New York: Library of America, 2012.

Cott, Nancy F. "Passionlessness: An Interpretation of Victorian Sexual Ideology, 1790–1850." In *Signs: Journal of Women in Culture and Society* 4 (1978): 219–36.
Cowell, Joe. *Thirty Years Passed among the Players in England and America.* 2 vols. New York: Harper, 1844.
Creahan, John. *The Life of Laura Keene.* Philadelphia, PA: Rodgers, 1897.
de Crevecoeur, J. Hector St. John. *Letters from an American Farmer.* Edited by Albert Stone. Penguin, 1981.
Curtis, George William. "Editor's Easy Chair." In *Harper's New Monthly Magazine* 28 (December 1863): 129–33.
Dana, James. *A Sermon, Preached before the General Assembly.* Hartford: n.p., 1779.
Davis, Andrew Jackson. *The Principles of Nature, Her Divine Revelation, and a Voice to Mankind.* Boston, MA: Colby and Rich, 1847.
Davidson, Cathy N. *Revolution and the Word: The Rise of the Novel in America.* Oxford: Oxford University Press, 1986.
Day, Charles William. *Hints on Etiquette and the Usages of Society.* Boston, MA: Otis Broaders, 1844.
Deloria, Philip J. *Indians in Unexpected Places.* Lawrence: University of Kansas Press, 2006.
———. *Playing Indian.* New Haven, CT: Yale University Press, 1999.
Denning, Michael. *Mechanic Accents: Dime Novels and Working-Class Culture in America.* New York: Verso, 1987.
Dodd, Jill Siegel. "The Working Classes and the Temperance Movement in Antebellum Boston." In *Labor History* 19 (1978): 51–31.
Dodge, Daniel Kilham. "Lincoln and Hamlet." In *The Mid-West Quarterly* 1 (April 1914): 220–22.
Douglas, Ann. *The Feminization of American Culture.* New York: Alfred A. Knopf, 1977.
Downer, Alan S. *The Eminent Tragedian: William Charles Macready.* Cambridge: Harvard University Press, 1966.
Dunlap, William. *Andre.* In *Early American Drama*, edited by Jeffrey H. Richards, 58–108. New York: Penguin Books, 1997.
———. *A History of the American Stage.* 2 vols. New York: J. Harper, 1832.
———. *Memoirs of George Frederick Cooke.* 2 vols. New York: D. Longworth, 1813.
Durang, Charles. "Life of Edwin Forrest." In Harvard Theatre Collection, 1864–1869.
Edgett, Edwin Francis. *Edward Loomis Davenport.* New York: Dunlap Society Publications, 1902.
Egan, Maurice Francis. *A Gentleman*, 2nd ed. New York: Benziger Brother, 1893.
Egan, Pierce. *Life in London, or, the Day and Night Scenes of Jerry Hawthorn, Esq.: And His Elegant Friend Corinthian Tom: Accompanied by Bob Logic, the*

Oxonian, in Their Rambles and Sprees through the Metropolis. London: Printed for Sherwood, Nealy, and Jones, 1821.
Emerson, Ralph Waldo. *The Complete Works of Ralph Waldo Emerson*. 12 vols. Boston, MA: Houghton Mifflin, 1903–04.
Farrar, Eliza Ware. *The Young Lady's Friend*. Boston, MA: American Stationers' Company, 1837.
Feasey, Rebecca. *Masculinity and Popular Television*. Edinburgh: Edinburgh University Press, 2009.
Fliegelman, Jay. *Declaring Independence: Jefferson, Natural Language, and the Culture of Performance*. Stanford, CA: Stanford University Press, 1993.
Fletcher, Richard M. *English Romantic Drama, 1795–1843: A Critical History*. Hicksville, NY: Exposition Press, 1966.
Foner, Eric. *Fiery Trial: Abraham Lincoln and American Slavery*. New York: W. W. Norton, 2010.
Foreman, Amanda. *A World on Fire: Britain's Crucial Role in the American Civil War*. New York: Random House, 2011.
The Forrest Divorce Case: Catherine Norton Forrest vs. Edwin Forrest before the Superior Court of New York, Chief Justice Oakley Presiding. Case Tried in December, 1851, and January, 1852. Boston, MA: n.p, 1852.
Forrest, Edwin. "Oration Delivered at the Democratic Republican Celebration, Fourth of July, 1838." New York: Jared W. Bell, 1838.
Fosdick, Henry Emerson. *The Power to See it Through*. New York: Harper, 1935.
Foster, George. *New York by Gaslight*. New York: Dewitt and Davenport, 1850.
Foust, Clement E. *The Life and Dramatic Works of Robert Montgomery Bird*. New York: Knickerbocker, 1919.
Fowler, Henry. *The American Pulpit*. New York: J. M. Fairchild, 1856.
Francis, John W. *Old New York, or, Reminiscences of the Past Sixty Years*. New York: Charles Roe, 1858.
Frick, John W. *Theatre, Culture, and Temperance Reform in Nineteenth-Century America*. Cambridge: Cambridge University Press, 2003.
Furtwangler, Albert. *Assassin on Stage: Brutus, Hamlet, and the Death of Lincoln*. Urbana: University of Illinois Press, 1991.
Gayler, Charles. *Our American Cousin at Home, or, Lord Dundreary Abroad*. New York, 1860.
Goddard, Henry P. "Recollections of Edward L. Davenport." In *Lippincott's Magazine* (April 1878): 463–68.
Goffman, Erving. *The Presentation of Self in Everyday Life*. Garden City, NY: Doubleday Anchor Books, 1959.
Goodale, Katherine [Kitty Molony]. *Behind the Scenes with Edwin Booth*. Boston, MA: Houghton Mifflin, 1931.
Gorn, Elliot. *The Manly Art: Bare-Knuckle Prize Fighting in America*. Ithaca, NY: Cornell University Press, 1986.
Gossett, Thomas F. *Uncle Tom's Cabin and American Culture*. Dallas, TX: Southern Methodist University Press, 1985.

Greenberg, Amy S. *Manifest Manhood and the Antebellum American Empire.* Cambridge: Cambridge University Press, 2005.

Greven, David. *Manhood, Sex, and Violation in American Literature.* New York: Palgrave Macmillan, 2005.

Grimsted, David. *American Mobbing, 1828–1861: Toward Civil War.* New York: Oxford University Press, 1998.

———. *Melodrama Unveiled: American Theater and Culture, 1800–1850.* Chicago, IL: University of Chicago Press, 1968.

Grose, B. Donald. "Edwin Forrest, *Metamora,* and the Indian Removal Act of 1830." In *Theatre Journal* 37 (May 1985): 181–91.

Hackett, James Henry. *Notes, Criticisms, and Correspondence Upon Shakespeare's Plays.* New York: Carleton, 1863. Reprint New York: Benjamin Blom, 1968.

Hall, Willis. *An Address Delivered August 14, 1844, before the Society of Phi Beta Kappa in Yale College.* New Haven, CT: Hamlen, 1844.

Halttunen, Karen. *Confidence Men and Painted Women: A Study of Middle-Class Culture in America, 1830–1870.* New Haven, CT: Yale University Press, 1982.

Hazlitt, William. *Hazlitt on Theatre.* Edited by William Archer and Robert W. Lowe. New York: Hill and Wang, 1957.

Heidler, David S. and Jeannie T. Heidler. *Henry Clay: The Essential American.* New York: Random House, 2010.

Hemphill, C. Dallett. *Bowing to Necessities: A History of Manners in America.* Oxford: Oxford University Press, 1999.

Hibben, Paxton. *Henry Ward Beecher: An American Portrait.* Foreword by Sinclair Lewis. New York: George H. Doran, 1927. Reprint New York: Press of the Reader's Club, 1942.

The History of Edwin Forrest, the Celebrated American Tragedian. Written by an Individual Who Has Known Him from His Boyhood. New York: n.p., 1837.

Hochman, Barbara. *Uncle Tom's Cabin and the Reading Revolution: Race, Literacy, Childhood, and Fiction, 1851–1911.* Amherst: University of Massachusetts Press, 2011.

Hochmuth, Marie Kathryn, ed. *A History and Criticism of American Public Address.* 3 vols. New York: Russell and Russell, 1955.

Hodge, Francis. *Yankee Theatre: The Image of America on the Stage, 1825–1850.* Austin: University of Texas Press, 1964.

Hofstadter, Richard. *American Political Tradition and the Men Who Made It.* New York: Alfred A. Knopf, 1948.

———. *Anti-Intellectualism in American Life.* New York: Alfred A. Knopf, 1963.

Hone, Philip. *The Diary of Philip Hone.* Edited by Allan Nevins. New York: Dodd, Mead, 1927.

Hutton, Laurence. "A Century of Hamlet." In *Harper's New Monthly Magazine* (November 1889): 866–884.

———. *Curiosities of the American Stage.* New York: Harper and Row, 1891.

Ireland, Joseph Norton. *Records of the New York Stage, 1750 to 1860.* 2 Vols. New York: T. H. Morrell, 1867.

Jefferson, Joseph. *The Autobiography of Joseph Jefferson.* New York: Century, 1889.

Jenkins, John S. *The Life of John Caldwell Calhoun.* Auburn, AL: James Alden, 1858.

Johnson, E. Patrick. *Appropriating Blackness: Performance and the Politics of Authenticity.* Durham, NC: Duke University Press, 2003.

Kasey, Rev. J. W. *The Young Man's Guide to True Greatness.* Big Springs, KY: J. W. Kasey, 1858.

Kasson, John F. *Rudeness and Civility: Manners in Nineteenth-Century Urban America.* New York: Hill and Wang, 1990.

Kaufman, Will and Heidi Slettedahl Macpherson, eds. *Britain and the Americas: Culture, Politics, and History.* Santa Barbara, CA: ABC-CLIO, 2005.

Keese, William L. *William E. Burton, Actor, Author, and Manager: A Sketch of His Career.* New York: G. P. Putnam's Sons, 1881

———. *William E. Burton: A Sketch of His Career Other Than That of an Actor.* New York: Dunlap Society, 1891.

Kemble, Frances Ann. *Records of a Later Life.* New York: Henry Holt, 1882.

———. *The American Journals.* Edited by Elizabeth Mavor. London: Weidenfeld and Nicolson, 1990.

Kendall, Amos. *Autobiography.* Edited by William Stickney. Boston, MA: Lee and Shephard, 1872.

Kete, Mary Louise. *Sentimental Collaborations: Mourning and Middle-Class Identity in Nineteenth-Century America.* Durham, NC: Duke University Press, 1999.

Kimmel, Michael. *Manhood in America: A Cultural History,* 2nd ed. New York: Oxford University Press, 2006.

Kippola, Karl M. "'The Battle-Shout of Freemen:' Edwin Forrest's Passive Patriotism and Robert T. Conrad's *Jack Cade.*" In *Journal of American Drama and Theatre* 13 (Fall 2001): 73–86.

———. "The Masculine Transformations of 'Genial John' McCullough." In *Theatre History Studies* 27 (2007): 22–38.

———. "Suppressing the Female Voice: Edwin Forrest's Silencing of Women in *Jack Cade.*" In *Theatre Symposium* 10 (2002): 8–19.

Kirk, John Foster. "Shakespeare's Tragedies upon the Stage: Remarks and Reminiscences of a Sexagenarian." In *Lippincott's Magazine* (June 1884): 598–607.

Knobel, Dale T. *Paddy and the Republic: Ethnicity and Nationality in Antebellum American.* Middletown, CT: Wesleyan University Press, 1986.

Knowles, Sheridan. *Lectures on Oratory, Gesture and Poetry.* London: n.p., 1873.

Lane, Roger. *Policing the City: Boston, 1822–1855.* Cambridge: Harvard University Press, 1967.

Leach, Joseph. *Bright Particular Star: The Life and Times of Charlotte Cushman.* New Haven, CT: Yale University Press, 1970.

Leggett, William. *A Collection of the Political Writings of William Leggett*. 2 vols. Edited by Theodore Sedgwick, Jr. New York: Taylor and Dodd, 1840.

Leman, Walter M. *Memories of an Old Actor*. San Francisco, CA: A. Roman, 1886.

Lester, Lisle. "Edwin Forrest. His Art and Manhood." In *Leslie's Popular Monthly* (December 1887): 684–690.

Levine, Lawrence W. *Highbrow/Lowbrow: The Emergence of Cultural Hierarchy in America*. Cambridge: Harvard University Press, 1988.

Lewes, George Henry. *On Actors and the Art of Acting*. New York: Holt, 1878.

Lhamon, Jr., W. T. *Raising Cain: Blackface Performance from Jim Crow to Hip Hop*. Cambridge, MA: Harvard University Press, 2000.

Lindfor, Bernth. *Ira Aldridge: The African Roscius*. Rochester, NY: University of Rochester Press, 2007.

———. *Ira Aldridge: The Early Years, 1807 to 1833*. Rochester, NY: University of Rochester Press, 2011.

Lippman, Monroe. "Uncle Tom and His Poor Relations: American Slavery Plays." In *Southern Speech Journal* 28 (1963): 183–97.

Lockridge, Richard. *Darling of Misfortune: Edwin Booth, 1833–1893*. New York: Century, 1932.

Longstreet, Abby Buchanan. *Social Etiquette of New York*. New York: D. Appleton, 1887.

Lott, Eric. *Love and Theft: Blackface Minstrelsy and the American Working Class*. New York: Oxford University Press, 1993.

Lowell, James Russell. *The Poetical Works of James Russell Lowell*. Boston, MA: Fields, Osgood, 1869.

Lunettes, Henry. *The American Gentleman's Guide to Politeness and Fashion*. New York: Derby and Jackson, 1857.

MacKaye, Percy. *Epoch: The Life of Steel MacKaye*. 2 vols. New York: Boni and Liveright, 1927.

MacKinnon, Kenneth. *Representing Men: Maleness and Masculinity in the Media*. London: Bloomsbury, 2003.

Macready, William Charles. *The Diaries of William Charles Macready*. 2 vols. Edited by William Thompson. New York: Putnam's, 1912.

———. *Macready's Reminiscences and Selections from His Diaries and Letters*. Edited by Frederick Pollock. New York: Harper, 1875.

Maginnes, F. Arant. *Thomas Abthorpe Cooper: Father of the American Stage, 1775–1849*. Jefferson, NC: McFarland, 2004.

Mahar, William J. *Behind the Burnt Cork Mask: Early Blackface Minstrelsy and Antebellum American Popular Culture*. Champaign: University of Illinois Press, 1998.

Marsh, John. *Temperance Recollections*. New York: Charles Scribner, 1866.

Marshall, Herbert and Mildred Stock. *Ira Aldridge: The Negro Tragedian*. Carbondale: Southern Illinois University Press, 1968.

Martin, Scott C. "Interpreting *Metamora:* Nationalism, Theater, and Jacksonian Indian Policy." In *Journal of the Early Republic* 19 (1999): 73–101.
Mason, Jeffrey D. *Melodrama and the Myth of America.* Bloomington: Indiana University Press, 1993.
Matthew, Jean V. *The Rise of the New Woman: The Women's Movement in America, 1875–1930.* Chicago, IL: Ivan R. Dee, 2004.
———. *Women's Struggle for Equality.* Chicago, IL: Ivan R. Dee, 1998.
Matthews, Brander and Laurence Hutton, eds. *Actors and Actresses of Great Britain and the United States from the Days of David Garrick to the Present Time.* 4 vols. New York: Cassell and Company, 1886.
McAllister, Marvin Edward. *White People Do Not Know How to Behave at Entertainments Designed for Ladies and Gentlemen of Color: William Brown's African and American Theater.* Chapel Hill: University of North Carolina Press, 2002.
———. *Whiting Up: Whiteface Minstrels and Stage Europeans in African American Performance.* Chapel Hill: University of North Carolina Press, 2011.
McArthur, Benjamin. *Actors and American Culture, 1880–1920.* Iowa City: University of Iowa Press, 2000.
McConachie, Bruce A. *Melodramatic Formations: American Theatre and Society, 1820–1870.* Iowa City: University of Iowa Press, 1992.
———. "New York Opera-going: 1825–1850." In *American Music* 6 (Summer 1988): 181–92.
———. "The Theatre of Edwin Forrest and Jacksonian Hero Worship." In *When They "Weren't" Doing Shakespeare: Essays on Nineteenth-Century British and American Theatre,* edited by Judith L. Fisher and Stephen Watt, 3–18. Athens: University of Georgia Press, 1989.
McDonough, Carla J. *Staging Masculinity: Male Identity in Contemporary American Drama.* Jefferson, NC: McFarland, 1997.
Miller, Marion M., ed. *Great Debates in American History.* 14 vols. New York: Current Literature Publishing, 1913.
Miller, Monica L. *Slaves to Fashion: Black Dandyism and the Styling of Black Diasporic Identity.* Durham, NC: Duke University Press, 2009.
Miller, Tice. *Bohemians and Critics: American Theatre Criticism in the Nineteenth Century.* Metuchen, NJ: Scarecrow Press, 1981.
Monaghan, Jay. *The Great Rascal: The Life and Adventures of Ned Buntline.* Boston, MA: Little, Brown and Company, 1952.
Moody, Richard. *The Astor Place Riot.* Bloomington: Indiana University Press, 1958.
———. *Dramas from the American Theatre, 1762–1909.* Cleveland, OH: World Publishing, 1966.
———. *Edwin Forrest: First Star of the American Stage.* New York: Alfred A. Knopf, 1960.
Moses, Montrose J. *The Fabulous Forrest: The Record of an American Actor.* Boston, MA: Little, Brown, and Co., 1929.

Moses, Montrose J. "Robert T. Conrad." In *Representative Plays by American Dramatists from 1765 to the Present Day*, Vol. 2, *1815–1858*, 427–38. New York: Benjamin Blom, 1929.

Moss, Sidney P. *Charles Dickens' Quarrel with America*. New York: Whitstone, 1984.

Mowatt, Anna Cora. *Fashion; or, Life in New York*, in *Early American Drama*, edited by Jeffrey H. Richards, 304–67. New York: Penguin, 1997.

Mullenix, Elizabeth Reitz. *Wearing the Breeches: Gender on the Antebellum Stage*. New York: Palgrave Macmillan, 2000.

Murdoch, James E. *The Stage, or, Recollections of Actors and Acting From an Experience of Fifty Years; a Series of Dramatic Sketches*. Philadelphia, PA: J. M. Stoddart, 1880.

Nagel, Paul C. *John Quincy Adams: A Public Life, a Private Life*. New York: Knopf, 1997.

Nathans, Heather Shawn. "'All of the Federalist?': Choosing Sides and Creating Identities in the Boston Theatre Wars." In *New England Theatre Journal* 11 (2000): 1–18.

———. *Slavery and Sentiment on the American Stage, 1787–1861: Lifting the Veil of Black*. New York: Cambridge University Press, 2009.

Nelson, Dana D. *National Manhood: Capitalist Citizenship and the Imagined Fraternity of White Men*. Durham, NC: Duke University Press, 1998.

Newcomb, Harvey. *How to Be a Man*. Boston, MA: Gould, Kendall, and Lincoln, 1847.

Newton, Sarah E. *Learning to Behave: A Guide to American Conduct Books before 1900*. Westport, CT: Greenwood Press, 1994.

Nicolay, John G. and John Hay. *Abraham Lincoln: A History*. 3 vols. New York: Century Company, 1890.

Niles, Hezekiah. *Principles and Acts of the Revolution in America*. Baltimore: William Ogden Niles, 1822.

Niven, John. *John C. Calhoun and the Price of Union: A Biography*. Baton Rouge: Louisiana State University Press, 1993.

Oberholtzer, Ellis Paxson. *The Literary History of Philadelphia*. Philadelphia, PA: George W. Jacobs, 1906.

Odell, George C. *Annals of the New York Stage*. 15 vols. New York: Columbia University Press, 1927.

Oggel, Lynwood Terry. *Edwin Booth: A Bio-Bibliography*. Westport, CT: Greenwood Press, 1992.

Oldstyle, Jonathan. "Letter IV—Audiences." In *Morning Chronicle*, December 4, 1802.

Page, Edwin L. *Abraham Lincoln in New Hampshire*. Boston, MA: Houghton Mifflin, 1929.

Paine, Thomas. *The Writings of Thomas Paine*. 4 vols. Edited by Moncure Daniel Conway. New York: G.P. Putnam's Sons, 1894.

Parsons, Lynn Hudson. *The Birth of Modern Politics: Andrew Jackson, John Quincy Adams, and the Election of 1828.* New York: Oxford University Press, 2009.

Paulding, James Kirke. *The Lion of the West and The Bucktails.* Edited by Frank Gado. Lanham, MD: Rowman and Littlefield, 1994.

Pease, William H. and Jane H. Pease. *Ladies, Women, and Wenches: Choices and Constraint in Antebellum Charleston and Boston.* Chapel Hill: University of North Carolina Press, 1990.

Peterson, Merrill D. *The Great Triumvirate: Webster, Clay and Calhoun.* New York: Oxford University Press, 1988.

Phelps, Henry P. *Players of a Century: A History of the Albany Stage.* New York: Joseph McDonough, 1880.

"Philadelphia Area Theatre Playbills." 28 vols. Library Company of Philadelphia.

Pugh, David G. *Sons of Liberty: The Masculine Mind in Nineteenth-Century America.* Westport, CT: Greenwood Press, 1983.

Quinn, Arthur Hobson. *A History of the American Drama from the Beginning to the Civil War.* New York: Harper and Brothers, 1923.

Rankin, Hugh F. *The Theater in Colonial America.* Chapel Hill: University of North Carolina Press, 1960.

Read, James H. *Majority Rule Versus Consensus: The Political Thought of John C. Calhoun.* University Press of Kansas, 2009.

Reaves, Wendy Wick. "Portraits for Every Parlor: Albert Newsam and American Portrait Lithography." In *American Portrait Prints: Proceedings of the Tenth Annual American Print Conference.* Edited by Wendy Wick Reaves. Charlottesville: University Press of Virginia, 1984.

Rebhorn, Matthew. "Edwin Forrest's Redding Up: Elocution, Theater, and the Performance of Frontier." In *Comparative Drama* 40 (Winter 2007): 455–81.

Reed, Thomas B., ed. *Modern Eloquence.* 15 vols. Philadelphia, PA: John D. Morris, 1903.

Reid, Marion. *A Plea for Woman.* Chester Springs, PA: Dufour Editions, 1989.

A Rejoinder to "The Replies From England, etc. to Certain Statements Circulated in this Country Respecting Mr. Macready." Together with an Impartial History and Review of the Lamentable Occurrences at the Astor Place Opera House, on the 10th of May, 1849. By an American Citizen. New York: Stringer and Townsend, 1849.

Remini, Robert V. *Andrew Jackson.* 3 vols. Baltimore: Johns Hopkins University Press, 1998.

———. *Andrew Jackson and His Indian Wars.* New York: Viking, 2001.

———. *At the Edge of the Precipice: Henry Clay and the Compromise That Saved the Union.* New York: Basic, 2010.

———. *Daniel Webster: The Man and His Time.* New York: W. W. Norton, 2009.

The Replies from England to Certain Statements Circulated in This Country Respecting Mr. Macready. New York: n.p., 1849.

Report of the Forrest Divorce Case, Containing the Full and Unabridged Testimony of All the Witnesses, the Affidavits and Depositions, Together with the Consuelo and Forney Letters. New York: n.p., 1852.

Review of *Bazar Book of Decorum*. By Robert Tomes. Reprinted in *Atlantic Monthly* 26 (July 1870): 121–123.

Reynolds, David S. *Mightier Than the Sword: Uncle Tom's Cabin and the Battle for America.* New York: W. W. Norton, 2011.

Richards, Jeffrey H. "Plays and Playwrights: 1800–1865." In *The Cambridge History of American Theatre*, Vol. 1, *Beginnings to 1970*, ed. Don B. Wilmeth and Christopher Bigsby, 250–302. Cambridge: Cambridge University Press, 1998.

Richardson, James. *The New York Police: Colonial Times to 1901.* New York: Oxford University Press, 1970.

Rinear, David L. *Stage, Page, Scandals, and Vandals: William E. Burton and Nineteenth-Century American Theatre.* Carbondale: Southern Illinois University Press, 2004.

Roach, Joseph. *The Player's Passion: Studies in the Science of Acting.* Ann Arbor: University of Michigan Press, 1993.

Roediger, David R. *The Wages of Whiteness: Race and the Making of the American Working Class.* Brooklyn, NY: Verso, 2007.

Rogers, Joseph M. *The True Henry Clay.* Philadelphia: Lippincott, 1905.

Rogin, Michael Paul. *Fathers and Children: Andrew Jackson and the Subjugation of the American Indian.* New York: Knopf, 1975.

Roorbach, Jr., O. A. *Actors As They Are; A Series of Sketches of the Most Eminent Performers Now on the Stage.* New York: O. A. Roorbach, Jr., 1856.

Rotundo, E. Anthony. *American Manhood: Transformations in Masculinity from the Revolution to the Modern Era.* New York: Basic Books, 1993.

Rourke, Constance Mayfield. *Trumpets of Jubilee.* New York: Harcourt and Brace, 1927.

Ruggles, Eleanor. *Prince of Players: Edwin Booth.* New York: W. W. Norton, 1953.

Ruyter, Nancy Lee Chalfa. *The Cultivation of Body and Mind in Nineteenth-Century American Delsartism.* Westport, CT: Greenwood Press, 1999.

Ryan, Halford, ed. *U.S. Presidents as Orators: A Bio-Critical Sourcebook.* Westport, CT: Greenwood Press, 1995.

Savran, David. *Take It Like a Man: White Masculinity, Masochism, and Contemporary American Culture.* Princeton, NJ: Princeton University Press, 1998.

Saxton, Alexander. *The Rise and Fall of the White Republic: Class Politics and Mass Culture in Nineteenth-Century America.* London: Verso, 1990.

Schanke, Robert A. and Kim Marra, eds. *Passing Performance: Queer Readings of Leading Players in American Theater History.* Ann Arbor: University of Michigan Press, 1998.

Scharnhorst, Gary and Gary Bales. *The Lost Life of Horatio Alger, Jr.* Bloomington: Indiana University Press, 1985.

Schecter, Barnet. *The Devil's Own Work: The Civil War Draft Riots and the Fight to Reconstruct America.* New York: Walker, 2003.
Schlesinger, Arthur M., Jr. *Learning How to Behave: A Historical Study of American Etiquette Books.* New York: Macmillan, 1947.
Schurz, Carl. *Reminiscinces of Carl Schurz.* 2 vols. New York: McClure, 1909.
Senelick, Laurence. *The Age and Stage of George L. Fox,* Hanover, NH: Tufts University by University Press of New England, 1988.
Shaffer, Jason. *Performing Patriotism: National Identity in the Colonial and Revolutionary American Theater.* Philadelphia: University of Pennsylvania Press, 2007.
Shattuck, Charles H. *The Hamlet of Edwin Booth.* Urbana: University of Illinois Press, 1969.
——. *Shakespeare on the American Stage.* 2 vols. Washington, DC: Folger Books, 1987.
Shaw, Warren Choate. *History of American Oratory.* 2 vols. Indianapolis, IN: Bobbs-Merrill Company, 1979.
Shenstone, N.A. *Anecdotes of Henry Ward Beecher.* Chicago, IL: R.R. Donnelly, 1887.
Skinner, Maud and Otis. *One Man in His Time: The Adventures of H. Watkins, Strolling Player, 1845–1863, from His Journal.* Philadelphia: University of Pennsylvania Press, 1938.
Skinner, Otis. *Footlights and Spotlights: Recollections of My Life on the Stage.* Indianapolis, IN: Bobbs, 1924.
Smith, William H. *The Drunkard; or, the Fallen Saved.* In *Early American Drama,* edited by Jeffrey H. Richards, 243–303. New York: Penguin, 1997.
St. George, Andrew. *The Descent of Manners: Etiquette, Rules and the Victorians.* London: Chatto and Windus, 1993.
Stanhope, Philip Dormer. *Letters to his Son by the Earl of Chesterfield on the Fine Art of Becoming a Man of the World and a Gentleman,* edited by Joseph R. Seabury. New York: Silver, Burdett and Company, 1902.
Stansell, Christine. *City of Women: Sex and Class in New York, 1789–1860.* Chicago: University of Illinois Press, 1982.
Staples, Robert. *Black Masculinity: The Black Man's Role in American Society.* San Francisco, CA: Black Scholar Press, 1982.
Stedman, E.C. "Edwin Booth." In *Atlantic Monthly* 17 (May 1866): 585–93.
Stephens, Alexander Hamilton. *A Constitutional View of the Late War between the States; its Causes, Character, Conduct and Results. Presented in a Series of Colloquies at Liberty Hall.* 2 vols. Philadelphia, PA: National Publishing, 1868–70.
Stone, Henry Dickinson. *Personal Recollections of the Drama; or, Theatrical Reminiscences, Embracing Sketches of Prominent Actors and Actresses, Their Chief Characteristics, Original Anecdotes of Them, and Incidents Connected Therewith.* Albany, NY: Charles Van Benthuysen, 1873.

Stone, John Augustus. *Metamora; or, The Last of the Wampanoags.* In *Dramas From the American Theatre, 1762–1909,* edited by Richard Moody, 199–228. Cleveland, OH: World Publishing, 1966.

Stott, Richard. *Workers in the Metropolis: Class, Ethnicity, and Youth in Ante-bellum New York City.* Ithaca, NY: Cornell University Press, 1990.

Stowe, Harriet Beecher. *The Life and Deeds of our Self-Made Men.* Hartford, CT: Worthington, Dustin, 1872.

———. *Uncle Tom's Cabin.* Edited by Elizabeth Ammons. New York: W. W. Norton, 1994.

Strand, Ginger. "'My Noble Spartacus': Edwin Forrest and Masculinity on the Nineteenth-Century Stage." In *Passing Performances: Queer Readings of Leading Players in American Theatre History,* eds. Robert A. Schanke and Kim Marra, 19–40. Ann Arbor: University of Michigan Press, 1998.

Strang, Lewis C. *Players and Plays of the Last Quarter Century.* 2 vols. Boston, MA: L. C. Page, 1903.

Styron, Arthur. *The Cast Iron Man: John C. Calhoun and American Democracy.* New York: Longmans, Green, 1935.

Sween, Gretchen. "Rituals, Riots, Rules, and Rights: The Astor Place Theater Riot of 1849 and the Evolving Limits of Free Speech." In *Texas Law Review* 81 (2002): 679–713.

Templeton, Joan. *Ibsen's Women.* New York: Cambridge University Press, 1997.

Thomas, Isaiah, ed. *The History of Printing in America,* 2nd ed. 2 vols. Albany, NY: n.p., 1874.

Thorpe, Francis Newton, ed. *The Statesmanship of Andrew Jackson as Told in his Writings and Speeches.* New York: Tandy-Thomas, 1909.

de Tocqueville, Alexis. *Democracy in America.* 2 vols. Trans. Henry Reeve. New York: A. S. Barnes, 1858.

Todd, John. *The Young Man: Hints Addressed to the Young Men of the United States.* Northampton, UK: J. H. Butler, 1845.

Tomes, Robert. *The Bazar Book of Decorum: The Care of the Person, Manners, Etiquette, and Ceremonials.* New York: Harper & Brothers, 1873.

Towse, John Rankin. *Sixty Years of the Theatre.* New York: Funk and Wagnall, 1916.

Trollope, Frances. *Domestic Manners of the Americans.* Edited by Donald Smalley. New York: Knopf, 1949.

Twain, Mark. "Lisle Lester on Her Travels." In *The Daily Dramatic Chronicle* (San Francisco), October 30, 1865.

Tyler, Royall. *The Contrast.* In *Early American Drama,* ed. Jeffrey H. Richards, 1–57. New York: Penguin Books, 1997.

de Valcourt, Robert. *The Illustrated Manners Book and Manual of Good Behavior and Polite Accomplishments.* New York: Leland, Clay, 1855.

Vorlicky, Robert. *Act Like a Man: Challenging Masculinities in America.* Ann Arbor: The University of Michigan Press, 1995.

Wallace, Anthony F. C. *The Long, Bitter Trail: Andrew Jackson and the Indians.* New York: Hill and Wang, 1993.
Wallace, Karl R., ed. *History of Speech Education in America.* New York: Appleton-Century-Crofts, 1954.
Waller, Altina L. *Reverend Beecher and Mrs. Tilton: Sex and Class in Victorian America.* Amherst: University of Massachusetts, 1982.
Ward, John William. *Andrew Jackson: Symbol for an Age.* New York: Oxford University Press, 1955.
Watermeier, Daniel J., ed. *Between Actor and Critic: Selected Letters of Edwin Booth and William Winter.* Princeton, NJ: Princeton University Press, 1971.
Watson, Elwood and Marc E. Shaw, eds. *Performing American Masculinities: The 21st-Century Man in Popular Culture.* Bloomington: Indiana University Press, 2011.
Weed, Thurlow. *The Life of Thurlow Weed.* Edited by H. A. Weed. 2 vols. Boston, MA: Houghton Mifflin, 1883.
Wells, Samuel Robert. *How to Behave: A Pocket Manual of Republican Etiquette.* New York: Fowler and Wells, 1856.
Wemyss, Francis Courtnay. *Theatrical Biography of Eminent Actors and Authors.* New York: William and Taylor, n.d.
———. *Twenty-Six Years of the Life of an Actor and Manager.* New York: Burgess, Stringer, and Co., 1847.
Wentworth, John. *Congressional Reminiscences: Adams, Benton, Calhoun, Clay, and Webster.* Chicago, IL: Fergus Printing, 1882.
Wheelan, Joseph. *Mr. Adams's Last Crusade: John Quincy Adams's Extraordinary Post-presidential Life in Congress.* New York: Public Affairs, 2008.
White, Jr., Ronald C. *A. Lincoln: A Biography.* New York: Random House, 2009.
Wiggin, Frederick A. *The Living Jesus: The Words of Jesus of Nazareth Uttered through the Medium Frederick A. Wiggin From February 11 to June 1, 1921.* New York: George Sully and Company, 1921.
Wilenz, Sean. *Andrew Jackson.* New York: Times, 2005.
———. *Chants Democratic: New York City and the Rise of the American Working Class, 1789–1850.* New York: Oxford University Press, 1984.
Willis, Nathaniel Parker. *Hurry-graphs; or, Sketches of Scenery, Celebrities and Society, Taken from Life.* Auburn, AL: Alden, Beardsley, 1853.
Wilmeth, Don B. *George Frederick Cooke: Machiavel of the Stage.* Westport, CT: Greenwood Press, 1980.
Wilson, Alexander. *American Ornithology; or the Natural History of the Birds of the United States.* Edited by Robert Jameson. 4 vols. Edinburgh: Constable and Company, 1831.
Wilson, Arthur Herman. *A History of the Philadelphia Theatre, 1835 to 1855.* Philadelphia: University of Pennsylvania Press, 1935.
Wilson, Garff B. *A History of American Acting.* Bloomington: Indiana University Press, 1966.

Winter, William. *Brief Chronicles*. New York: Dunlap Society, 1889.
———. *Edwin Booth in Twelve Dramatic Characters*. Boston, MA: Osgood, 1872.
———. *In Memory of John McCullough*. New York: De Vinne, 1889.
———. *The Life and Art of Edwin Booth*. New York: Macmillan, 1893.
———. *Other Days*. New York: Moffat and Yard, 1908.
———. *Shakespeare on the Stage*. 2nd series. New York: Moffat, Yard, 1915.
———. *The Wallet of Time*. New York: Benjamin Blom, 1913.
Wollstonecraft, Mary. *A Vindication on the Rights of Woman: With Strictures on Political and Moral Subjects*. Cambridge: Cambridge University Press, 2010
Woodruff, Bruce E. "'Genial' John McCullough: Actor and Manager." Ph.D. diss., University of Nebraska, 1984.
Woods, S. D. *Lights and Shadows of Life on the Pacific Coast*. New York: Funk and Wagnalls, 1910.
Wyllie, Irvin G. *The Self-Made Man in America: The Myth of Rags to Riches*. New Brunswick, NJ: Rutgers University Press, 1954.
Young, William C. *Famous Actors and Actresses on the American Stage: Documents of American Theatre History*. 2 vols. New York: R. R. Bowker Co., 1975.

Index

acting style
   classical, 10, 14, 15, 43, 60, 65, 94, 99, 122, 124, 145, 159
   romantic, 10, 12, 15, 60–61, 94, 95, 145, 149, 199
Adams, John Quincy, 196
   1828 presidential election and, 5, 7, 24–29
   Clay and, 32
   Hackett and, 181
   intellectualism and, 30, 43–44, 62
   Jackson and, 22, 24–29
   masculinity and, 29, 60, 145
   National Republican Party and, 196
   as orator, 35, 199
   Paine and, 23
   public perception of, 24–25, 30
   Webster and, 33–34
Addams, Augustus A., 61, 75
Addison, Joseph, 18
Aiken, George L., 178–79, 226
Albion, 62, 66, 132
Alda, Alan, 189
Alger, Horatio Jr., 54
Alger, William Rounseville, 54, 58, 64, 66, 75, 176
Allen, Tim, 173, 190
American Gentleman's Guide to Politeness and Fashion, 46, 50
American Indians
   Choctaw, 61
   Jackson and, 173–75, 197, 224
   portrayal in dramas, 70, 73, 175–76, 180
   Trail of Tears, 174
   white masculinity and, 76, 173–75
   see also Indian Removal Act of 1830
American Pulpit, The (Fowler), 41
American Revolution, *see* Revolutionary War
Ammons, Elizabeth, 179, 226
Andre (Dunlap), 17–18
Arch Street Theatre, 95, 120, 215
Art of Good Behavior, The, 47
Astaire, Fred, 189
Astor Place Riot
   aftermath, 113–16
   American theatre and, 64, 67
   background, 92–95
   description of riot, 108–13
   description of theatre, 95–97
   Forrest and, 8, 36, 53, 55, 82, 99–101, 104–16
   Hackett, 181
   Macready and, 8, 64, 90, 92, 97–99, 113–16
   lead-up to, 89–92
   masculinity and, 46, 64, 108–13
   viewed as U.S. vs. England, 101–4
Aylmere (Conrad), 69, 77–82, 84–87, 208

Badeau, Adam, 123, 128, 216, 217
Baker, Benjamin A., 91
Barker, James Nelson, 70
Barnum, P. T., 42–43
Barrett, Lawrence, 65, 122–24, 126
Barrymore, John, 42

246 Index

Beckford, William, 55
Beecher, Henry Ward, 22, 40–44, 47–48, 56–57, 61–62, 64–65, 90, 143, 145
Bell, John, 34
Belle Lamar (Boucicault), 159
Benton, Thomas Hart, 35, 199
Bernard, William Bayle, 100
Bird, Robert Montgomery, 68–69, 74, 207
Bishop, Charles, 151, 153, 170
Blackhawk War, 174
Booth, Edwin
  Civil War and, 43
  Delsarte system and, 147
  femininity and, 8–9, 117, 122, 141–42
  Forrest and, 117–21, 139–46
  Hamlet and, 130–39, 188–89, 200
  intellectualism, 5, 44
  masculinity and, 8–9, 170, 183
  McCullough and, 152–53, 159–60, 163–66, 170–71
  popularity, 5, 98
  restraint in performances, 8
  Sinclair and, 56
  tragedy's influence on his craft, 122–30
Booth, John Wilkes, 61, 125, 136, 152
Booth, Junius Brutus, 5, 13–15, 61
Boucicault, Dion, 159, 179–80
Bowery Theatre, 95
Brando, Marlon, 134, 189
Breckenridge, John C., 34
Brooke, Henry, 19
Brougham, John, 175, 180
Buchanan, James, 35
Bulwer-Lytton, Edward, 105, 137–38
Buntline, Ned (pseudonym of E. Z. C. Judson), 112
Burr, Aaron, 196
Burton, William Evans, 93, 120, 180–82, 215
Bush, George W., 189

Caitlin, George, 174
Calhoun, John C., 22, 29–31, 35, 198
Calvinism, 40
Carboy, John, 55
Carter, Jimmy, 189
Cato (Addison), 17–18
Chanfrau, Francis S., 91, 109
Cherokee Nation v. Georgia, 174
Chesterfield, Earl of, 17, 50, 110, 171
Chestnut Street Theatre, 16, 120–21, 132, 175, 179, 215
Christy Minstrels, 177
Civil War
  aftermath, 7, 56, 188
  American theatre and, 43, 128, 147, 159–60, 162, 176, 179
  Edwin Booth and, 5, 8, 43, 117, 134, 136, 141–42, 144
  class tension and, 115
  Delsarte system and, 156
  efforts to avert, 33–34
  fragmentation of America and, 4
  Great Triumvirate and, 29–30
  Lincoln and, 39
  literature and, 45
  masculinity and, 134, 141, 148, 170, 182
  middle class and, 8, 144
  perception of masculinity following, 7
  spiritualism and, 186
Clark, Susie Champney, 185–87
Clarke, Charles, 133, 218
Clarke, Joseph, 157
Clay, Henry, 22, 24–25, 29–32, 35, 38, 42
Clinton, George, 198
Cmiel, Kenneth, 23, 25, 28, 197
Cochrane, John, 119
Cohen, Patricia Cline, 86, 209–10
Common Sense (Paine), 23
Congdon, Charles, 57

Conrad, Robert T., 8, 44, 53, 69, 74–87, 208
Contrast, The (Tyler), 16, 19, 37, 90–91, 171
Cooke, George Frederick, 12–13, 15, 61
Cooper, Gary, 189
Cooper Institute, 118–19, 122
Cooper, James Fenimore, 197
Cooper, Thomas Abthorpe, 11–13, 15, 60
Cowell, Joe, 62
Crawford, William H., 24
Crèvecoeur, Hector St. John de, 1, 23
Crockett, Davy, 27, 100
Cruise, Tom, 189
Curtis, George William, 118–19

Dana, James, 17
Davenport, Edward L., 122–24
Davis, Andrew Jackson, 186
Davis, Jefferson, 56
De Niro, Robert, 189
Dean, James, 134, 189
Declaration of Independence, 21, 23, 53, 101
Delsarte system, 9, 147, 154–58, 162, 170–71
Democratic Eloquence (Cmiel), 23, 25
Democratic Party, 3, 6, 25, 28, 34, 37, 54, 69, 76, 87
Democratic-Republican Party, 65–66, 196
Depp, Johnny, 189
DiCaprio, Leonardo, 189
Dickens, Charles, 101, 109
Dodge, Daniel Hilham, 142
Douglas (Home), 20
Douglas, Ann, 119
Douglas, Stephen A., 34, 37, 199
Douglass, Frederick, 36, 44, 177, 199, 225
Dowton, Will, 91

Draft Riots, 115, 215
Drunkard, The (Smith), 42–43, 48–49, 91
Dunlap, William, 12, 18–19
Durang, Charles, 60

Eaton, Charles, 61
Edwards, Henry, 165
Edwards, Jonathan, 40, 48
Egan, Pierce, 91
Emerson, Ralph Waldo, 21, 28, 101, 186
Era of Good Feelings, 24
etiquette, 46–50, 58, 61–62, 127, 190

Fillmore, Millard, 33, 35
Fliegelman, Jay, 22
Florence, W. J., 169
Fonda, Henry, 189
Forrest, Edwin
  Astor Place Riots and, 108–16
  Booth and, 5, 117–21, 124–25, 128–29, 131, 134, 136–46
  Cooper and, 11–12
  early life, 53–55
  as father of American drama, 67–74
  Hamlet and, 64, 104, 143
  intellectualism, 44
  Jack Cade and, 74–75, 77–82
  Macready and, 8, 55, 64, 90, 92–95, 100–12
  masculinity and, 8, 36, 56–59, 82–88, 170–71, 188–89
  McCullough and, 9, 147–52, 154–55, 157–62, 165–67
  Metamora and, 173–76, 179
  performance style, 188–89
  popularity, 5, 16, 20, 29, 56, 59–67
  Catherine Sinclair and, 55–56
  Spartacus and, 184
  as working-class hero, 59–67
Forster, John, 100, 105–6
Foster, George, 97

248   Index

Fowler, Henry, 41–42
Francis, John, 14
Fugitive Slave Act, 33, 134, 178

Garrick Club, 101, 126
Garrick, David, 10, 42
Gayler, Charles, 91
Gentleman, A, 47
Gladiator, The (Bird), 63, 68–70, 74–75, 78, 111–13, 168, 184
Glory of Columbia, Her Yeomanry, The (Dunlap), 18
Goddard, Henry P., 123
Goodwin, Nat, 127
Gore, Al, 189–90
Gough, John Bartholomew, 42, 43
Grant, Cary, 189
Grant, Ulysses S., 36, 44
Gray, Mark, 129
Great Awakening, 40
Great Triumvirate, 22, 29–34, 43
Greeley, Horace, 97
Greenberg, Amy S., 3
Gustavus Vasa (Brooke), 17, 19–20

Hackett, James H., 93, 95, 100, 112, 180–81
Halttunen, Karen, 49, 127, 134
Hamblin, Thomas S., 95, 111
Hamlet
  Astor Place Riot and, 106
  Edwin Booth and, 5, 44, 117, 123, 125, 127, 129–40, 142, 188
  burlesque performance of, 127
  Thomas Abthorpe Cooper and, 11
  Edwin Forrest and, 64, 104, 143
  Hackett and, 181
  William Charles Macready and, 14, 106
  John McCullough and, 154, 163–64, 185
Hanks, Tom, 189
Harrison, Gabriel, 62

Harrison, William Henry, 33, 35, 76, 199
Hazlitt, William, 13
Hinton, Henry, 126
Hints on Etiquette and the Usages of Society, 50
Hoffman, Dustin, 189
Holmes, Oliver Wendell, 101
Home, John, 20
Hone, Philip, 111
Houdini, Harry, 186
How to Be a Man, 48
How to Behave: A Pocket Manual of Republican Etiquette, 49
Humphreys, David, 90
Hutton, Laurence, 128, 143
Hyer, Tom, 89

Illustrated Manners Book, The, 48, 50
Indian Removal Act of 1830, 174, 224
  see also American Indians
Ingersoll, David, 61
Irish immigrants, 89, 91, 107, 112, 148, 173, 179–80, 226
Irving, Henry, 126, 137, 144
Irving, Washington, 1, 111

Jack Cade (Conrad), 8, 44, 53, 56, 68–72, 74–87, 102, 159–60, 188, 208
Jackson, Andrew
  John Quincy Adams and, 5, 196
  Calhoun and, 198
  criticism of, 46
  decorum and, 142, 245–46
  election, 5, 7, 24
  Forrest and, 53–55, 57–60, 65–67, 69–70, 75–76, 78, 83–84, 87–88
  Great Triumvirate and, 29–32
  influence, 22, 29–32, 53–55, 57
  masculinity and, 8, 36, 43, 142, 145–46, 148
  Native Americans and, 173–74, 197

popular appeal, 35–36, 39–40, 43–44, 49
presidential election of 1928, 24–29
rhetorical impression, 35, 199
scholarship on, 197
Webster and, 199
Jefferson, Joseph, 122–23
Jefferson, Thomas, 23, 84, 196, 198, 199
Jim Crow, 176
Johnson, Andrew, 188
Johnson, Samuel, 17
Johnson, William F., 183–84
Judson, E. Z. C., 112

Kasson, John, 144
Kean, Charles, 126, 143, 182
Kean, Edmund, 10, 12–15, 60–61, 65, 98, 100
Keene, Laura, 144
Keene, Thomas, 169, 187
Kemble, Charles, 123
Kemble, Fanny, 46
Kemble, John Philip, 10–14, 60
Kimmel, Michael S., 2, 16, 188–89
Kirby, J. Hudson, 61
Kirk, John Foster, 57, 65
Knowles, J. Sheridan, 14, 185

Leggett, William, 66, 68, 76–77, 87, 101, 206
Lester, Lisle, 57, 64
Letters from an American Farmer (Crèvecoeur), 23–24
Lewes, George Henry, 15
Lewis, Sinclair, 42
Lhamon, W. T. Jr., 177
Lincoln, Abraham, 152, 178, 186, 188, 199, 200
  Edwin Booth and, 5, 117, 119, 125–26, 130, 132, 135–36, 142–43, 145–46, 188
  Clay and, 32
  death, 22, 125, 130, 132, 152
  forgiveness and, 142
  gentility, 142–43, 145
  Hamlet and, 117, 135–36, 142
  intellectualism, 9, 43–44
  masculinity and, 22, 34–39
  religious eclecticism, 186
  rhetorical impression, 199
  second inaugural address, 142, 200
  slavery and, 178, 200
Lott, Eric, 177

Macbeth, 137, 141
MacKaye, Steele, 155–56, 158, 162, 184
Macready, William Charles
  Astor Place Riot and, 8, 64, 90, 92, 97–99, 113–16
  Booth and, 122, 143
  classical style, 100, 122
  final trip to America, 108–13
  first American tour, 97–99
  Forrest and, 8, 55, 64, 90, 92–95, 100–1, 104–8
  Hackett and, 181
  popularity, 14–15
  second American tour, 101–4
  Virginius and, 185
Madison, James, 24, 198, 199
Manifest Destiny, 3
masculine performance
  intellectual self-control, 3, 29, 39, 43, 44, 115–16, 124, 128, 144–45, 188–190
  passionate action, 3, 21, 29, 39, 58–61, 66, 108–9, 115–16, 143, 188–190
Mason, Jeffrey, 42, 201, 206
McConachie, Bruce, 45, 69, 192
McCullough, John
  Booth and, 159–67
  critical reaction to, 149–51
  early life, 147–48

McCullough, John—*Continued*
  Forrest and, 148–49, 176
  illness and death, 167–71
  Lincoln assassination and, 152–53
  masculinity and, 9, 183–88
  perpetual self-improvement, 153–59
  popularity, 151–52
  private life, 152
McDonough, Carla J., 3
McVicker, Mary, 129
Melville, Herman, 111
Metamora (Stone), 62, 68–73, 75, 94, 113, 173–76, 188, 206, 207, 224
Mexican-American War, 6, 30
Mitchell, John, 105
Monroe, James, 24
Moody, Richard, 55, 59, 102
Moses, Montrose, 56
Mowatt, Anna Cora, 47, 123
Murdoch, James E., 11–12, 62, 122–24

Native Americans, *see* American Indians
Niblo, William, 112
Niles, Hezekiah, 21
Noah, Mordecai, 70
Norton, George Chapple, 85

O'Connor, Charles, 56
Octoroon, The (Boucicault), 179
Oldstyle, Jonathan (pseudonym of Washington Irving), 1, 111
O'Sullivan, John, 6

Pacino, Al, 189
Paine, Thomas, 16, 23
Panic of 1837, 76
Phelps, Henry P., 149
Pierce, Franklin, 29, 35
Poe, Edgar Allan, 74, 77–79
Polk, James K., 6, 12, 29, 35
Power of Sympathy, The (Brown), 86
Pratt, William W., 42

reconstructed manhood, 40, 90, 195
Reconstruction, 142, 162, 188
Reid, Marion, 85
religious eclecticism, 185–86
Republican Party, 3, 37
Revolutionary War, 2, 11, 18, 23–24, 40, 175
Rice, Thomas D., 176–77
Rollins, Edward H., 37
Roorbach, O. A., 123
Roosevelt, Theodore, 35, 189
Rynders, Isaiah, 112

Schwarzenegger, Arnold, 189
self-made manhood, 16, 20, 22, 28, 32, 53–54, 57, 71, 88, 123, 129, 145, 199
Seminole War, 174
Shaw, Warren Choate, 200
Shays' Rebellion, 1
Shurz, Carl, 35
Sinclair, Catherine, 55–56, 85, 125
Skinner, Otis, 139
slavery, 16, 25, 30–34, 37, 39, 41, 43, 70–71, 83, 90, 116, 134, 177–80, 186
Smith, Richard Penn, 68–69
Smith, Sidney, 53
Smith, William H., 42–43
Social Etiquette of New York, 50
Spartacus (character), 63, 70–72, 112–13, 150, 160–61, 163, 168, 184, 188
Stallone, Sylvester, 189
Stanhope, Philip Dormer, 17
Stedman, E.C., 128, 133, 141, 145
Stephens, Alexander Hamilton, 39
Stewart, Jimmy, 189
Stone, Henry Dickinson, 11, 123
Stone, John Augustus, 68–69, 74, 175–76
Stowe, Harriet Beecher, 134, 178–79, 226

Strang, Lewis, 166
Sullivan, Yankee, 89

Tammany Hall, 112
Taylor, Tom, 137–38
Taylor, Zachary, 29, 33, 35, 199
Thoreau, Henry David, 6
Tilton, Elizabeth, 43
Tocqueville, Alexis de, 5, 47, 87
Towse, John Rankin, 128, 135–37, 139, 141, 150, 184–85
Tracy, Helen, 152, 220
Trail of Tears, 174
Tremont Theatre, 95
Trollope, Frances, 46, 101
Twain, Mark, 57
Tyler, John, 12, 33, 35
Tyler, Royall, 1, 16–17, 19, 90, 171
Tyler, Wat, 75

Uncle Tom's Cabin (Stowe), 134, 178–79, 226

Van Buren, John, 56
Van Buren, Martin, 29, 35, 56, 65, 76
Vietnam War, 134, 189–90
violence, 3, 59, 81, 84, 91, 95, 110, 113, 116, 175
Virginius (Knowles), 147, 152, 154, 159, 163, 168, 184–185
Vorlicky, Robert, 3

Walnut Street Theatre, 12, 20, 55, 95, 102, 113, 121
War of 1812, 24, 32, 45, 60, 196
Ward, John William, 142
Washington, George, 18–20, 23, 109, 212

Wayne, John, 189
Webster, Daniel, 22, 29–30, 33–35, 56, 65, 199
Wells, Samuel Robert, 49
Wemyss, Francis, 12, 77, 89, 91, 98, 181–82
Wentworth, John, 31
Wheeler, A. C., 131, 157, 160–64, 222
Whig party, 3, 6, 25–28, 34, 37, 75–77, 80, 87, 112, 196, 205
White, Lemuel G., 61, 148
Wignell, Thomas, 18
William Tell (Knowles), 14, 65, 98
Williams, Mr and Mrs. Barney, 179–80
Williams, Tennessee, 189
Willis, Bruce, 189
Willis, N. P., 55
Winter, William, 74, 117, 124, 128, 130, 132, 136–38, 142, 147, 149–50, 154, 157, 160, 162–63, 170, 180, 185
Winter Garden Theatre, 118, 125–26, 129, 143
Wollstonecraft, Mary, 85
Woodhull, Caleb Smith, 112
Woods, Samuel D., 152
Woodville, Richard Caton, 6
Worcester v. Georgia, 174
World War I, 187
World War II, 134, 189–90, 192

Young Man: Hints Addressed to the Young Men of the United States, 48
Young Man's Guide to True Greatness, The, 47

GPSR Compliance
The European Union's (EU) General Product Safety Regulation (GPSR) is a set of rules that requires consumer products to be safe and our obligations to ensure this.

If you have any concerns about our products, you can contact us on

ProductSafety@springernature.com

In case Publisher is established outside the EU, the EU authorized representative is:

Springer Nature Customer Service Center GmbH
Europaplatz 3
69115 Heidelberg, Germany

www.ingramcontent.com/pod-product-compliance
Lightning Source LLC
LaVergne TN
LVHW011811060526
838200LV00053B/3738